Between 1690 and 1715, well over one hundred literary fairy tales appeared in France, two-thirds of them written by women. This book explores why fashionable adults were attracted to this new literary genre and considers how it became a medium for reconceiving literary and historical discourses of sexuality and gender. Integrating socio-historical, structuralist, and post-structuralist approaches, Seifert argues that these fairy tales use the "marvelous" (or supernatural) to mediate between conflicting cultural desires, particularly between nostalgia and utopian longings.

The first part of the book considers how the marvelous is used to legitimize the genre, to espouse waning aristocratic ideals, to exemplify theories of "modern" (as opposed to ancient classical) culture, and to reaffirm women's potential as writers. The second part examines how specific groups of tales both reiterate and unsettle late seventeenth-century discourses of love, masculinity, and femininity, through literary and/or folkloric conventions such as the romantic quest, the marriage closure, chivalric heroes, and good and evil fairies. Seifert's study sheds new light on the development of the literary fairy tale and proposes a new approach to understanding sexuality and gender both in this genre and the *ancien régime* as a whole.

CAMBRIDGE STUDIES IN FRENCH 55

FAIRY TALES, SEXUALITY, AND GENDER IN FRANCE, 1690–1715

Recent titles in this series include

A complete list of books in the series is given at the end of the volume.

FAIRY TALES, SEXUALITY, AND GENDER IN FRANCE

1690–1715

Nostalgic Utopias

LEWIS C. SEIFERT

Department of French Studies, Brown University

CAMBRIDGE
UNIVERSITY PRESS

CAMBRIDGE UNIVERSITY PRESS
Cambridge, New York, Melbourne, Madrid, Cape Town, Singapore, São Paulo

Cambridge University Press
The Edinburgh Building, Cambridge CB2 2RU, UK

Published in the United States of America by Cambridge University Press, New York

www.cambridge.org
Information on this title: www.cambridge.org/9780521550055

First published 1996
This digitally printed first paperback version 2006

A catalogue record for this publication is available from the British Library

ISBN-13 978-0-521-55005-5 hardback
ISBN-10 0-521-55005-X hardback

ISBN-13 978-0-521-02627-7 paperback
ISBN-10 0-521-02627-X paperback

For Cathy

Contents

Acknowledgments

Storytelling is impossible without a network of other story-tellers, an audience, and a stock of tales. For reading my story at an early stage, I offer special thanks to Floyd Gray, Anne Herrmann, and Bill Paulson. For encouraging me to keep on spinning this tale, my heart-felt gratitude goes to Patricia Hannon, Beth Goldsmith, Gretchen Schultz, and Abby Zanger. For guiding me through the intricacies of the publication process, I express my appreciation to Ed Ahearn and Henry Majewski. For reading my manuscript and responding to my tale-telling, I am grateful to Catherine Velay-Vallantin and Jack Zipes. For convincing me early on that this story was worth telling and for showing me the excitement and challenges of tale-spinning, I am indebted to Domna Stanton.

Portions of chapter 3 appeared in very different form in my "Tales of Difference: Infantilization and the Recuperation of Class and Gender in 17th-Century *Contes de fées*," *Actes de Las Vegas*, ed. Marie-France Hilgar, Biblio 17, 60 (Paris, Seattle, Tübingen: Papers on French Seventeenth-Century Literature, 1991) 179–194 and "*Les Fées Modernes*: Women, Fairy Tales, and the Literary Field in Late Seventeenth-Century France," *Going Public: Women and Publishing in Early Modern France*, eds. Elizabeth Goldsmith and Dena Goodman (Ithaca: Cornell University Press, 1995) 129–145.

This book would never have been finished without the support and encouragement of Catherine Gordon-Seifert.

Note on translations and quotations

At present, many of the primary sources studied in this book are not readily available either in modern editions or in most libraries. Accordingly, I have quoted primary sources from the original French in both the text and the notes and have given English translations for all such quotations in the text. Secondary French sources, which are more accessible, are quoted exclusively in English translation. I have modernized the spelling and punctuation (but not the capitalization) of all quotations from seventeenth- and eighteenth-century French sources. Unless otherwise noted, all translations are my own.

Introduction

Bien souvent les plaisirs de l'imagination
valent mieux que les plaisirs réels.
Charlotte-Rose Caumont de La Force

Paradox is no stranger to fairy tales. They are at once among the most marginal and the most central of all cultural forms. On the one hand, they are only occasionally included in literary canons, if indeed they are understood to be "literature" at all. On the other hand, fairy tales are immediate, almost universal cultural references that reveal in succinct form some of the most significant of all psychic and social phenomena. Even more paradoxical, the reasons for the marginality of fairy tales are, at the same time, indications of their centrality. Consider but three of these reasons. (1) If a wide-spread prejudice holds fairy tales to be simplistic and unsophisticated, it is equally widely accepted, in the wake of structuralist theorists such as Propp, Greimas, and Brémond, that the repetitive and predictable features of the genre offer a highly condensed model of more elaborate narrative forms. (2) The escapism or retreat from reality prevalent in supernatural tales blatantly contravenes the dominant literary esthetic of realism and, by this standard, accords them less prestige. As fantasy literature, however, fairy tales can be said to outline the very contours and solidity of what we take to be "reality." (3) Since fairy tales – even so-called literary fairy tales[1] – are fully synonymous in our time with children's literature, they are usually not considered to be of primary interest to adults. In fact, literary fairy tales *were* intended for adult readers in the seventeenth and eighteenth centuries. More significant, their classification as children's literature is at least in part a mimetic transposition of content onto intended readership since they depict, by and large, the conflicts of childhood or adolescence and its resolution into adulthood. As such, fairy tales specify with extraordinary precision and economy a culture's prototypical quest for identity; they are *par excellence* narratives of initiation, becoming, and maturity; they are themselves susceptible to becoming (and have become) powerful instruments of socialization and acculturation.

Hence, it is hardly an exaggeration to conclude that fairy tales, both in spite and because of their liminal status as literary works, present major cultural themes more succinctly and more accurately than many if not most other literary forms. Among these themes, sexuality has come to occupy an important place in the interpretation of fairy tales. From Freud and his disciples to Bruno Bettelheim's influential book, *The Uses of Enchantment*,[2] the characters and plot situations of individual tales have been deciphered as symbols of sexual desires and conflicts. Most of all, the primacy of sexuality depends on the recognition (which is *not* specific to psychoanalytic perspectives) that, more often than not, fairy-tale plots concern the dynamics of a family. For the hero or heroine, this means progressing from an initial situation of disequilibrium within his or her family (resulting from the death of a parent, expulsion from the family, etc.) to a situation of restored equilibrium (in which the family is reunited or a new family is begun). Following many critics, we might even interpret the hero's or heroine's helpers (such as fairies) or opponents (such as ogres) as parental figures.[3] Of course, familial structures and the sexual dynamics they entail are most obvious in the stereotypical marriage closure of so many fairy tales. However, what is often left unexplored or unstated is the fact that these familial adventures always position the characters as males or females within that unit.[4] Their adventures force them to assume what turn out to be highly codified attributes of sexual and gender identity.

In spite of their lesser prestige compared to "high" literature, fairy tales are a particularly apt means of studying the construction of sexuality and gender differences. As narratives that are highly economical and widely diffused, they present many of our most central myths about what divides the sexes and what constitutes desire. By that same token, they reveal more explicitly than other texts the conflicts, contradictions, and tensions on which those myths are founded – both within dominant and among competing ideologies. It is the aim of this book to show how a specific corpus of fairy tales reveals some of the most central myths or ideologies of the culture in which it was produced. The 114 *contes de fées* (fairy tales) published in France between 1690 and 1715, by their very marginality, reveal as do few other sources (literary or otherwise) both dominant ideologies of sexuality and gender in late seventeenth-century France, as well as rival ideologies that resist and define them.

The analyses in this book begin with what is perhaps the fundamental insight of feminist theory: namely, that sexual and gender identities are not essential, biological givens but rather derived from culturally constructed "sex/gender systems."[5] From this recognition, there result two rather paradoxical conclusions. Bound as they are to specific contexts, "sex/gender systems" are fundamentally unstable and susceptible to change. At the same time, since they are ideological formations that by definition legitimize themselves as "natural" or "commonsensical," these systems are extremely resilient. And in the West, of course, the patriarchal system or group of systems that has repressed women and valorized reproductive over other forms of sexuality has shown just such longevity. While it is very difficult to think of any "sex gender system" paradoxically – as both stable and unstable – such a perspective is imperative if we are to define the capacity of patriarchy as a system to perpetuate itself. Unchanging in its repression, this social and conceptual force is not a transhistorical monolith.[6] Always recognizable as a patriarchal "sex/gender system," its different chronological and cultural inflections reveal the extent to which it is ideological and, thus, subject to internal contradictions, adaptation to new circumstances and conditions, or outright recasting. Charting the intricacies of patriarchy's unstable yet relentless development necessarily involves a consideration of tendencies that threaten or disrupt, in however minimal a way, the hegemonic regulation of sexuality and gender. But these tendencies can only be assessed by placing them within the larger paradox of patriarchy.

What, then, is the role of fairy tales in the construction and socialization of sexuality and gender differences? Rather than elucidate the aforementioned paradoxes, feminist work on fairy tales has been primarily concerned with demonstrating this genre's overwhelming complicity with patriarchal gender roles. Considering a wide range of collections, feminist folklorists and literary critics have drawn attention not only to our culture's predilection for tale-types[7] that feature passive and victimized heroines, but also to the expectations that such characterizations instill (or have instilled) in children, especially in girls.[8] Ultimately, this work has not clarified how the genre contributes or responds to moments of instability in the historical elaboration of patriarchal systems. And yet, the contemporary reception and production of fairy tales illustrate the genre's complex role in this regard. A number of authors (including Angela Carter and Anne Sexton) have either rewritten or invented tales so as to empower heroines, attenuate male aggression, and/or problematize the traditional marriage closure.[9] In spite of these alternative versions, however, the fairy tales popularized for the mass market (the most obvious example being the films made by the Walt Disney Studios) continue to valorize generic structures such as the marriage closure that reinforce highly conservative gender norms, even while featuring more active heroines.[10] Of course such fairy tales are themselves signs of the paradoxes within the patriarchal "sex/gender system(s)" of our own time.

The effects that the pre-modern and pre-capitalist fairy tale had in constructing sexuality and gender are no less complex, although this question remains largely unexplored. The example of the *contes de fées* published between 1690 and 1715 is particularly noteworthy in this regard. For, as I will argue, they relate a complex story about the persistence but also the instability of patriarchy at a decisive moment in the history of French literature and culture.

It is no accident that the *Petit Robert* indicates 1698 as the year
the words *"conte de fée"* entered the French language, for that
year saw the publication of six volumes totaling some thirty-one
tales. In all, more than 250 were published in seventeenth- and
eighteenth-century France. Only a fraction of the tales in this
vast corpus are regularly read or even reprinted. Among these,
however, are some of the best known of all fairy tales, such as
"Beauty and the Beast," "Cinderella," "Little Red Riding
Hood," and "Sleeping Beauty," which appeared in their first
written and most influential form during this period. Beginning
in 1690, with the publication of a tale in d'Aulnoy's novel
Histoire d'Hypolite and running through almost the entire
eighteenth century, *contes de fées* intended for a *mondain* adult
readership were published and, in many instances, republished
(including the massive forty-volume collection of tales *Le Cabinet
des fées* [1785–1789])[11].

Specialists of French fairy tales generally acknowledge that
there were two major "waves" or "vogues" of publication
between 1690 and 1789: the first extending through approxi-
mately 1715 and the second from 1730 to 1758.[12] The present
study concentrates on the tales of the first vogue. Both thematically and structurally, the seventeenth-century *contes de fées*
constitute a much more cohesive corpus than those of the
eighteenth century.[13] Most important, as I will show, they also
arose within and as a response to a specific cultural climate, in
contrast to the eighteenth-century tales, which are characterized by extremely varied contexts of production and reception.
Enormously popular long after their original appearance, the
texts of the first vogue were the quintessential models that the
eighteenth-century fairy-tale writers sought to imitate and/or
parody, that editors of the *Bibliothèque bleue* republished well into
the nineteenth century, and that Romantic writers took as
models for their own tales.

Since the mid-nineteenth century, the notoriety of a single
fairy-tale writer, Charles Perrault (1628–1703), has eclipsed that
of all the others. And yet, Perrault was but one of sixteen
writers who participated in the first vogue, including both
women – Marie-Catherine d'Aulnoy (c. 1650–1705), Louise

d'Auneuil (?–c. 1700), Catherine Bernard (1662–1712), Catherine Bédacier Durand (c. 1650–c. 1715), Charlotte-Rose Caumont de La Force (c. 1650–1724), Marie-Jeanne Lhéritier de Villandon (1664–1734), and Henriette-Julie de Murat (1670–1716) – and men – Jean-Paul Bignon (1662–1743), François-Timoléon de Choisy (1644–1724), François de la Mothe-Fénelon (1651–1715),[14] Eustache Le Noble (1643–1711), Jean de Mailly (?–1724), François-Augustin de Moncrif (1687–1770), Paul-François Nodot (?–?), and Jean de Préchac (1676–?).

The first vogue of *contes de fées* is a part of the cultural crisis that marked the final years of Louis XIV's reign, and as such confirms Fredric Jameson's observation that romance literature becomes especially appealing in moments of historical transition or crisis.[15] The phrase *"crise de la conscience européenne"* (crisis of European consciousness), coined by Paul Hazard in his classic book of the same title, has often been applied to the period 1680–1715. Hazard demonstrates this period's consolidation of sceptical and rationalist thought, accomplished by Bayle and Fontenelle (among others), that was to provide the foundation for Enlightenment philosophy. In Hazard's account, this philosophical shift was only part of a larger *Zeitgeist* that privileged and was typified by real and imagined voyages, religious heterodoxy, scientific and artistic progress, and a psychology of *sensibilité*. Within this period of transition, the *contes de fées* are more of a symptom or by-product than a contribution to the important epistemological and esthetic shifts that were taking place. In a few short paragraphs devoted to these fairy tales, Hazard suggests that they functioned as an outlet for the "feeling of great decline" which, in his view, pervaded this period.[16] In this respect, they are similar in function to the travel narratives, utopian novels, and comic opera of this same moment in that they all provide an imaginary compensation for (what was perceived to be) the depressing reality of the present.

Although undeniable, Hazard's view of the fairy tales within the *crise de la conscience européenne* is nonetheless highly reductive. Beyond a response to a psychological and/or cultural need for escape, the first vogue is also (part of) a strategic *production* of meanings within late seventeenth-century French culture. This is perhaps most obvious with regard to the *Querelle des Anciens et des Modernes* (Quarrel of the Ancients and the Moderns) which pitted the "Ancients," who espoused the inimitability of classical Greek and Roman models against the "Moderns," who advocated the relativity of cultural models from all periods while conceiving the possibility of historical progress. As an elegantly stylized imitation of peasants' folktales, an "indigenous" French source, the *conte de fées* offered the Moderns both an example and a weapon in their struggle with the Ancients. Perrault and Lhéritier in particular exploited the marginal status of this genre without classical precedent to argue the "modernist" cause in explicit terms. The vogue of fairy tales as a whole endorses this outlook, if only implicitly, through a shared basis in *mondain* literary culture.

This *fin de siècle* culture was also marked by controversies concerning the proper boundaries of male and female gender roles, and the fairy tales of the first vogue are part of this debate. At stake was the role of women in the production of literature, if not culture in general. Joan DeJean and Timothy Reiss, for example, have chronicled the late seventeenth-century hostility to women as creative agents of culture and specifically literature,[17] which is itself part of a broader movement that has been termed the *"grand renfermement"* (great confinement).[18] Relegating women to the domestic sphere and strictly regulating their matrimonial status (among other things), this legal and discursive trend also manifested itself through increased attacks on polite society during the final years of the century. The best known of these came from Fénelon and Madame de Maintenon (Louis XIV's second wife by morganatic marriage) whose writings and efforts on behalf of the education of women[19] denounced the moral corruption of aristocratic culture in general and, especially, women's role in it through the acquisition and display of *bel esprit* (worldly wit).[20] In its stead, both preached the virtues of domesticity and motherhood for women in view of a regeneration of French society, and especially the nobility of the blood.

Given this climate, it is striking to note the predominance of women among the writers of the first fairy-tale vogue. Since work on French fairy tales has to date concentrated overwhelmingly on Perrault, the fact that women were the most prolific writers of *contes de fées* has been obscured.[21] Combined, the tales of the seven *conteuses* (female fairy-tale writers) account for seventy-four of those published between 1690 and 1715, as opposed to the thirty-eight tales written by the nine *conteurs* (male fairy-tale writers).[22] The high proportion of *contes de fées* authored by women is somewhat less startling if we consider that the 1690s saw a dramatic increase in the percentage of novels written by women. For the period 1687 to 1699, for instance, at least 33 percent of all novels published in France were by women (DeJean, *Tender Geographies*, 128). Yet, this fact does not explain why women wrote in excess of two-thirds of all the fairy tales in the first vogue. Even more significant, there is some evidence to suggest that the *conteuses* – and not Perrault, as is commonly asserted – initiated the first vogue.[23] D'Aulnoy, Bernard, and Lhéritier had all published prose tales before the appearance of Perrault's *Histoires ou contes du temps passé, avec des moralités* in 1697.[24]

The prominence of women as initiators and writers of fairy tales in a period when their role in the cultural sphere was a hotly debated issue raises the question of what functions the genre may have served for the *conteuses*. The *conte de fée* originated in the mid-seventeenth-century salon,[25] which, under the direction of women, had fostered many literary forms, including the novel. This fact is notable for several reasons. It is, of course, further evidence of women's preeminent role in the production and development of the genre. But at a time when polite society was under direct attack by moralist writers and when the salon had turned into decline or at least was undergoing profound changes, the fairy tales, and especially those of the *conteuses*, inscribe and advocate the creative potential of both those gatherings and women's participation in them, all the more so because the tales are themselves often given as examples of salon storytelling within longer narrative frames.[26] Finally, the *conteuses*, distinct from the *conteurs*, refer to the intertextual network that connects them as storytellers and writers; so doing, they indicate the extent to which the *conte de fées* is an example of what Joan DeJean has called "salon writing" *(Tender Geographies*, 94–97), the usually anonymous group production of texts in the salon. Thereby the *conteuses* deliberately identify themselves as *salonnières* (salon women).[27] While all of this suggests that the genre served as a compensation for the increasing pressure on women in late seventeenth-century France to retreat from the public sphere, it also suggests that the vogue of fairy tales enabled the *conteuses* to assert and demonstrate their own vision of women's role in literary culture and society at large. The fairy-tale form was particularly well suited to this task because of its ambivalent marginality. It was at once an unthreatening genre that was far from approaching the elite status of tragedy or epic poetry and a *mondain* form that signified the sociable ideal of aristocratic culture. It was at once a genre that women could appropriate without threatening male literary figures and a form that enabled them to defend and perpetuate their own *locus* of cultural authority.

To be sure, many if not all of the *conteurs* doubtless saw in the fairy tale a means of defending a cultural milieu and ideal that they too advocated. With the obvious exception of Fénelon, all of the male fairy-tale writers were participants in *mondain* society and produced works for its consumption. Further, attacks on polite society were by no means exclusively aimed at women, and men were always part of salon gatherings. The fact remains, however, that the male fairy-tale writers do not demonstrate anything approaching the group consciousness of the *conteuses*, several of whom met regularly in salons.[28] Moreover, they tend to put their tales to more specialized uses than do the female fairy-tale writers and/or assign them a distinctly subordinate role within a larger text.[29] Whereas the *conteurs* tended to write isolated tales, the *conteuses* on the whole produced collections of fairy tales. To the extent that multiple production is an indicator of personal investment, the women demonstrate, relatively speaking, a greater attachment to the genre or, to put it another way, they seem to have had more to say with/through fairy tales than do the men.

Comparing the texts of the *conteurs* and those of the *conteuses* reveals similarities, but a certain number of differences as well. Thematically, the narratives of both groups of writers are most often structured around a romantic plot that bears close resemblance to the earlier seventeenth-century prose forms (such as the *romans héroïques*).[30] Yet, consideration of formal features reveals several differences as well. Compared to those of the *conteurs*, the tales of the *conteuses* are, on average, considerably longer,[31] prominently feature heroines and especially fairies, and, on the level of plot structure, often include complications or revisions of the male-centered quest for a female object (ie. the hero encountering and overcoming numerous obstacles in pursuit of his beloved). However, even if less frequent, these latter features are not entirely absent from the tales of the *conteurs* and, thus, do not completely resolve the question of the specificity of the men's or women's corpus.

In view of these ambiguities, my critical approach to this corpus is two-fold. On the one hand, I will be arguing throughout this book that the seventeenth-century *conte de fées* can and should indeed be interpreted as a form of gendered writing, that is, writing in which the gender of the author is inscribed as a distinguishing feature of textual production and meaning. Consequently, I seek at various points in the analyses that follow to draw distinctions between the textuality of men's and women's fairy tales, particularly in those based on the same or similar tale-types. On the other hand, I will argue that this approach must also take into account the differences within groups of male- and female-authored texts, and within those of individual authors. Attention to these differences, alongside those corresponding to authorial gender, reveals the complexity of this corpus, one that shows itself to be an expression of collective as well as individual desires. The readings I give of selected tales and groups of tales by no means exhaust the richness of this corpus. My objective, however, is to highlight, through emblematic examples, the conflicting longings, both individual and collective, that traverse the vogue.

Precisely how the *contes de fées* form could serve such varied desires can only be understood by considering the role of the marvelous *(merveilleux)*. Throughout this study, I argue that it is this facet that distinguishes the genre from other seventeenth-century cultural forms by allowing the expression of desires otherwise less immediately representable. The chapters in Part I probe the specific textual and contextual functions of the marvelous within the vogue. Chapter 1 suggests that the marvelous maintains an ambivalent relation to the dominant literary/esthetic category of *vraisemblance* (verisimilitude). Its inherent rejection of empirical reality results in a reaffirmation, but also a questioning of dominant ethical and social codes, which are themselves encompassed by *vraisemblance*. Chapter 2 considers the marvelous as a central feature of the fairy tale's readability or interpretability. As a whole, the vogue is predicated on an ironic distancing from the supernatural through what I call the "infantilizing" and "moralizing" pretexts. However, this irony is itself subject to irony since the presumed distance from the childish and pedagogical narrative in fact fosters an even more fundamental investment in the marvelous. Finally, chapter 3 considers the historically specific uses of the fairy-tale marvelous in late seventeenth-century France. In the context of the Quarrel of the Ancients and the Moderns, the increasing attacks on *mondain* culture, and the growing barriers against women in the public sphere, this brand of fantasy rewrites folkloric and literary tradition in order to imagine a discursive counter-reality, an imaginary compensation for particular lived constraints of the present.

In all of the *contes de fées*, the marvelous plays a crucial role in representing sexuality and gender. In Part II, I explore the profoundly ambiguous treatment of heterosexual passion, masculinity, and femininity in this corpus. If the supernatural settings most often celebrate the supposed complementarity of masculine and feminine desires, they sometimes privilege different types of male–female relations and, in extreme cases, question the very possibility of happiness through love and marriage (chapter 4). Similarly, the marvelous powers accorded to or used against male (chapter 5) and female (chapter 6) characters most readily reinforce patriarchal gender stereotypes. And yet, the marvelous can also serve to expose the lack at the center of masculine subjectivity and to blur the binary

construction of femininity typical of folk- and fairy-tale narratives. By means of the marvelous, then, the *contes de fées*
(re)define the cultural boundaries of sexual desire, masculinity,
and femininity. They reveal the instability of a particular "sex/
gender system."

To explore sexuality and gender in the fairy tale is to probe the
more general question of how the genre represents the "real."
Aspects of reality among others, notions of sexuality and gender
in the fairy tale are deliberately bracketed from the constraints
of the ordinary and the everyday. Yet, the fairy tale's own
seemingly distinct world acts to define what its readers conceive
as "normal" and "real." As Michel Butor has concluded: "it is
because of the fairy tale that reality presents itself as something
certain and solid, something easily distinguished, something
one masters and understands."[32] Emphasizing the unreality of
the supernatural setting, fairy tales stereotypically reaffirm their
readers' sense of both what reality is and what it is not. They
would seemingly offer the comfort and reassurance that the
world is unchanging, uncomplicated, and unfrightening.

Yet, fairy tales can only impart stability by opposing and
undermining dominant cultural understandings of reality. Most
obvious is the case of the marvelous which, in the tales that rely
on it, supercedes and contradicts the natural order of the "real"
world. From a structuralist perspective, folk- and fairy tales,
and most *all* forms of narrative, embody moments of both
revolt and accommodation. The movement from disequilibrium to equilibrium so basic to narrative structure is in fact a
movement from a situation of disruption in the social order to a
situation in which this order or its equivalent is (re)affirmed.
This same ambivalence is at work in the familial dynamics
around which the prototypical fairy-tale narrative is constructed. If, on the one hand, the hero or heroine rejects or is
rejected by his or her parents, there is always in the end an
effacement of this rejection, often through a reconciliation with
the parents. Drawing parallels between the child's rejection *qua*
idealization of the parents in both Freud's family romance and
the structure of fairy tales and novels, Marthe Robert has

argued that "this duplicity of the fairy tale, which is, we might say, double...allows revolt to pass itself off as conformity, and then, by attenuating or negating all negative feelings, to return to conformity and piety."[33]

Now, in all of these perspectives, the fairy tale's revolt against "reality" or the social order is, in the end, always dissolved into accommodation. François Flahault, however, has proposed a more ambiguous model for understanding the ways oral folk- and fairy tales represent "reality." Unique to these texts and the contexts of their production and reception, he contends, is a refusal of the transcendent salvational perspective that typifies the written narrative (what he calls the "things must get better" [*ça doit s'arranger*] answer to existential dilemmas) in favor of an acceptance of the "positivity of lack" (what he calls the "we have to live with the ways things are" [*il faut faire avec*] answer). Thus, rather than resolve the opposing points of view or forces within conflicts, folk- and fairy tales play two contradictory dynamics off each other: "one works to reduce the distance between positions [and] the other...moves in the direction of discerning differences, of maintaining or reestablishing them."[34] Flahault perceives the tension between these two dynamics within many structural and thematic aspects of the genre, including the conflicts between alterity and identity, duty and transgression, desire and satisfaction, among several others. By allowing for mediation without the resolution of contradictory or opposing tendencies, Flahault's model openly defies finality and closure.

Although Flahault considers his theory most applicable to the oral folktale, it is not without pertinence to the literary fairy tale as well. In fact, as I will argue, the seventeenth-century *contes de fées* define aspects of reality, and specifically norms of sexuality and gender, in profoundly ambivalent ways that recall Flahault's dual dynamic. When the corpus is considered as a whole, dominant conceptions of "reality" are neither completely rejected nor reaffirmed, neither absolutely redefined nor reiterated. Rather, both individually and as a group, these fairy tales reveal a central ambivalence or tension between nostalgia on the one hand and utopia on the other. Throughout this study, I concentrate on the ambivalence between these two desires in order to come to terms with the cultural and social instability that obtains in late seventeenth-century France. More specifically, I posit that the ambivalence between nostalgic and utopian desires corresponds to the ambiguity or ambivalence between conservative notions of gender roles on the one hand and more or less unconventional gender roles on the other. I have coined the seemingly paradoxical, if not contradictory expression "nostalgic utopias" to designate my corpus as a whole so as to explore *how* this historically specific use of fantasy (which Rosemary Jackson aptly called the "literature of desire")[35] wavers between romanticized past traditions and unacknowledged future possibilities. By this expression, I mean to delimit the two boundaries of the culturally conceivable. Before considering the notion of "nostalgic utopias" any further, it is necessary to explain what I mean by "nostalgia" and "utopia," both of which are used widely, and often quite vaguely.

A particularly useful analysis of nostalgia has been proposed by Susan Stewart.[36] For her, nostalgia (or what she also terms "longing") is not so much an emotional state arising in individuals as a social disease characterized by the desire for authentic reality or experience; it is a desire that rejects the present by seeking to fuse lived and mediated experience and to erase the gap between nature and culture. Paradoxically, the authenticity that is sought can only be achieved through *mediated* experience, of which narrative is doubtless the most important form. In whatever guise, nostalgia or longing can manifest itself in three different ways. First, it is what Stewart has called a "future-past" – it denies the present as decadent and inauthentic even as it turns to an idealized vision of the past as the hope for the future *(On Longing,* x). Second, nostalgia imagines a location of origin for authentic experience or reality in either the immortal transcendent or the immanent earthly *(On Longing,* x). Third, nostalgia often attempts to create significant objects, especially through narrative and its capacity to "both generate and engender a significant other" *(On Longing,* xi).

Considered as a corpus and literary form, the seventeenth-century *contes de fées* amply demonstrate all three of these manifestations of nostalgia. First, they (like many folk- and fairy tales) are structured so as to denounce the present and refer back to a mythical, non-existent past, most notably in their formulaic openings (such as "il était une fois" [once upon a time]) and final *moralités* (morals). Moreover, formally and thematically, many of the tales hark back to the pastoral and heroic novels from the early part of the seventeenth century, in stark contrast to novelistic conventions of the 1690s.[37] Most prominent among these is the use of pastoral settings as well as heroes and heroines of noble birth who adhere to a feudal *ethos*. Second, the *contes de fées* also (re)create an enunciative origin not only in a revitalized salon, as I have discussed above, but, most strikingly, in the person of the peasant woman storyteller. In chapter 3, I discuss how this (phantasmatic) guarantor of narrative authenticity serves to legitimate certain constructions of class and gender. Finally, based on the pretense that they rewrite popular folkloric traditions (either in a direct or an implicit way), these literary fairy tales belong among what Stewart has called "distressed genres" or "new antiques" that are both in and out of time because they recontextualize a "natural," oral past as/within a mediated, written form. So doing, they, like all "distressed genres," enable the literary tradition "to create an idealization of itself through a separation of speech and writing" ("Notes," 7) or, what Stewart calls, "a counterfeit materiality and an authentic nostalgia" ("Notes," 24).

Temporally speaking, nostalgia, which is a fantasized recuperation of the past, is diametrically opposed to utopia, which is oriented toward the future, or at least away from both the present and the past. However, by using the term "utopia," I do not mean to imply that fairy tales are elaborately organized spatial and political systems (similar to Thomas More's, for instance) that theorize themselves as historical negativity, nor do I mean to suggest that these texts are ever devoid of ideology.[38] Rather, what I will be referring to as the "utopian function" of the tales in my corpus is derived from the philosopher Ernst Bloch's extensive reflections on the relations between ideological and esthetic value. In his rather unorthodox version of Marxist thought, Bloch makes a distinction within ideology between false consciousness and utopian surplus. With this latter term (obviously derived from Marx's notion of surplus value), Bloch refers to that part of a work of art that outlives its historical context of production. Ideological surplus is utopian in that it is an inkling or consciousness within humans of what they might become in the future. This surplus or not-yet-conscious is assimilable to a daydreaming that is driven by hope but never loses sight of concrete possibilities. It is this inkling or consciousness that a work of art can produce. It is, to use Bloch's terminology, the latency of being in the present that looks forward to and propels individuals toward the future. At the same time, of course, it contests the existing social order or *status quo*. What works of art and literature provide, then, according to Bloch, are not so much "concrete" utopias as the "anticipatory illumination" *(Vor-Schein)* of such utopias. Anticipatory illumination, as Jack Zipes has succinctly defined it, "is an image, a constellation, a configuration closely tied to the concrete utopias that are lit up on the frontal margins of reality and illuminate the possibilities for rearranging social and political relations so that they engender *Heimat*, Bloch's word for the home that we have all sensed but have never experienced or known" ("Introduction," *The Utopian Function*, xxxiii). It is important to realize, however, that these "anticipatory illuminations" never aspire to definitive closure, but are instead the effects of a *drive toward* the future, *toward* the realization of concrete utopias. As such, the utopian function of the text or artwork simultaneously uncovers the incompleteness of its own anticipatory illuminations.[39]

In elaborating his notion of the utopian function, Bloch himself gives special attention to folk- and fairy tales. Because they speak to the desire of the masses to escape the oppressive confines of the ordinary and the everyday, in his view these narrative forms are illustrative of the utopian function. In the fairy tale, the creative potential of the marvelous gives expression to ideological surplus. "Play and magic together have carte

blanche in the fairy tale. Wish becomes a command. There is
no difficulty in carrying it out. Neither is space or time divisive"
("Better Castles," *The Utopian Function*, 171). Although Bloch's
treatment is somewhat marred by the fact that he does not
consider fairy tales as historically specific texts,[40] his understanding of utopia as ideological surplus and anticipatory
illumination is valuable for analyzing the corpus of seventeenth-
century *contes de fées*. I will be contending throughout this study
that it is especially through ideologies of sexuality and gender
that these tales serve a utopian function. The transformation
and, even, rejection of the purportedly natural complementarity of masculine and feminine desires (chapter 4), the questioning of masculine self-sufficiency (chapter 5), and binaristic
definitions of femininity (chapter 6) suggest that many of the
tales are new inflections of literary conventions. They represent
a forward-looking impulse, an anticipatory illumination of
different "sex/gender systems."

As I have suggested, it is impossible to isolate the utopian
function of the *contes de fées* or any artwork from what Bloch
would call ideological false consciousness. Indeed, Bloch understands utopian surplus to be fundamentally tied to the deceptive
and repressive force of ideology. On the one hand, false
consciousness depends on the utopian potential of all ideology
to smooth over its constituent contradictions:

> False consciousness alone would not be capable of producing one of
> the most important characteristics of ideology, i.e., the premature
> harmonizing of the social contradictions. Ideology is less comprehen-
> sible as the medium of a continuous cultural substratum without an
> encounter with the utopian function. All this obviously exceeds the
> capacity of the false consciousness that cannot invigorate or apologize
> for the specific social basis. Therefore, without the utopian function,
> the class ideologies would have only managed to achieve an ephem-
> eral delusion and not the models of art, science, and philosophy.
> ("The Conscious and Known Activity," *The Utopian Function*, 117–118)

On the other hand, the utopian function is capable of drawing
on the resources of the past, in spite of false consciousness.
"The productive utopian function...draws images from the still
valid past insofar as they ambiguously fit for the future, despite

all the spells within them, and it makes these images useful since they are the expression of what has still not happened" *(The Utopian Function,* 126). Thus, the utopian function enables *contes de fées* to recuperate "images" of a different social organization (especially with respect to sexuality and gender) from within the archaic, often nostalgic setting typical of the genre.

Ultimately, the corpus of seventeenth-century fairy tales evinces a tension between both nostalgia and utopia (in the sense of the utopian function); they are, in other words, "nostalgic utopias." As the logical tension of this oxymoron suggests, they represent an unstable middle ground between Bloch and Stewart, between ideological surplus and anticipatory illumination on the one hand and nostalgia and distressed genres on the other. Although there *are* fairy tales in the first vogue that conform wholly to Stewart's definition, this corpus both conforms to it and exceeds it. Nostalgia and the utopian function are bound together, constantly interacting and constraining each other. If we remember Flahault's observation about the folktale's mediation of contradictory positions or tendencies – a tendency toward differentiation and a tendency toward reconciliation – the coupling of these two opposing desires or forces is perhaps less puzzling. If nostalgia pines for a blurring of the present into a phantasmatic past, utopia on the contrary distinguishes a partial future solution from an inadequate present. Of course, Flahault's model also suggests that an interpretive resolution to the tensions between nostalgia and utopia is impossible in the long run, at least as concerns the corpus as a whole. The non-finality or non-closure of my own storytelling is perhaps the product of our own, late twentieth-century moment of crisis and transition. In this sense, the *contes de fées* may well suggest that nostalgia and utopia are central not only to late seventeenth-century France, but to all critical moments of cultural and epistemological change.

PART I

Marvelous storytelling

CHAPTER I

Marvelous realities: toward an understanding of the merveilleux

Based either directly or indirectly on folkloric material, literary fairy tales very often transcend national, ethnic, and historical confines. Many of today's best known fairy tales, such as "Beauty and the Beast" or "Cinderella," have been found to exist in the folklore not only of Europe but of several non-Western cultures as well. But the wide-spread diffusion of certain oral narratives with the same basic structure can be deceptive. In spite of the striking similarities among different traditions, tale-tellers and their audiences always put stories to historically and culturally specific uses. "As soon as an ethnic group adopts the main themes of a tale type, it imbues them with local interests and tastes," concludes the noted folklorist Lutz Röhrich.[1] Often, literary fairy tales too are appropriations of pre-existing stories that were fashioned to accommodate the preferences and preoccupations of specific tale-spinners and readers. Folk- and fairy tales are closely related genres because of the important continuities they share, such as similar or recurring thematic and structural devices (motifs, stock characters, formulaic openings and endings, etc.). At the same time, the wide-spread diffusion of these devices enables individual storytelling communities to adapt tales to their own needs and desires.

Anyone even remotely familiar with folk- and fairy tales will recognize that one of their most prominent features is the use of marvelous (ie. supernatural) characters and settings. Perhaps nowhere is this more obvious than in the colloquial use of "fairy tale" as an adjective to denote an excessively unrealistic situation or idea. Of course, the marvelous is by no means a feature

of all folk- and fairy tales. It does, however, recur with great
frequency in literary fairy tales and, as we will see in a moment,
is an intrinsic feature of the seventeenth-century *contes de fées*.
Moreover, in spite of its wide-spread use, the marvelous serves
specific functions according to the particular storytelling communities that use it.

Compared to their oral prototypes, literary fairy tales are not
only more prone to use the marvelous,[2] they also inscribe it
within a larger project of nostalgic recuperation and recreation
of (what is perceived to be) a lost social cohesion and interaction. So doing, they belong to the tradition of prose fiction,
represented by Boccaccio's *Decameron*, Chaucer's *Canterbury
Tales*, Marguerite de Navarre's *L'Heptaméron*, among others, in
which the narrative frame and its intercalated tales depict a
contractual "give-and-take" between storytellers and listeners.
From their inception with Giovan Francesco Straparola's *Le
Piacevoli Notti* (1550–1553), literary fairy tales highlight their
desire to recover an immediacy and instrumentality thought to
exist in a past or inaccessible storytelling.[3] From this perspective, the marvelous is an extension of the nostalgic tale-spinning
on which the genre is predicated. It functions as does fantasy
literature generally, as an attempt "to compensate for a lack
resulting from cultural constraints: it is a literature of desire,
which seeks that which is experienced as absence and loss."[4]

In all of the seventeenth-century *contes de fées*, as in most of the
folk- and fairy tales that employ it, the marvelous is perhaps
best described as a context that suspends the rules and constraints of reality. Along these lines, Tzvetan Todorov has
provided a useful definition of the marvelous in his *Introduction à
la littérature fantastique* by contrasting it with fantastic literature.
Whereas this latter hesitates between a natural (ie. empirical,
scientific) and a supernatural (ie. inexplicable, transcendent)
explanation of narrative events, marvelous literature assumes
that only a supernatural or, rather, that *no* explanation is
possible.[5] Of course, Todorov's definition in no way precludes
the existence of "realistic" traits alongside marvelous ones. In
folk- and fairy tales, kings and queens coexist with ogres and

fairies. And yet, the melding of so-called realistic and marvelous features within these genres is part of the contradictory dynamics that François Flahault has theorized is the structural basis for folkloric narratives.[6] On the one hand, the marvelous is an estrangement of empirically defined reality since it is either an exaggeration of the real or an assertion of the impossible. On the other hand, folk- and fairy tales attenuate this impulse toward estrangement and transgression. Not only does the repetitive use of a limited number of supernatural features make them predictable (if not acceptable), but most important, the marvelous also reproduces and reaffirms familiar social structures and values. In what follows, I will argue that this tension within the marvelous is crucial to our understanding of the seventeenth-century *contes de fées* as nostalgic utopias. The *merveilleux* is capable of reproducing familiar realities, but also of revealing their incoherences and suggesting, in however schematic a way, a different future. The marvelous, then, produces both a monologic return to a mythic past and a dialogic critique of the past and the present with a view toward the future.

MARVELOUS (IM)PLAUSIBILITY

In her important work on the seventeenth- and eighteenth-century French literary fairy tale, Raymonde Robert proposes a definition that accounts for both the specificity of her corpus and the narrative structure of the *merveilleux* within it. Elaborating on Propp's observation that "villainy or ... lack are the only ... obligatory elements [of all tales],"[7] by which he means that their plot structure is predicated on the need or misfortune of the protagonist(s) at the hands of the antagonist(s), Robert outlines three basic elements that constitute the *écriture féerique* (fairy-tale writing) of her corpus:

(1) *Explicit guarantees that the villainy or lack will be liquidated;* formulated in diverse but redundant ways, they establish the certainty of the failure of aggression even before the intervention of the aggressors.

(2) *The highlighting of the heroic couple's exemplary destiny* by a

particularly economical system that attributes moral or physical characteristics according to the opposed categories of heroes and adjuvants on the one hand and anti-heroes and antagonistic characters on the other.

(3) *The establishment of an exclusive fairy-tale order* ("ordre féerique exclusif") by which the micro-universe of the marvelous tale ("conte merveilleux") is constituted as an absolute and sufficient reference (*Le Conte de fées*, 36–37).

Consider Perrault's well-known version of "Cendrillon" (Cinderella) as a brief illustration of this definition. According to Robert, the first criterion of fairy-tale writing – explicit guarantees that the misdeed will be redressed – is most often carried out by a character endowed with supernatural powers (*Le Conte de fées*, 39). In Perrault's tale, it is the heroine's fairy god-mother who fulfills this role. Later, of course, the magical glass slipper resolves any remaining doubt about the outcome of this story. More significant still, Cinderella testifies to these guarantees herself by displaying a measure of self-assurance. When she is given the opportunity to try on the slipper, "Cendrillon ... qui reconnut sa pantoufle, dit en riant: 'Que je voie si elle ne me serait pas bonne!' " (Cinderella ... who recognized the slipper, said with a smile, "Let me see if it will fit me").[8] In this moment, she shares with the narrator and the readers an omniscience denied to the other characters and, thus, affirms the resolution of the misdeed or act of villainy. If we slightly modify Robert's second criterion to include the exemplary destiny of single protagonists as well as heroic couples, then it is possible to see how an absolute moral dichotomy is invoked at the very beginning of the tale and reiterated throughout. On the one hand is Cinderella's stepmother, "la plus hautaine et la plus fière qu'on eût jamais vue" (the haughtiest and proudest woman in the world) and her two daughters "qui lui ressemblaient en toutes choses" (who resembled her in every way) and, on the other, the heroine, who was "d'une douceur et d'une bonté sans exemple" (of a gentleness and goodness without parallel [171]). Further, her physical appearance is no less exemplary than her moral stature. The tale points out early on that, in spite of her rag-like clothes, she is "cent fois plus belle que ses sœurs" (one hundred times more beautiful than her sisters [172]). It is clear that Cinderella is unquestionably on the side of supreme good and beauty, and that she is the perfect match for the prince. Finally, the third criterion, the establishment of a self-sufficient fairy-tale universe, requires a dichotomous value system such as the one that opposes Cinderella on the one hand and her stepmother and stepsisters on the other. According to Robert, the *contes de fées* deploy particular structural elements so as to legitimize or motivate the Manichean binarism of good and evil (*Le Conte de fées*, 45). And in this tale, there are at least three parts to this internal legitimation. Most obvious perhaps are the two versed *moralités* (morals) that conclude the tale. Extracting a lesson from Cinderella's good example, they legitimize (at least ostensibly) the moral context presented in the narrative. Second is what might be termed the heroine's moral genealogy since, as the tale indicates, Cinderella inherits her sweetness and goodness from her deceased mother, "qui était la meilleure personne du monde" (who had been the best person in the world [171]). Third is the extent of her goodness: in the end, she forgives her stepsisters, brings them to the palace, and marries them to "deux grands Seigneurs de la Cour" (two great Noblemen of the Court [177]). And, finally, there is the marriage closure itself, which serves as the ultimate sanction for Cinderella's virtue and beauty. Legitimating indications such as these are widely used in the *contes de fées* (and indeed in many literary fairy tales) to indicate the closure and self-sufficiency of their narrative universe.

The three characteristics of Robert's *l'écriture féerique* are particularly useful for delineating not only the relative specificity of this corpus, but also the nature of the marvelous. Going beyond *thematic* features, this tri-partite definition of the *conte de fées* accounts for the *narrative* or *structural* function of the marvelous. Moreover, by recognizing the crucial role of the heroic couple, this definition reveals, if only implicitly, the importance of sexuality and gender in this corpus. Finally, drawing attention to the mechanisms by which the fairy tales legitimize their "micro-universe," Robert's third criterion allows us to consider how these texts construct ideological systems.

There are, however, two general limitations to this model. First, Robert explicitly excludes from her definition those tales that are either "cautionary" (eg. Perrault's "Le Petit Chaperon rouge") or "tragic" (eg. d'Aulnoy's "L'Isle de la félicité") since in both the misdeed is not redressed, but left intact at the end. Although such tales are in the minority, they are nonetheless significant limit-cases of the use of the marvelous and, as such, deserve to be considered.[9] Second, and more problematic, this definition does not explain the extent to which the *contes de fées* contribute to an estrangement of accepted notions of reality; that is, it does not provide a way of analyzing how these fairy tales can critique or subvert ideological systems and how they can serve a utopian function. Instead, it emphasizes the internal coherence of the "magical order" and the restoration of order – the liquidation of villainy or lack – in the fairy tale's overarching narrative structure. While Robert is absolutely correct, in my view, to underscore the preeminence and redundancy of these two features, her definition does not allow for the contradictory dynamics that are so central to all folk- and fairy tales and, specifically, to the marvelous.

To understand the ambivalent effects of the *merveilleux*, we must first consider its relationship to the esthetic principle of *vraisemblance*.[10] Although often translated as "verisimilitude" or "plausibility," this term had very precise meanings in the context of seventeenth-century France. *Vraisemblance* was the result of the *ut pictura poesis* representational system that dominated artistic practice and theory in early modern Europe. According to this system, imitation was, above all, artful (if not artifice) in that it employed analogy or allegory rather than direct reference. Since the relation between art and nature was mediated by use of specific codes, such as mythology, the result was not truth, but verisimilitude.[11] Accordingly, as Aron Kibédi-Varga has astutely observed, *vraisemblance* could have at least three meanings.[12] First, *vraisemblance* was called to uphold the moral objective of art by refusing the chaos of history in favor of an ideal world in which right always triumphs over wrong. Second, *vraisemblance* served the social order as "tout ce qui est conforme à l'opinion publique" (all that conforms to public opinion [Rapin, quoted in Kibédi-Varga, *Les Poétiques*, 38]), that is, the codification of what is taken for good or common sense. Third, *vraisemblance* could also have ontological ramifications since it implied perfecting real individual species in accordance with a true original. "Extending what is true, bringing it to perfection, these were the goals assigned to *vraisemblance*" (Kibédi-Varga, *Les Poétiques*, 39).

It is fairly obvious that these definitions of plausibility or verisimilitude do not automatically preclude marvelous literature. In other words, the *contes de fées* can indeed be *vraisemblables*. If we recall Robert's three-part definition, only the first criterion, which relies on the intervention of supernatural forces, contradicts *vraisemblance* since it goes against an empirical understanding of reality upheld by "public opinion" or "common sense." The two remaining criteria allow for moral, social, and ontological verisimilitude. Moral *vraisemblance* is affirmed through the highlighting of the heroic couple's destiny (the second criterion), which involves a polarization of characters according to moral and physical traits (eg. good vs. bad, industry vs. laziness, beauty vs. ugliness, and so on). The fact that the physical traits valorized are hyperbolically superlative confirms ontological verisimilitude. Finally, what these traits consist of and how they manifest themselves – be it by birth, education, marriage, or something else – is the domain of the narrative's exclusive fairy-tale order (the third criterion), justified by implicit and explicit social maxims.

Vraisemblance, whether or not it pertains to marvelous literature, is fundamentally ideological. It is determined by dominant public opinion and, thus, serves the interests of the most powerful by construing to their own advantage what is perceived as truth. Not surprisingly, the history of this critical notion in seventeenth-century France is that of an overtly political construct by which the absolutist state exerted control over cultural production. Perhaps the most notorious example of this control occurred with the *Querelle du Cid* (1637), which was largely fought around what was and was not considered to be *vraisemblable* in Corneille's play. This debate also marked the decisive moment when the concept of verisimilitude came to designate obligation, rather than mere plausibility as an abstract referential notion. As Thomas DiPiero has concluded, "the fact that the Académie Française labeled *invraisemblables* sequences in *Le Cid* that are perfectly plausible from a material point of view drives home the point that the literary text was charged with reproducing not extratextual reality in the referential sense ... but an ideology."[13] *Vraisemblance* played no less important a role in the development of prose fiction in this period. Since the novel and other narrative prose genres lacked a clear antecedent in classical literature, not to mention a theoretical justification, their moral utility appeared dubious at best to many critics.[14] *Vraisemblance* was to become the first theoretical concept used to defend prose fiction against accusations of moral depravity by assigning it a fully political function. Most notable in this regard were the heroic novels (*romans*) of the 1640s and 1650s, in which verisimilitude upheld the essential legitimacy of the hereditary nobility and its central place in the conservation and transmission of culture.

By the 1690s and the appearance of the first vogue of fairy tales, the dominance of both *vraisemblance* and *ut pictura poesis* as models of artistic imitation were showing signs of considerable stress. The gradual rejection of these ideals is often attributed to the rise to prominence of the *bourgeoisie*, who were increasingly unable to identify with an esthetic that served the interests of an elite aristocracy.[15] Although the reliance on *vraisemblance* and *ut pictura poesis*, as defined above, did not completely wane until the fall of the *ancien régime*, the second half of the seventeenth century witnessed dramatic shifts away from these esthetic principles. In prose fiction, to cite but one example, many of the *nouvelles* that flourished presented themselves as demystifications of aristocratic and especially court privilege by revealing what was purported to be the secret lives of prominent historical figures. "The *nouvelle* betrayed an undeniably democratizing tendency in its break with the traditions of the *roman* ... If noble readers of the *roman* felt privileged to identify with fictional characters so exclusive as to be locked into a world of their own, readers of the *nouvelle* were called upon to identify with characters whose different stations in life merely dramatized their common humanity" (Harth, *Ideology and Culture*, 190–191). Of course, the changes in the novel correspond to a broader epistemological change that affected all aspects of cultural production. For, the very meaning of what was considered to be "truth" as a general perceptual category was undergoing profound changes in this period. Gradually, truth proclaimed itself objective and renounced the rhetorical trappings of *ut pictura poesis*. *Vraisemblance* was giving way to the *vrai*.

Appearing in the midst of these changes, the *contes de fées* are themselves implicated in the *malaise* about the place and function of *vraisemblance* in literary representation. How this *malaise* manifested itself in the first vogue of fairy tales and, more specifically, the ambivalent impact of the marvelous on verisimilitude can be elucidated by reference to the *Querelle du Merveilleux* (Quarrel of the Marvelous) that arose within theoretical discussions about epic poetry during the seventeenth century. At first glance, the *contes de fées* would seem to have little if anything to do with *Querelle du Merveilleux*. Involving one of the most prestigious literary forms as well as theoretical questions about the very nature of literary representation, this debate seems far removed from a fleeting *mondain* vogue for stylized versions of folk narratives. In spite of the obvious differences, however, the two opposing positions in the Quarrel shed light on what is at stake in the fairy-tale marvelous and the extent to which it is compatible with notions of *vraisemblance*.

The Quarrel of the Marvelous (which actually consisted of a number of incidents) opposed two main points of view concerning the use of the *merveilleux* in epic poetry. On one side were the proponents of the Christian marvelous (*le merveilleux chrétien*) who sought to revive and promote the use of supernatural characters and events from biblical and hagiographic sources (including God, Satan, angels, demons, saints, and sorcerers) while, generally but not always, condemning the use of gods and other figures from Greek and Roman mythology as incompatible with Christian belief.[16] Some of the most vocal advocates for this position were themselves authors of epic

poems that glorified either biblical figures or personages
from French history, including Chapelain (*La Pucelle*, 1655),
Desmarets de Saint-Sorlin (*Clovis, ou la France chrétienne*, 1657;
Marie-Madeleine, 1669), Le Moyne (*Saint Louis*, 1658), and
Perrault (*Saint Paulin, évêque de Nole*, 1686; *Adam*, 1697). On the
other side were the defenders of the so-called pagan marvelous
(*le merveilleux païen*) who either tolerated both the mythological
and Christian traditions (Rapin, Segrais) or promoted the
exclusive use of mythological gods and characters in the epic
(Le Bossu, Boileau).

Central to this quarrel were two very different considerations
of what constituted a plausible *merveilleux*. Whereas the theoreticians of the Christian marvelous posited religious belief as the
necessary condition for *vraisemblance*, those who defended the
pagan marvelous saw in the use of mythological figures the
esthetic beauty that lent essential coherence to the text. More
precisely, advocates of the Christian *merveilleux*, and particularly
Perrault, argued that the plausibility of the marvelous was
relative to the culture in which it was produced. Thus, the
deities of Greek and Roman mythology, they argued, were not
necessary features of the epic, which could accommodate supernatural powers of Christian traditions.[17] Opposing this point of
view were those critics, most notably Boileau, who asserted the
universal value of *la fable* (mythology) not only for the epic but
for literary production as a whole. Yet, contrary to their
opponents', this line of argument justified the mythological
marvelous less as the representation of supernatural events than
as the allegorical transposition of natural and human traits.[18]
Most important, as Boileau warned, was the recognition that
without this symbolic code and the esthetic beauty it afforded
there would be no poetry.[19] For the epic poets and other
defenders of the *merveilleux chrétien*, then, the marvelous was
culturally variable and, consequently, an article of faith concerning Christian and nationalistic dogma. The *vraisemblance* of
the marvelous was first and foremost a matter of religious and
political truth. For the champions of the *merveilleux païen*, by
contrast, the marvelous, although compatible with the "truth"
of moral verisimilitude, was by its very abstraction a universal

trait of poetic beauty rather than a system that required belief. The *merveilleux* was *vraisemblable* primarily because it was esthetically pleasing.

In several respects, the marvelous employed by the *contes de fées* resembles that proposed by theoreticians of the *merveilleux chrétien*. Like the Christian epics, the vogue of fairy tales is a recognition and exploitation of a culturally specific type of marvelous that arises from indigenous French traditions (as opposed to the purported universality of the mythological *merveilleux*).[20] The association of folkloric marvelous with the lowest classes was an important strategic maneuver that afforded a self-affirmation for *mondain* writers and readers, as well as a defense of the "modernist" cause in the *Querelle des Anciens et des Modernes*.[21] Furthermore, both fairy-tale and Christian epic forms of the marvelous depict literal (rather than allegorical) supernatural characters and events. And in both cases, this emphatic use of the *merveilleux* strains and often transgresses the generally accepted bounds of *vraisemblance*. Even the most ardent supporters of Christian epic poetry were wary about "excessive" use of the supernatural on the grounds that it led to falsifying biblical and Christian history or, even worse, making Christian figures conform to mythological models. Of course, the *contes de fées* were hardly in danger of flouting the verisimilitude of religious *doxa*. Nonetheless, critics of the first vogue often expressed disdain for the blatant *invraisemblance* that they associated with the *contes merveilleux* told to children – a criticism, as we will see, that the genre anticipates and plays upon.[22]

In the final analysis, however, the use of the marvelous in the *contes de fées* differs from that in both the mythological and the Christian epic. In these latter forms, the *merveilleux* ultimately conforms to verisimilitude. The mythological marvelous can claim to be plausible on moral and esthetic grounds because its supernatural characters are either widely used conventions or abstract allegories. And even if the Christian epic attempts to uphold moral *vraisemblance* by means of supernatural effects deemed *invraisemblables* from a strictly empirical point of view, it nonetheless makes implausibility a matter of belief in the divine order, and consequently *vraisemblable*. By contrast, the *contes de fées* do not reduce the marvelous to allegorical systems of esthetic, moral, or religious plausibility. Although they do have recourse to a moralizing pretext with the use of interspersed maxims and/or appended final morals, these serve to motivate the representation of individual characters or traits which are thereby plausible, and not the marvelous setting as a whole, which remains *invraisemblable*. Even further, the fairy tales make deliberate use of the marvelous and are, thus, deliberately implausible. This self-conscious and playful use of both the supernatural setting and the moralizing pretext distances any real belief in fairy magic, but also contributes to the readability of the text.

The difference of fairy-tale marvelous from the more prestigious epic reveals the ambivalent function of the first vogue within the late seventeenth-century crisis of *vraisemblance*. On the one hand, the *contes de fées* shore up and remotivate the embattled notion of *vraisemblance*. This is not unlike the reconciliation of the marvelous and plausibility by theoreticians of the epic, which, according to Kibédi-Varga, enabled these latter to counteract the reduction of verisimilitude to the truth of dominant public opinion, expressed as "clarity, the natural, but also banality and monotony."[23] In this sense, the fairy-tale vogue espouses out-dated esthetic and ideological positions. On the other hand, the seventeenth-century *contes de fées* defy norms of *vraisemblance* in their use of an unmotivated marvelous. So doing, they participate in the on-going critique of verisimilitude (in the sense of a restrictive set of ideologies) in late seventeenth-century literary practice.

TEXTS AND BODIES

The textual features of the marvelous both produce and attenuate an estrangement of accepted reality, especially in its literary guise of *vraisemblance*. These contradictory dynamics are apparent in the two distinct traditions of the marvelous on which this corpus draws – the national/folkloric and the "pagan" or mythological.[24] Although elements of the national/folkloric traditions (including tale-types, motifs, and characters) clearly dominate the *contes de fées*, reminiscences of the mythological marvelous (including gods, such as Jupiter and Cupid, and lesser figures, such as Zephyr, who perform supernatural deeds) are also present. Few other literary or artistic forms use marvelous elements from more than one tradition to the extent that do the fairy tales.[25] More important, the contrast between the "high" repertory of mythological figures and the "low" inventory of folkloric types becomes one between esthetically plausible and implausible traditions. The diegetic and rhetorical uses of Greek and Roman mythology appear as part of a widely acknowledged code whose supernatural content is fully *vraisemblable* for the elite readers of the first vogue.[26] The same is not true, however, for the national/folkloric traditions since they represent a culture that is largely alien or at least marginal in relation to the period's canonical literary intertexts. Fairies and other supernatural figures of national origin do appear in poetry, opera, and plays during the seventeenth century, most notably in *pièces à machines* (especially those of the Théâtre Italien before Louis XIV ordered it closed in 1697).[27] In such genres, as in the fairy tales, the national/folkloric *merveilleux* never attains the prestige or esthetic *vraisemblance* of mythology. However, unlike the other genres, the *contes de fées* intensify the implausibility of the national/folkloric tradition by using it to form a context that transcends a "realistic" setting.

Although the marvelous can take the form of characters, objects, or physical elements, supernatural powers are usually attributed to an agent, principally fairies, but also ogres, giants, gnomes, sorcerers, anthropomorphic animals, and mythological figures. In those few tales without an agent, an object with "marvelous" qualities (such as the magic key in Perrault's "La Barbe bleue" [Blue Beard]) creates the requisite misfortune or lack and/or liquidates it. The agents of the marvelous in the *contes de fées* can serve any of four basic functions as either "helpers" or "opponents" to the hero/heroine:[28] (1) to predict his/her future; (2) to serve as advisors to the hero/heroine; (3) to impose a hindrance or obstacle that prevents the hero/heroine from reaching the goal of his/her quest; (4) to personally help him/her overcome the obstacle. This last function can be performed in two ways, by giving a "gift" (magical object or powers) to the hero/heroine and/or by intervening directly on his/her behalf. Throughout the 114 *contes de fées*, the specific roles played by the agents vary widely. In some tales, such as Perrault's "La Belle au bois dormant" (Sleeping Beauty), fairies appear only briefly at the beginning of the story to endow the princess with gifts that determine her future. In others, such as d'Aulnoy's "Le Nain jaune" (The Yellow Dwarf), all four of the above functions are fulfilled and hardly a moment passes without recourse to marvelous characters – the yellow dwarf himself, a good syren, twenty-four nymphs guarding a steel tower, a mysterious voice – as well as a magical (and *almost* invincible) sword. Of course, marvelous agents and the four narrative roles they play not only defy reality and *vraisemblance*, they are also the most powerful means by which these norms can be reaffirmed. The moral dichotomy that divides "helpers" from "opponents" is itself a consequence of such norms, but these agents also actively impose a familiar social order within the narrative. Helpers, for instance, often return kingdoms to their "rightful" rulers or arrange the marriage of the hero and heroine, to name but two of the most common fairy-tale closures.

Just as there is a wide variety of marvelous agents, so too are there numerous types of marvelous actions and events. Magical modes of travel (eg. Petit Poucet's seven-league boots), gifts enhancing physical traits (the senses, intelligence, strength) and manipulation of space (eg. magical construction or destruction of castles) are but a few of the many manifestations of the marvelous. Of all these, however, metamorphosis is among the most prominent. Not only are main characters transformed into other beings or given the power to transform others, but the marvelous agents often use their powers to change their own appearance. In the majority of cases, metamorphosis is used as an obstacle – the misfortune or lack – central to the tale's narrative structure, as when a hero or heroine is transformed into another being as part of an evil spell (eg. d'Aulnoy's "Serpentin vert" [Green Serpent] or "La Biche au bois" [The Doe in the Woods]) or when an opponent transforms him- or herself into a monstrous figure to overpower the hero/heroine (eg. Le Noble's "L'Apprenti magicien" [The Magician's Apprentice]).[29] Yet, metamorphosis can also be used to overcome the obstacle, as when the hero and heroine in d'Aulnoy's "L'Oranger et l'abeille" (The Orange Tree and the Bee) use a wand to disguise themselves three times in order to elude their captors. Common to all of these uses of metamorphosis is a positing of the marvelous as an abnormal state that leads to or results in (what is presented as) normalcy. For instance, when the hero and heroine in "L'Oranger et l'abeille" transform themselves into an orange tree and a bee, respectively, they lose the magic wand and are unable to regain their human form. Their adventures in this guise represent an integral part of their quest, leading finally to their marriage. When metamorphosis is imposed on the hero/heroine as an obstacle or a means of overcoming it, the altered physical state serves an initiatory function since it prepares him/her to assume a preordained place in the reestablished order of the tale's conclusion. These two most common uses of metamorphosis are, then, dramatic illustrations of the fairy tales' ambivalent treatment of *vraisemblance*. The abnormal masks the normal, but the abnormal also paves the way for the normal. *Vraisemblance* is inseparable from *invraisemblance*.

More important still, metamorphosis highlights the importance that the body acquires in the *contes de fées*, and indeed in all fantasy literature. As forms of writing predicated on manipulating what is ordinarily considered to be inexorable, fantasy, and particularly the seventeenth-century French fairy tales, display a singular fascination with the body as a "natural" essence that imparts meaning and truth. Paradoxically, by positing the body as the inherent site of identity, these genres reveal the extent to which identity is itself a necessary differentiation from otherness in its physical form. In other words, they show the body to be a socially constructed unit of significance lacking an inherent essence. As such, representations of the body become a fundamental means by which moral, social, and ontological *vraisemblance* are both upheld and transgressed. What constitutes the acceptable and the unacceptable body is part and parcel of the same dominant social consensus that determines what is and is not plausible. By extension, then, the body is the point at which the ambivalent nostalgic and utopian impulses of the *contes de fées* converge and come into conflict. And, as we will see, this conflict is centered around the ways in which the marvelous defines the gendered body as both essence and social construct.

Since fairy-tale narratives are structured around a central misfortune or lack, it is not surprising that the bodies of heroes and heroines are often subjected to violence. In fact, the supernatural deeds performed by opponents (evil fairies, ogres, magicians, etc.) are usually intended to make the protagonist(s) suffer. Although the seventeenth-century *contes de fées* are generally considered to contain less violence than many other literary fairy tales,[30] violence and the physical suffering it induces are nonetheless portrayed in this corpus, most notably in tales by d'Aulnoy, La Force, Lhéritier, and Perrault.[31] Except in the case of cautionary or tragic tales, suffering is always overcome, and usually by supernatural means that are the obverse of violence and suffering, namely bodily comfort and pleasure. Accordingly, their representation might be thought to expel the fear they inspire, the fear of the body's vulnerability. Through their representation, such fears are banished and replaced by the assurance of marvelous pleasures.

This process of representation and expulsion is part of a broader mechanism of fantasy literature that Rosemary Jackson has linked to desire:

In expressing desire, fantasy can operate in two ways (according to the different meanings of "express"): it can *tell of,* manifest or show desire (expression in the sense of portrayal, representation, manifestation, linguistic utterance, mention, description), or it can *expel* desire, when this desire is a disturbing element which threatens cultural order and continuity (expression in the sense of pressing out, squeezing, expulsion, getting rid of something by force). In many cases, fantastic literature fulfills both functions at once, for desire can be "expelled" through having been "told of" and thus vicariously experienced by author and reader. (*Fantasy*, 3–4)

There are at least two reasons why Jackson's model of desire in fantasy literature is useful for understanding the representations of the body in the *contes de fées*. First, the expulsion of culturally disruptive desires by their representation can be extended to the way the depiction of (good and evil) supernatural powers abate fears about the body. As both a source and an object of desire, the body of "normal" human proportions can only be understood or reaffirmed as such when it has been subjected to or put into contact with superhuman forces. Second, this model posits that the desires represented and/or expelled in fantasy literature have a connection with readers and writers as wish-fulfillment or what Jackson terms vicarious experience. Representations of the body in the marvelous context of the fairy tale are, thus, imbued with desires as well as fears. However, in its emphasis on the *expulsion* of desires, this model does not account for the ambivalent effects of the marvelous on these representations. Far from simply reaffirming normal (or plausible) conceptions of the body (as Jackson's model would imply), the *contes de fées* are also capable of revising if not contesting these conceptions. A specific example will help to illustrate the complex ramifications of these representations in the vogue.

La Force's tale "Plus Belle que Fée" (More Beautiful than a Fairy), named for the heroine, expels the fear of physical suffering and replaces it with the pleasures of the marvelous. Plus Belle que Fée is ordered to carry out three seemingly fatal tasks by the evil fairy Nabote; but each time, her magical admirer Phraates intervenes to accomplish the task for her and to offer her innumerable pleasures – magnificent feasts, beautiful apartments, pastoral retreats – not to mention a magic wand to liberate the Reine du pays des fées, who in turn defeats Nabote. Not only are each of Nabote's plans to inflict suffering and death on Plus Belle que Fée immediately cut short, but the "marvelous" pleasures given to the heroine make her simultaneously human and superhuman. Her very name echoes the ambiguous state of her body, for she is, as the text repeatedly emphasizes, a human, born to ordinary mortals; yet her beauty surpasses even that of the most beautiful fairies. But the story does not end here. For Plus Belle que Fée is guaranteed eternal life and beauty when she acquires some *eau de vie immortelle*

(water of immortal life) and *fard de jeunesse* (youth cream).
With the assurance of an unchanging body, her superhuman
humanity becomes, finally and quite simply, superhuman.

Throughout the *contes de fées*, the body is represented in its
metonymic relations to various sorts of pleasure. For Plus Belle
que Fée, immortality is desirable because it ensures continued
pleasures like those her magical lover provides throughout her
imprisonment. In La Force's tale and in many others (especially
by the *conteuses*), the protagonist's pleasures are described in
spatial terms, thus further linking him/her to the marvelous
context of the tale. Instead of concentrating on the heroine's
own reactions, the narrative transposes these onto the superlative objects in space, which are described in detail. Consider,
for instance, the following passage in which Plus Belle que Fée
and her companion Désirs enter a room provided for them by
Phraates:

Il y avait à un des bouts de cette charmante chambre, une table
couverte de tout ce qui pouvait contenter la délicatesse du goût, et
deux fontaines de liqueurs qui coulaient dans des bassins de porphyre.
Les jeunes princesses s'assirent dans deux chaises d'ivoire, enrichies
d'émeraudes; elles mangèrent avec appétit, et quand elles eurent
soupé, la table disparut, et il s'éleva à la place où elle était un bain
délicieux, où elles se mirent toutes deux. A six pas de là on voyait une
superbe toilette, et de grandes mannes d'or trat, toutes pleines de
linge d'une propreté à donner envie de s'en servir. Un lit d'une forme
singulière, et d'une richesse extraordinaire, terminait cette merveilleuse chambre, qui était bordée d'orangers dans des caisses d'or
garnies de rubis, et des colonnes de cornaline soutenaient tout autour
la voûte somptueuse de cette chambre: elles n'étaient séparées que
par de grandes glaces de cristal, qui prenaient depuis le bas jusques
en haut. Quelques consoles de matières rares portaient des vases de
pierreries pleins de toutes sortes de fleurs.

At one end of this charming room were a table covered with
everything that could satisfy the most delicate taste and two fountains
of liqueurs that flowed into porphyry basins. The young princesses sat
down on two ivory chairs that were inlaid with emeralds. They ate
heartily. When they had finished, the table vanished, and in its place
there appeared a delightful bath, which they both stepped into. Just
six paces away stood a magnificent washstand and large golden wicker
baskets completely filled with linen so clean it made one want to use

it. A bed of singular shape and extraordinary richness finished off this marvelous room, which was surrounded by orange trees in golden boxes garnished with rubies. This room's sumptuous vault was supported all around by cornalin columns which were only separated by large crystal mirrors that stretched from the floor to the ceiling. Jewel vases filled with a variety of flowers rested upon several consoles of rare material.[32]

In hyperbolic passages such as this one, the objects described stand in a metonymic relation to the characters who observe them and for whom they are intended. The superlative nature of the objects is presumed to indicate the physical pleasure they offer, such as the description of "linen so clean it made one want to use it." The table of food, the fountains of liqueurs, the jewel-encrusted chairs, the bathtubs, linen, and mirrors are all concrete extensions of the princesses' bodies. They are pleasures that firmly anchor the two women in the marvelous context literalized in the room offered by Phraates. Sumptuous descriptions such as this one situate the body within the self-enclosed fairy-tale order created by the marvelous.

To the twentieth-century reader, such descriptions are admittedly tedious; but to the late-seventeenth-century reader, they were decidedly nostalgic. Micheline Cuénin and Chantal Morlet-Chantalat have shown that detailed narrative depictions of châteaux and spatial settings drop off sharply in prose fiction after 1660.[33] While such descriptions figure prominently in the pastoral and heroic novels of the first half of the seventeenth century and often allegorize the moral qualities of inhabitants, dwellings and other locations appear much less frequently in the *nouvelles* and *histoires* of the second half of the century. When they do, they serve primarily as *effets de réel* with direct relevance to the plot structure (Cuénin and Morlet-Chantalat, "Châteaux et romans," 111). Hence, "Plus Belle que Fée" and other seventeenth-century *contes de fées* go against the trend toward fewer and more realistic descriptions and, at first glance, appear to return to the spatial allegorizations of the earlier *romans*. In contrast to these latter forms, the fairy tales portray not moral qualities, but the material and physical pleasures intended for the hero/heroine. More than signs of class elitism or even the superlative nature of the heroic couple, however, spatial descriptions like the one in "Plus Belle que Fée" represent a nostalgic conception of the body, made possible by the manipulation of reality in the marvelous. Following Susan Stewart's observation that nostalgia is capable of "generat[ing] significant objects" that in turn "transform ... the very boundary, or outline of the self" (*On Longing*, xi), we can conclude that the sumptuous presentation of Plus Belle que Fée's room is a nostalgic extension and material grounding of the heroine's body that also fuels desires and fantasies.

In addition to the pleasures that replace the intended suffering from her tasks, the narrative repeatedly describes Plus Belle que Fée's astonishment at the marvels that surround her (indeed, *étonnée* [astonished] becomes the most common epithet to describe her in the text). Expressions of surprise at the supernatural are commonplace in the *contes de fées*. By contrast, such reactions are much less frequent or totally absent in most other folk- and fairy tales, where the marvelous context is taken for granted.[34] By acting out the etymological sense of "marvelous" (>*mirabilia*) as amazement, the fairy-tale protagonists point to what exceeds the "normal" body of the fairy-tale order. The depiction of astonishment, then, indicates the role the marvelous plays in transporting the body beyond the realm of the human and the marvelous. It suggests that when the body is transformed by the marvelous, it is infused with utopian surplus or potential, which is first of all transcendence, however limited and illusory, from the limits – the violence, suffering and death – of the real body.

In "Plus Belle que Fée," the utopian excess of the heroine's body is also expressed in terms of gender difference. To be sure, heroines of superlative beauty are synonymous with fairy tales, and the emphasis on female beauty is hardly utopian in and of itself. In the context of seventeenth-century salon circles, however, the name "Plus Belle que Fée" would have had particular resonance for readers, since the title "fée" was often used to compliment *hôtesses* (Delaporte, *Du Merveilleux*, 45–46). In one sense, then, the name of La Force's heroine is a humorous conceit that recuperates from sociable conversation a title itself taken from fantasy literature (Delaporte identifies the principal source as *Amadis de Gaule* [*Du Merveilleux*, 44]). In another sense, however, this name identifies the heroine with salon women and then both literalizes and exaggerates the physical powers and pleasures designated by the metaphoric title "*fée*." Understood in the context of attacks against sociable society and women's role in it, Plus Belle que Fée's superlative body provides a possible compensation or even vicarious experience for readers desiring a rebirth of the heyday of the salon.[35]

Yet, the representation of Plus Belle que Fée's body is simultaneously tinged with nostalgia. We have already seen how the spatial descriptions, which are metonymic extensions of the heroine, reflect an archaic fantasy. Just as nostalgic is her gendered role in relation to Phraates, her helper who, in the end, becomes her husband. Although Plus Belle que Fée does liberate the Reine du pays des fées, throughout most of the tale she assumes the role of the beloved who is served by a diligent courtly lover. In La Force's tale, the courtly love model, a central nostalgic topos of the vogue, is intimately connected with the utopian excess of the heroine and her body. The pleasures that Plus Belle que Fée enjoys, and the immortality she acquires, are offered to her by Phraates. The heroine's utopian potential is inseparable and indeed dependent upon her suitor's nostalgic role.

Arguably, all manifestations of fantasy literature, from whatever historical period and artistic medium, involve a rethinking of the body as that which is unimaginable and unattainable, feared and desired. At the same time, representations of the body reveal the full extent of the powers as well as the constraints of fantasy and, more specifically, the marvelous. In both defying and reaffirming literary codes of reality, the marvelous both reconceives and reproduces, first of all, what a culture defines as the body. Thus, within the seventeenth-century fairy tales, the ambivalence of the *merveilleux* toward *vraisemblance* is also an ambivalence toward representations of the body. The marvelous always begins as an explicit subversion of plausibility, and thus of what is physically possible. But the uses to which this subversion is put vary. The implausibility of the marvelous can dissolve into plausibility of one kind or another, flout plausibility, or do both at the same time. The representations of the body can, ultimately, conform to the prevailing moral, social, and ontological codes of verisimilitude, defy them, or maintain an uneasy tension between conformity and resistance. Of course, the social construction of the body invokes both desires and fears. Thus, when imagining the body, the marvelous expresses desires and expels fears – it expresses desires in order to expel fears, but it also expresses desires in order to satisfy them. In short, it provides a wish-fulfillment of which the body is the chief subject and object. By exploring the ambiguous potential of the marvelous to "produce" bodies, and more generally the "real," we can begin to glimpse the attraction of late seventeenth-century France for the *contes de fées*.

CHAPTER 2

Reading (and) the ironies of the marvelous

What does the marvelous mean? How is one to interpret the marvelous? These questions are at the heart of many studies devoted to folk- and fairy tales. From the numerous folkloristic approaches to structuralist methodologies and from traditional literary history to psychoanalytic perspectives, the question of how to interpret the marvelous is a central and often contentious issue. Yet, common to all these critical tendencies is the assumption that the marvelous presents itself as meaning "otherwise," as meaning something other than what it designates literally. Of course, from this perspective, marvelous literature is no different from any other literary text in that it can be read simultaneously in two different ways – *referentially* (as referring to its own fictional context) and *figuratively* (as meaning something other than its reference and, thus, requiring interpretation). Within the seventeenth-century fairy tales, it is the marvelous that highlights the possibility of figurative readings. As such, the marvelous becomes an emphatic sign of the readability, that is, the figurability or interpretability, of the text.[1]

In chapter 1, I argued that the links between the marvelous and *vraisemblance* are highly ambivalent: the *merveilleux* can both uphold and disrupt the social outlook that literary plausibility came to signify in seventeenth-century France. To discern this ambivalence, however, is to acknowledge at least tacitly the readability of this corpus and, specifically, the marvelous that characterizes it. The *merveilleux* is what provides a new or at least different cover for the plausible; yet, it can also point toward what exceeds this literary (and thus ideological) code. In the first case, interpretation distinguishes the familiar within the supernatural setting; in the second, interpretation takes this setting as the figure of something other than what is codified by *vraisemblance*. The nostalgic and utopian longings which I argue are so central to the seventeenth-century fairy tales are, then, effects of reading or interpretation. They are produced when the fairy tales' marvelous universe is understood (ie. interpreted) as being more than the literal structure of the narrative.

Throughout the vogue, irony is one of the most important means by which readability is produced, and this irony is directed above all at the marvelous, the sign *par excellence* of all that is unacceptable in the *conte de fées* for an elite readership – its *invraisemblance*, and specifically its childishness and roots in peasant folklore. Among the fairy tales, use of explicit irony varies considerably. Although some writers, especially d'Aulnoy, Lhéritier, and Perrault, create an ironic (and humorous) distance from traditional folkloric *merveilleux*, most do not, or at least not overtly. Nonetheless, I will argue in this chapter that the readability of the entire vogue is predicated in part on what I will term the infantilizing and moralizing pretexts of the genre.[2] These pretexts function ironically by mimicking a discourse so as to subvert it and reinvest it with a different meaning. They are alibis to tell something other with the marvelous than childish tales and moral lessons and are integral parts of the "horizon of expectations" within which the vogue was read. To date, however, relatively few critics have recognized the importance of irony in the corpus of *contes de fées* as a whole (over and beyond Perrault's tales).[3] And yet, irony, and specifically, the ironic pretexts are crucial to the interpretation of the marvelous. Since it presupposes an ironic reading that extends to the fairy-tale text as a whole, the marvelous is a crucial part of what might be called the genre's self-marginalization, the autoreferential undercutting of its literary and social status that paradoxically legitimizes its (albeit liminal) existence. As we will see, irony not only vindicates the writing and reading of fairy tales, it also reveals the role of the marvelous in *expressing* (in the two senses of the word) desires and fears.[4]

INFANTILE TEXTS AND ADULT CONTEXTS

From our own cultural vantage-point, in which fairy tales are synonymous with children's literature, it is rather difficult to imagine adults wanting to read fairy tales. From all appearances, this awareness was far from alien to seventeenth-century consciousness, which readily associated *contes de fées* with tales told to children. In Molière's *Le Malade imaginaire*, for instance, little Louison offers to tell her grandfather, Argan, "le conte de *Peau d'Ane*, ou bien la fable du *Corbeau et du Renard*" (the tale of *Donkey-skin* or the fable of the *Crow and the Fox* [Act 2, Scene 8]), thus adding to the humor of the scene by inverting the usual storytelling positions – by suggesting that her grandfather, an adult, listen to and she, a child, recite texts generally told *to* children (and in the case of "Peau d'Ane" a tale about incestuous desire to boot). Moreover, it appears that the association of folk- and fairy tales with an archetypal storytelling for children was an integral part of the salon game from which the first vogue (probably) originated. In La Force's *Les Jeux d'esprit*, the Princess of Conty seems to be inspired by the child-like quality of the games (which include the telling of fairy tales) she proposes for her salon: "Il n'y a pas un de nous qui ne s'y soit amusé mille fois en son enfance, mais je voudrais que dans ces jeux il y eût de l'esprit et du plaisir" (Each of us enjoyed them in our childhood, but I would like there to be wit and pleasure in these games).[5] Central to both the oral and written vogue of fairy tales, then, is an infantilizing pretext that couches the stories told in irony, and even humor. In other words, the "horizon of expectations" governing the reception of the *contes de fées* in seventeenth-century France stipulated that readers recognize infantilization and its irony.

At first glance, only the inaugural *contes de fées* explicitly highlight the genre's infantilizing pretext. The fact that the fairy tales published thereafter almost entirely refrain from overt irony about infantilizing storytelling is in part a sign of the genre's increased popularity and legitimacy. But whereas the signs of an ironic reading (more or less) disappear, the reception of the *contes de fées* continues to be predicated implicitly on an ironic infantilization, as suggested by allusions to children's storytelling as well as frontispieces depicting adult storytellers with an audience of children.[6] However, in the inaugural tales of the vogue by d'Aulnoy, La Force, Lhéritier, and Perrault the play on the genre's association with children is accomplished through such devices as vocabulary and parenthesis.[7] Two brief examples will make my point here.

While infantile vocabulary is found in the works of all four writers, it is most frequent and visible in d'Aulnoy's narratives. Childish words are often substituted for their standard equivalents (eg. *"maman"* and *"papa"* for *mère* and *père)*,[8] and their comic potential is exploited. In "La Princesse Rosette" (Princess Rosette), for instance, after the mutinied crew throws the sleeping heroine overboard with her mattress, the narrator intervenes to explain:

Mais ce qu'il y a d'heureux, c'est que son lit de plume était fait de plumes de phénix, qui sont fort rares, et qui ont cette propriété, qu'elles ne vont jamais au fond de l'eau; de sorte qu'elle nageait dans son lit, comme si elle eût été dans un bateau. L'eau pourtant mouillait peu à peu son lit de plume, puis le matelas; et Rosette sentant l'eau, elle eut peur d'avoir fait pipi au dodo, et d'être grondée.

Fortunately, her bed was stuffed with phoenix feathers, which are extremely rare and are known to never sink in water. Consequently, she swam in her bed as if she were in a boat. Little by little, however, the water soaked her featherbed and then the mattress. And when Rosette felt the water, she was afraid she'd gone pipi in her sleep and that she'd be scolded.[9]

In the larger structure of the tale, this passage ultimately counteracts any definitive infantilization by emphasizing its role as extraneous detail.[10] For this brief instant, though, even a fairy-tale heroine cannot escape the terrors of childhood, and this playful thought reaffirms adult readers' sense of superiority.

Ironic distancing is also produced by parentheses, which create the impression of a closed storytelling event by evoking child-like expectations. In Lhéritier's "Les Enchantements de l'éloquence" (The Enchantments of Eloquence), the narrator comments on the anachronistic rifle with which a young prince (the hero) accidently shot the heroine:

Quelque critique va dire apparemment que ce chasseur n'avait point de fusil, puisque du temps des fées, on n'avait pas encore l'usage de l'artillerie. Je connais des savants si scrupuleux qu'ils ne laisseraient pas finir un conte sans se récrier sur cet anachronisme; mais ... mesdames les fées pouvaient bien avoir fait là quelqu'un de leurs coups. On va voir bien d'autres merveilles: elles auraient bien pu encore faire celle-là ...

Some critic will surely point out that this hunter did not have a rifle since at the time when fairies lived the use of firearms didn't exist yet. I know some scholars who are so scrupulous that they wouldn't wait until the end of a tale to denounce this anachronism. But ... Mesdames the fairies could very well have accomplished one of their deeds here. We shall see many other marvels: they would have been more than capable of doing that one ...[11]

Referring to a hypothetical oral storytelling scene, the narrator defends her tale by stressing the verisimilitude of its *merveilleux*. But this attempt to rationalize the story's implausibility is designed to draw attention to itself, and is further undercut by the narrator later: "Cependant il est vrai que l'arme dont Blanche fut blessée n'était point une arme à feu, car un historien doit toujours dire la vérité, quoique j'en sache assez qui y manquent ..." (However, it is true that the weapon that wounded Blanche was not a firearm, for a historian must always tell the truth, even if I know plenty who fail to do so [251]). Valorizing her own purported adherence to historical truth, the narrator foregrounds and, thus, pokes fun at the fairies' supernatural powers. The reader is presumed to follow the narrator's allusions to her adversaries (the scrupulous scholars and the untrustworthy historians) and to participate in the game mocking the belief in fairy magic.[12]

Whether or not the infantilizing pretext is explicitly highlighted and subverted (as it is in the preceding examples), the ironic reception it presupposes results in a strategic marginalization of the *contes de fées*. It allows readers to enjoy but also to disavow, to advocate but also deny the genre's playfulness. More precisely, it allows readers to disavow *in order to* enjoy, to deny *in order to* advocate a narrative form thought to exist for children alone. Proof of this defensive posture and the appropriation it allowed adult readers is to be found in an excoriating critique of the fairy-tale vogue by the Abbé de Bellegarde on grounds that it is utterly childish:

> Nous avons à nous reprocher la fureur avec laquelle on a lu en France pendant quelque temps les Contes des Fées ... Ce qui n'avait été inventé que pour divertir les enfants, est devenu tout à coup l'amusement des personnes les plus sérieuses. La Cour s'est laissée infatuer de ces sottises; la ville a suivi le mauvais exemple de la Cour, et a lu, avec avidité, ces aventures monstrueuses.

> We should be ashamed of the fury with which Fairy Tales have been read in France during the last few years ... What had been invented for the sole purpose of entertaining children has all of a sudden become the amusement of the most serious of people. The Court let itself be infatuated with these stupidities; the city followed the Court's bad example and avidly read these monstrous adventures.[13]

Ironically, this critique is more interesting for what it fails to do than for what it does. In his haste to reject the genre, Bellegarde does not pause to consider *why* it appeals to so many readers, and even less so to conceive that the tales' supposed "stupidities" and "monstrous adventures" might have other meanings. This critic, then, does not (wish to) see that adults *want* to read child-like texts and that they purport to do so ironically. Since he does not perceive the possibility of irony, Bellegarde cannot entertain the idea that the genre's infantilization contributes to a rereading of the marvelous, to a reimagining or even a rejection of reality and *vraisemblance*.

Yet, Bellegarde may not have been completely off the mark in his assessment of the fairy-tale vogue. For, even if adults read the infantilizing pretext ironically, they cannot, I will argue, totally extricate themselves from an infantile point of view. This ambiguity appears in several of the manifestoes for the *contes de fées*. In what is perhaps the most elaborate but also the most ironic of the theoretical justifications for the seventeenth-century fairy tale, the *Préface* to Perrault's *Contes en vers* defends French folk tales, the "contes que nos aïeux ont inventés pour leurs Enfants" (the tales that our forefathers invented for their Children[14] by describing how these young listeners convert stories into moral value:

Quelques frivoles et bizarres que soient toutes ces Fables dans leurs aventures, il est certain qu'elles excitent dans les Enfants le désir de ressembler à ceux qu'ils voient devenir heureux, et en même temps la crainte des malheurs où les méchants sont tombés par leur méchanceté. N'est-il pas louable à des Pères et à des Mères, lorsque leurs Enfants ne sont pas encore capables de goûter les vérités solides et dénuées de tous agréments, de les leur faire aimer, et si cela se peut dire, les leur faire avaler, en les enveloppant dans des récits agréables et proportionnés à la faiblesse de leur âge? ... Ce sont des semences qu'on jette qui ne produisent d'abord que des mouvements de joie et de tristesse, mais dont il ne manque guère d'éclore de bonnes inclinations.

However frivolous and bizarre all these Fables may be in their adventures, it is certain that they arouse in Children the desire to resemble those whom they see become happy, and at the same time, the fear of the misfortunes into which the wicked have fallen, because of their wickedness. Is it not praiseworthy for Fathers and Mothers, when their Children are not yet capable of appreciating solid truths which are stripped of any ornamentation, to make the children like them, and if one might say, to make them swallow them, by wrapping them in tales which are enjoyable and proportioned to the weakness of their young age? ... These are seeds that one sows, which at first produce only feelings of joy or sorrow, but which do not fail to bloom into good inclinations. (52; 122)

Hardly a more efficient model of moral instruction through literature could be imagined. The effect of the tale is immediate: just as soon as children are captivated, they are initiated into ideological norms. While this reception "proves" the moral efficacy of folk- and fairy tales, it also purports to explain how children read. Children experience the pleasures and fears of the heroes and heroines they hear/read about because they cannot help but identify with these characters. The text has an immediate, if not intuitive effect on them. But what of the adult readers for whom this theoretical explanation and, indeed, the entire corpus of *contes de fées* were intended?

Perrault concludes his *Préface* with a poem attributed to "une jeune Demoiselle de beaucoup d'esprit" (a young Lady of great wit [52; 122]), who is none other than his niece, the *conteuse* Marie-Jeanne Lhéritier de Villandon.[15] In this concluding

poem, Lhéritier compares the pleasure she felt as an adult and
a child when told "Peau d'Ane" (which, in the seventeenth
century designated not only a particular literary and folkloric
motif, but folktales in general):

> Le Conte de Peau d'Ane est ici raconté
> Avec tant de naïveté,
> Qu'il ne m'a pas moins divertie,
> Que quand auprès du feu ma Nourrice ou ma Mie
> Tenaient en le faisant mon esprit enchanté.

The Tale of Donkey-skin is here told / With such naïveté, / That it
did not entertain me less / Than when, near the hearth, my Nurse or
my Governess / Held my mind enchanted by telling it. (52–53; 122)

Because of the tale's *naïveté* – its "natural" simplicity of expression – the adult admits to having felt as if she were a child while
reading the tale. But since she recognizes – and exposes – the
conte's seductiveness, she assumes a critical distance that is
further confirmed in the second part of the poem when she
acknowledges the satire in Perrault's tale.[16] Ostensibly, this
critical distance makes the child-like pleasure of the tale
accessible and acceptable to the adult reader. It is ironic
because the position of the narratee is a site of child-like
pleasure that is transcended by and converted into adult
pleasure. However, there is an irony of the irony of critical
distance and the (adult) pleasure it procures: ultimately it
cannot be differentiated from children's pleasure. The "pas
moins" in "il ne m'a point moins divertie" is a sign of this
ambiguity: it can indicate the difference as well as the similarity
of the two storytelling scenes.

   This ambiguity or irony is crucial in the oft-cited final verses
of La Fontaine's "Le Pouvoir des fables" (VIII, 4), in which an
orator, unable to capture the attention of his audience by
rhetorical eloquence, resorts to a child's tale:

> Si *Peau d'Ane* m'était conté,
> J'y prendrais un plaisir extrême.
> Le monde est vieux, dit-on; je le crois, cependant
> Il le faut amuser encor comme un enfant.

If *Donkey-skin* were told me, / I would take great pleasure in it. / The world is old, they say; I believe so, and yet / It still needs to be amused like a child.[17])

Given the opportunity to hear a fairy tale, the narrative voice would gladly slip into an infantile persona. But the fabulist tells us this to demonstrate that adults can only be persuaded rhetorically if they are treated like children. Now within the fable, this final moral has a strategic oppositional function.[18] Yet, it also reveals a duplicity within the psyche of the fabulist: he affirms the capacity of fairy tales like "Peau d'Ane" to sway adult readers because he is himself swayed by infantile narratives such as these. He counsels adults on how to persuade other adults by treating them like the children they resemble, which he proves by admitting his own infantile penchant for "Peau d'Ane".

The narrative voice in La Fontaine's fable dramatizes the irony of the irony of the infantilizing pretext that conditions the reception of the vogue of *contes de fées*. Adults read child-like texts ironically; however, the pleasure they afford assimilates adults to children. Adults distance themselves but do not and cannot escape from the infantilizing narration of fairy tales and the pleasure it procures. Since this pleasure is inseparable from (if not synonymous with) the marvelous, it follows that adult readers are simultaneously disdainful of it and drawn to it. Or, as it would be more accurate to say, adults reject a *merveilleux* that is marginal, because infantile, the better to remain seduced by it. Interpreted ironically, the infantilizing pretext is a justification for writing and reading fairy tales. But this very justification is itself ironic since, for adult writers and readers, the infantile marvelous has the potential for wish-fulfillment. If irony is the sign of adult identity in these texts, is it perhaps because it is also the sign of the contingency of adulthood on childhood, and the adult's inescapable desire to "regress" to that state?

IRONIC MORALS

Perhaps the most direct way that the *contes de fées* appeal to adult readers is through the moralizing pretext represented by final versed morals as well as maxims interspersed throughout the text. Roughly half of the tales contain a final versed moral. Among those writers who do not make use of this convention – most notably, d'Auneuil, Mailly, and Nodot – maxims inter-calated at various points in the narrative often serve a function similar to the final moral. As signs of the tales' "literariness," these devices perform an ironic reading of the marvelous narrative by extracting from it a non-marvelous *exemplum* applicable above all to adults. From the *invraisemblance* of the marvelous, they derive, at least ostensibly, a moral and/or social *vraisemblance*. At the same time, of course, these devices supercede the marvelous by suggesting its instrumentality.[19]

Now the use of morals and maxims in this way is not unlike that in the more famous example of La Fontaine's *Fables*, and, more generally, a long tradition of justifying literature by emphasizing its didactic and/or pedagogical value. The presence of these devices indicates that the genre is founded on the critical ideal of *dulce et utile*, according to which the work of art was to be both pleasing and instructive, pleasing in order to be instructive. But in the case of the *contes de fées*, the reliance on such a commonplace is fraught with ambiguity. In the *Préface* to his *Contes en vers*, Perrault relies on the commonplace of *dulce et utile* in order to counter the attacks on the fairy tale by the Ancients with the opinions of the "gens de bon goût" (persons with good taste), who "ont été bien aises de remarquer que ces bagatelles n'étaient pas de pures bagatelles, qu'elles renfer-maient une morale utile, et que le récit enjoué dont elles étaient enveloppées n'avait été choisi que pour les faire entrer plus agréablement dans l'esprit et d'une manière qui instruisît et divertît tout ensemble" ([who] have been pleased to notice that these *bagatelles* were not pure *bagatelles*, that they incorporated a useful moral, and that the light story in which they were enveloped was chosen only to make them enter more agreeably into the imagination, and in a manner which both instructs and entertains [49; 120–121]). Following this formulation, the final moral (about which nothing is ever explicitly mentioned in this preface) would be a "natural" restatement of the implicit moral embedded in the tale. In this account, then, the marvelous is but a cover for this moral, it is nothing more than an accessory to the "real" meaning of the tale. Related to the *dulce et utile* motif is the assertion that the tales depict the triumph of virtue over vice, an assertion found repeatedly throughout the *contes de fées* as a defense of the genre on moral grounds.[20] "Partout la vertu y est récompensée, et partout le vice y est puni" (Everywhere virtue is rewarded, and everywhere vice is punished [51; 121–122]), declares Perrault in his *Préface*. In both of these critical commonplaces, the marvelous as literal meaning is deemphasized in deference to a superior moral (and, one should add, figurative) meaning. According to the logic of these clichés, the morals and maxims extract and distance the exemplary meaning from the marvelous setting. Yet, the use of final morals and maxims in the *contes de fées* is considerably more complex than the theoretical justifications lead one to believe. Contrary to Perrault's claims, these devices are arbitrary (not "natural") and in fact tend to emphasize their arbitrariness, rendering problematic the privileging of moral value over the marvelous and any separation of the literal and figurative readings, of the *merveilleux* and its (supposed) *exemplum*.[21]

The *moralités* that conclude Perrault's "Le Chat botté" (Puss in Boots) will serve as an illustration of these ironies. In this tale, an anthropomorphic cat, the entire inheritance of a miller's youngest son, promises to help his master escape poverty after hearing that he is about to be eaten and skinned. Through a series of crafty moves, the cat is able to kill an ogre, secure his château and, most significant of all, obtain the hand of a king's daughter in marriage for his master. The success of the cat's adventures depends on duping the king and everyone else he encounters into believing that his master is the fictive Marquis de Carabas. In the end, he succeeds in giving his master this new identity and in becoming a "grand seigneur" himself. The tale then concludes with two morals:

MORALITÉ
Quelque grand que soit l'avantage
De jouir d'un riche héritage
Venant à nous de père en fils,
Aux jeunes gens pour l'ordinaire,

> L'industrie et le savoir-faire
> Valent mieux que des biens acquis.
>
> AUTRE MORALITÉ
> Si le fils d'un Meunier, avec tant de vitesse,
>   Gagne le cœur d'une Princesse,
> Et s'en fait regarder avec des yeux mourants,
>   C'est que l'habit, la mine et la jeunesse,
>   Pour inspirer de la tendresse,
> N'en sont pas des moyens toujours indifférents.

MORAL
However great the advantage / Of enjoying a fat inheritance / That comes to us from father to son, / For young men ordinarily, / Industry and ingenuity / Are preferable to acquired wealth.

ANOTHER MORAL
If the Miller's son, with such speed, / Wins the heart of a princess, / And makes her look at him with longing in her eyes, / It is because clothes, good-looks, and youth, / For inspiring tenderness, / Are not always immaterial. (161)

The fact that this tale ends with not one but two *moralités* is itself an indication of the interpretive complexity of the story. There is not one "point," but two. But if there is, beyond the moral, another moral, could there not be still others? Even this cursory glance at the morals leads back to the narrative, to a figurative reading of the text. On closer observation, the *moralités* highlight the readability of the story in other ways as well. To examine these, it is first necessary to consider how the *contes de fées* use the moral (or the maxim) as *exempla*.

The use of examples (*exempla*) in early modern texts was perhaps the most fundamental way of justifying the moral value of literature. Just how the rhetoric of example functions in this period is the subject of a comprehensive study by John Lyons,[22] who outlines seven general characteristics of exemplarity.[23] Of these, the most relevant to my discussion of the fairy-tale morals and maxims here are the following: discontinuity ("the status of example as fragment of another whole" [31]), rarity ("a complex system of values and expectations based on both extratextual and textual ideas about frequency of occurrence or normal behavior" [32]), artificiality ("the fact that an example is made by 'inventing' significance out of the continuum of experience or of prior statement" [33]), undecidability ("the always insufficient quality of example as proof," the fact that "example is not meant to offer certainty but only probability" [33]), and excess (the fact that "any fiction adduced to support a generalization will have characteristics that exceed what can be covered by the generalization" [34]). These characteristics provide a framework for analyzing the ironic function of the morals in "Le Chat botté."

What is perhaps most apparent, upon examining the *moralités* in light of the above characteristics, is the extent to which exemplarity here is (what I designated earlier as) arbitrary. To be sure, all of these characteristics are themselves exposed as discursive strategies that manipulate the tale as moral meaning. Yet, these morals tend to highlight this artificiality. This is evident first of all in the discontinuity of the morals, their representation of parenthetical asides or extrapolations from the actual plot. In the "Moralité" (henceforth M1), it is neither the situation of the cat nor that of his master that is the subject of discussion, but rather their antitheses ("industrie" and "savoir-faire" instead of what would be more properly called the cat's *ruse*, and a "riche héritage" instead of the cat as his sole and unique inheritance). Further, in the "Autre Moralité" (M2), the love of the princess for the Marquis de Carabas, a detail relegated to a few lines in the tale, becomes a significant aspect. Discontinuity is at work in both cases, because details from the narrative are excised and placed in different, although related contexts. The morals display rarity not by demonstrating the unusual or uncommon nature of the examples, but rather by implying that they are presented in an unusual or uncommon way. Indeed, both *moralités* underscore (what are posited as) general "laws" of human behavior. In M1, by contrast to the prospect of a "riche héritage," generality is emphasized by designating, in the plural, "jeunes gens" as the beneficiaries of the encapsulated wisdom, and this situation is further generalized by the adverbial phrase "pour l'ordinaire." In M2, the oddity of a princess marrying a miller's son is reduced to a not-so-uncommon cause by a humorous litotes.

Clothes, good-looks, and youth are decidedly *not* "des moyens *toujours* indifférents" for inspiring love because, as the *moralité* would have it, women are *always* seduced by them. Thus, both MI and M2, beginning with the uncommon in order to state the common, demonstrate the rarity of example as hyperbolic commonality, if not banality (MI) and (misogynistic) humor (M2). To recognize that the *exempla* in the morals of "Le Chat botté" display discontinuity and rarity is to recognize, further, that they are a result of artificiality. Both *moralités* aim to construct moral meaning for the tale, which they can only do by isolating certain aspects of the narrative and demonstrating both their particular and general significance. And yet, the fact that there are two morals, combined with their highlighted discontinuity and rarity, makes the artificiality of the stated examples self-reflexive. The morals foreground themselves as *discursive* markers of the tale's meaning.

This self-reflexive arbitrariness also extends to the relation between the *moralités* and the narrative text. In fact, it is this interaction that is most consequential for the production of possible figurative readings on the tale as a whole. Undecidability and excess are the two characteristics of exemplarity that pertain to the relation between narrative and moral(s), and both are of particular importance in "Le Chat botté." Undecidability or open-endedness is especially apparent in MI, which, in what is a more than oblique reference to the cat's adventures, states the desirability of "industrie" and "savoir-faire" over "biens acquis." While the cat does display a good amount of "savoir-faire," to call his ruses "industrie" in the typical sense of hard work is incongruous at best. Furthermore, the polarization of mental/physical activity and material possessions is itself never established in the narrative, where the new Marquis de Carabas happens upon wealth – not unlike aristocrats, who are born into it. A significant feature of the narrative's excess is that neither of the *moralités* mention the cat or his magic in the examples they draw from the text. As a result, the morals enjoin a rereading of the tale that, at least in part, considers the marvelous as that which is strange or other within a non-marvelous ("realistic") context. The social *arrivisme* of the miller's son/Marquis de Carabas does not rely on "industrie" and "savoir-faire," but on his good fortune to possess an inheritance just as desirable as a "riche héritage." The marvelous qualities of this inheritance (the cat), conspicuously absent from MI, expose the radical similarity of nobility as wealth (and thus appearance) to nobility as essence, the similarity of the Marquis de Carabas to the king. It is the rereading prompted by MI that frames the marvelous as the capacity of discourse to co-opt power.[24] The conferral of social status by a speech-act (based on a lie) cannot be realized without the marvelous abilities of the cat and the *moralité*'s insistence on it by negation. When the miller's son becomes the Marquis de Carabas (via the ruse of his cat and, consequently, the acquiescence of the king), he also gains the hand of the king's daughter in marriage. In M2, however, this chain of causality is reversed. It is the princess's desire, her "yeux mourants" and her privileging of appearance that make a miller's son her sexual object, and as a consequence, her social equal. The centrality of sexuality in this *moralité* contrasts with its marginal status in the narrative, but it also contradicts the attribution of the hero's rise to nobility. Sexual desire, and specifically, feminine desire, is what can be read *into* the tale. It is what is missing from it, according to M2; and yet, it is what can take the place of the marvelous. It is homologous to the cat's disruption of social distinctions and, in the end, deserves to be distanced or even negated by humor as much as does an anthropomorphic cat in magic boots. In the final analysis, then, this *moralité* ironizes the marvelous and, thereby, converts it into a nostalgic longing for the essentialism of class and gender but, simultaneously, into a potentially utopian demystification of the power of language to produce social status, and thus disrupt essentializing social categories.

The *exempla* formulated by the *moralités* at the end of "Le Chat botté," like all the morals and maxims in the seventeenth-century fairy tales, are *not* (as Perrault theorizes) the condensation and generalization of the narrative's purported moral value. Rather they use the *dulce et utile* formula to reveal the "hidden" values of the moral. On the surface, the pleasure of the narrative gives way to the instructional value of the moral.

But, as we have seen, this is but the first, most obvious reading, after which the exemplarity of the moral invites a rereading of the story and a *re*formulation – a different understanding – of the tale's moral value. The new understanding can take the form of nostalgic and/or utopian (re)readings of the marvelous, which, I would argue, afford a pleasure of their own. The initial pleasure of the marvelous *does* cover for moral value, but only so that moral value as exemplarity can create the possibility for pleasure as the stuff of figurative readings. There is an irony of the irony of the marvelous in the *contes de fées*. What is relegated to the realm of non-consequential pleasure turns out to be a pleasure more consequential than moral value. And while this irony of irony can be seen as a feature of all fiction,[25] in combination with the marvelous it constitutes a defining aspect of the seventeenth-century literary fairy tales.

If the infantilizing and moralizing pretexts create an ironic distance from the marvelous, it is in order to preserve the appearance of *vraisemblance*. The association of *contes de fées* with children becomes a humorous game for adult readers in the know, who can always justify their penchant for these stories by pointing to the well-worn dictum *dulce et utile*. If, as I have argued, the irony of these pretexts is itself ironic, then *vraisemblance* is not the "natural" or inherent effect of the marvelous narrative, but an overtly arbitrary construction of meaning. The claims that adults read fairy tales ironically and that these stories transmit moral value are, in the end, exposed for what they really are: the manipulation of literary and social plausibility so that readers can engage with the marvelous, so that they can read in it the fulfillment of their own desires. Finally, then, it is not the marvelous that is ironic as much as it is the position of the readers (and writers) themselves. They maintain their mastery of the marvelous when in fact quite the opposite appears to be the case. To read the seventeenth-century fairy tales is to read ironically, to read the irony of the marvelous, to read irony into reality and *vraisemblance*. It is also, we might conclude, to subject oneself to irony.

CHAPTER 3

The marvelous in context: the place of the contes de fées in late seventeenth-century France

Praising the restraint with which Perrault uses the marvelous, Mary-Elizabeth Storer asserts that in his tales "fairy magic (féerie) is made plausible, contemporary so to speak, and an atmosphere of reality is created by details to which a La Fontaine or a La Bruyère could not have given more attention" (*La Mode*, 103). Storer's statement relies on what continues to be a fundamental and largely unchallenged assumption in much criticism on the *contes de fées*: the marvelous is acceptable to the extent that it is used sparingly and plausibly. But in so far as fantasy literature, by its very definition, defies an empirical or realistic explanation of narrative action, observations such as Storer's are bewildering. Why should fairy tales be expected to minimize their use of the marvelous? Why should a fundamentally *implausible* narrative effect be judged in terms of *plausibility*? At least part of the answer can be found in critical stereotypes that take rationality to be the defining feature of French "classical" literature. In this perspective, the *contes de fées* are an aberration to be ignored, explained away, or at best subjected to this standard. To be sure, much recent work militates against a simplistic view of "reason" and even "classicism" as the hallmarks of seventeenth-century French literature.[1] The fact remains, however, that the first vogue of fairy tales, because of its *merveilleux*, is strikingly original in the history of seventeenth-century French literary forms. And it is perhaps this originality or specificity that has caused critics to underscore the genre's implausibility.

Over and beyond its potential to subvert prevailing notions of verisimilitude (chapter 1) and to define the text's readability (chapter 2), the marvelous leads to questions about why the genre appeared when it did as well as its roles in the social and cultural forces of the 1690s and early 1700s. To date, the explanations offered by critics have failed by and large to account for the specific historical moment of the vogue. In her groundbreaking study, Mary-Elizabeth Storer mentions without extensive analysis five conditions that in her view contributed to the explosion of *contes de fées*: readers' boredom with the long *romans* from the middle of the century; the tradition of fantasy literature extending back to the Middle Ages; the use of the *merveilleux* in seventeenth-century court pastimes, opera, and salons; the sentiment of decline at the end of Louis XIV's reign; and the personal misfortune of many of the *conteurs* and *conteuses* (Storer, *La Mode*, 9–13, 252–253). While any or even all of these factors doubtless contributed to the first vogue of fairy tales, they do not necessarily explain why so many writers were attracted to this specific genre at this particular time.[2] By contrast, Raymonde Robert offers a considerably more complex picture. She concentrates at length on the ways that the *contes de fées* "mirror" (the term is Robert's) late seventeenth-century society and culture – not only the elite pastimes evoked by Storer, but also architecture, the decorative arts, attitudes of the privileged classes toward *le peuple* (the lower classes), and the ideals of *mondain* culture (Robert, *Le Conte de fées*, 327–430). Central to Robert's understanding of the genre is the assertion that it "is framed as the ideal space for complete self-recognition and thus plays a sociological role as a mirror intended to reinforce the image that the social group claims for itself" (*La Mode*, 327). However, by insisting that the fairy tales simply *reflect* a set of predetermined values, Robert tends to exclude from consideration the complex ways that they *produce* and, especially, alter ideological meanings.[3] What Robert leaves unstated, then, is that the fairy tales' purported "realism" is both a reflection of and a response to a precise social and cultural context. Moreover, she does not explain how the "mirroring" of the *contes de fées* differs from that of other art forms. The seventeenth-century novel, as many critics have shown, also reinforced the ideological underpinnings of the aristocracy and in some instances the bourgeoisie.[4] As a result, Robert's otherwise magisterial analysis begs the question as to why a plethora of *contes de fées* appeared and why contemporaries found fairy tales so attractive during the final years of the seventeenth century.

In the current state of research on late seventeenth-century French culture, it is admittedly difficult to explain the rise of the genre in great detail. In particular, much remains to be explored concerning the transition from the seventeenth- to the eighteenth-century salon and, more generally, the changes within the reading public during the final decades of Louis XIV's reign. Far from resolving these questions or claiming exhaustive treatment of the appearance of the *contes de fées*, I will nonetheless argue that the fairy-tale vogue had strategic meanings in the context of the Quarrel of the Ancients and the Moderns as well as the *fin de siècle* attacks against *mondain* society. This chapter will also demonstrate that women writers found in the fairy-tale form a means of defining and defending their own stake in these conflicts. The meanings the genre assumed as an exemplar of "modernist" and *mondain* culture help us understand why it became so popular.

ANCIENT TALES/MODERN STORYTELLING

Why would readers of the literate elite become interested in narratives they associated with the illiterate masses? Why would they desire to tell and write stories they treated with condescension not unlike that reserved for the popular tale-spinners themselves? What purposes did this recuperation or rewriting of such stories serve? Answers to these questions concern first of all the status of folklore in the seventeenth-century *contes de fées*. The link between folklore and this literary vogue is a matter of discernible traces of tale-types and motifs as well as the perception of folklore at the time.

Literary fairy tales are usually defined as written narratives based, in however minimal a way, on folktales, the oral narratives preserved and told by literate and non-literate groups alike. However, to conclude that the folkloric tradition was exclusively oral would be an over-generalization, for the historical study of folkloric tale-types and motifs has revealed that it is often impossible to separate written from oral versions.[5] As they were told and retold, tales were transformed, truncated, and combined with other motifs or tale-types in accordance with both printed and oral narratives. The reception of many of the seventeenth-century *contes de fées* proves this point quite clearly. Mainly through the *Bibliothèque bleue*, many of these versions of tale-types (re)entered the oral folkloric tradition, only to be collected later by folklorists.[6]

Unlike the Grimms and other nineteenth-century German fairy-tale writers in particular, none of the seventeenth-century *conteurs* and *conteuses* endeavored to transcribe folkloric narratives out of anything resembling ethnographic interest. This does not mean that folkloric tale-types (collected and indexed in the early twentieth century) are not to be found in many of the seventeenth-century *contes de fées*. Indeed, one of the most significant aspects of the seminal studies by both Marc Soriano and Raymonde Robert is their painstaking research into how and to what extent folkloric tale-types and motifs are used in the seventeenth-century *contes de fées*. Soriano shows that complex intertextual (literary and folkloric) networks inform the *Contes en vers* and the *Histoires ou contes du temps passé, avec des moralités* and that Perrault himself was an avid but unsentimental observer of popular folkore. Synthesizing the work of folklorists and literary historians, Robert concludes that fully one-half of the *contes de fées* published between 1690 and 1715 were based at least in part on tale-types (*Le Conte de fées*, 71).[7] As we will see in a moment, several *conteurs* and *conteuses* explicitly acknowledge their debt to folkloric sources. Of those who do not, several nonetheless display a thoroughgoing knowledge of traditional tale-types in their narratives.[8] These tales might be said to exploit a *direct* recuperation of folklore.[9]

In a general sense, the entire vogue represents what can be termed an *indirect* recuperation of folklore since the *contes de fées* were read as a derivation of folktales and, more importantly, as a genre that bore the imprint of the lower classes.[10] Indeed, the fairy tales were predicated on the presumption that they could

be traced to folklore, that is, stories whose social indignity was
sealed by their association in the minds of aristocratic and
bourgeois readers with the superstition of the marvelous.
Certain textual features, and especially marvelous characters
such as fairies, ogres, dwarfs (among others) were associated,
correctly or incorrectly, with folkloric tradition and served to
remind readers of the popular "origins" of the vogue. It is the
evocation of these purported origins more than the actual
rewriting of folkloric narratives that is put to strategic uses in
the social and cultural conflicts of the late seventeenth century.

The presumed folkloric origins of the *contes de fées* take on
precise meanings within the *Querelle des Anciens et des Modernes*
(Quarrel of the Ancients and the Moderns). Although various
incarnations of this debate appeared from the sixteenth to the
eighteenth centuries, its most famous battles in France took
place during the second half of the seventeenth century,
especially between 1687 (the year Perrault's poem "Le Siècle de
Louis le Grand" was read in the Académie Française) and 1694
(when Boileau and Perrault were publicly reconciled). Complex
in its aims and ramifications, this Quarrel centered around the
status of modern cultural artifacts in relation to those inherited
from Greek and Roman antiquity. Whereas the Ancients maintained that the latter were a universal benchmark against which
all artistic endeavors should be measured, the Moderns promoted the ideal of progress, which allowed the possibility that
modern artistic creation could surpass that of antiquity. Where
the Ancients saw a fundamental *stasis* and unchanging essence
as the norm for cultural production, the Moderns perceived
historical and cultural relativity.

Developed, at least ostensibly, from indigenous French and
not ancient classical sources, fairy tales constituted a somewhat
radical *exemplum* of the Moderns' theses. In their "theoretical"
discussions, both Lhéritier and Perrault explicitly compared
French folktales to the myths and fables of antiquity. In the
context of the Quarrel, such comparisons required a good deal
of audacity and polemic motivation. The ancient "tales"
enjoyed the legitimacy of educational institutions not to

mention a privileged place in the hierarchy of literary values. Folktales, by contrast, were accessible to anyone, but were above all the province of the uneducated and the illiterate. To compare folkloric narratives to ancient myths and fables was to drive home the relativity of the latter prestigious forms. For both Lhéritier and Perrault, it was also to make a strategic attack on the Ancients. With only a few exceptions, Boileau and other partisans of the Ancients virtually ignored the fairy tales published by Perrault and the other *conteurs* and *conteuses*. In all likelihood they could not take the vogue seriously, given its association with folklore and children's literature, nor would they want to dignify it by openly denouncing it.[11]

Safe from counterattacks, then, Lhéritier and Perrault aggressively defended the value of folkloric tales and, thus, the capacity of a heretofore neglected generic form to serve the lofty goals of literature. "Contes pour contes" (Tales for tales), concludes the narrator in Lhéritier's "Les Enchantements de l'éloquence" (The Enchantments of Eloquence), "il me paraît que ceux de l'antiquité gauloise valent bien à peu près ceux de l'antiquité grecque; et les fées ne sont pas moins en droit de faire des prodiges que les dieux de la Fable" (it seems to me that those of Gallic antiquity are more or less comparable to those from Grecian antiquity; and fairies are no less capable of miracles than the gods of mythology).[12] To make this comparison, both Perrault and Lhéritier must show that their *contes* have every bit as much moral value as the classical *fable* (mythology, but also tales and fables). In the *Préface* to his *Contes en vers*, Perrault goes even further and argues for the moral superiority of the *conte de fées*: "Je prétends même que mes Fables méritent mieux d'être racontées que la plupart des Contes anciens, et particulièrement celui de la Matrone d'Ephèse et celui de Psyché, si l'on les regarde du côté de la Morale, chose principale dans toute sorte de Fables, et pour laquelle elles doivent avoir été faites" (I even claim that my Fables deserve more to be told than most of the ancient Tales, and particularly those of the Matron of Ephesus and Psyche, if one looks at them from the perspective of Morality, a principal aspect of every kind of

Fable, and for which they ought to have been created [50; 121]). Calling his own tales "*fables*" and the "ancient" fables "*contes*," the advocate for the *Modernes* makes his genre even more canonical than the canon itself. Perrault gives his tales a name of prestige and official sanction, the better to emphasize their moral quality. Later in the *Préface*, Perrault does not hesitate to attribute the moral value of folktales to their "originary" storytellers:

Tout ce qu'on peut dire, c'est que cette Fable de même que la plupart de celles qui nous restent des Anciens n'ont été faites que pour plaire sans égard aux bonnes mœurs qu'ils négligeaient beaucoup. Il n'en est pas de même des contes que nos aïeux ont inventés pour leurs Enfants. Ils ne les ont pas contés avec l'élégance et les agréments dont les Grecs et les Romains ont orné leurs Fables; mais ils ont toujours eu un très grand soin que leurs contes renfermassent une moralité louable et instructive.

All that one can say is that this Fable, like most of the Fables remaining to us from the Ancients, was created only to please, without regard for good morals, which they greatly neglected. It is not the same with the tales that our forefathers invented for their Children. They did not tell them with the same elegance and embellishment with which the Greeks and the Romans ornamented their Fables; but they always took great care that their tales should incorporate a praiseworthy and instructive moral. (51; 121)

What the folkloric narratives lack in elegance and ornament, they gain through their "moral" developed by the anonymous "forefathers" to edify their children. Significantly, then, Perrault substantiates the superiority of the French "fables" by evoking both the moralizing and infantilizing pretexts we saw in the previous chapter. So doing, he idealizes not only the folkloric tales but also the archetypal tale-spinners. Popular narratives and narrators lose their brute reality to become worthy models of modern culture. Moreover, the decidedly non-literary form of folklore – its lack of "elegance and embellishment with which the Greeks and the Romans orna- mented their fables" – becomes the guarantor of its exemplary content. By contrast, the form of the ancient *fables*, Perrault argues, pleases "without regard for good morals." The very literariness of these "tales" is tied, at least implicitly, to moral dissolution.

In her "Lettre à Madame D.G**," Lhéritier presents a considerably more complex justification of folklore and its use in literature. Rather than deliver a frontal attack on the Ancients, as does Perrault, she concentrates on (what she perceives to be) the history and forms of folklore, which she traces to the Middle Ages. It was the troubadours, Lhéritier claims, who created what were to become folktales (*contes*), but also the epic novels (*romans*) of the mid-seventeenth century. Over the course of time, both of these offspring of the medieval poets became corrupted. Referring to the *nouvelles* of the second half of the century, Lhéritier declares that, with the notable exception of *La Princesse de Clèves*, "les Romans ont perdu beaucoup de leurs beautés: On les a réduits en petit, et dans cet état, il y en a peu qui conservent les grâces du style et les agréments de l'invention" (Novels have lost much of their beauty: they have been reduced in size, and in this state, there are few that preserve stylistic grace and the charms of innovation).[13] Similarly, many (but not all) folktales were filled with "aventures scandaleuses" (scandalous adventures), which Lhéritier attributes to the social standing of their popular storytellers. "Je crois ... que ces Contes se sont remplis d'impuretés en passant dans la bouche du petit peuple, de même qu'une eau pure se charge toujours d'ordures en passant par un canal sale" (I think ... that these Tales were filled with impurities by passing through the mouths of lowly people, just as pure water is laden with garbage when it passes through a dirty gutter [312–313]). Other popular storytellers are responsible for obscuring the moral function of folktales (313). By contrast, the fairy tales told/written for polite society attempt to recapture the inherent moral purity of the troubadours' storytelling and, thereby, simultaneously regenerate both the novel and folklore (306–307). More than a return to an indigenous intertext, the "Contes au style des troubadours" (Tales in the style of the troubadours), as Lhéritier calls them, are rewritten to exemplify the perfection of modern literary expectations, which only adds to the original stories: "la bienséance des mots n'ôte rien à la singularité des choses; et si le peuple ou les Troubadours s'étaient exprimés comme nous, leurs Contes n'en auraient que mieux valu" (the propriety of the words takes nothing from the singularity of things; and if the people or the Troubadours had expressed themselves as we do, their Tales would only have been better for it [314–315]).

Whether they rely on the storytelling of the popular masses or the troubadours, both Perrault and Lhéritier convey nostalgic and, thus, idealized visions of folklore. However, their nostalgia has less to do with a conviction for the pedagogical value of folklore than with strategic polemical interest. If the fundamental role of the literary text is to please and instruct (*plaire et instruire*), or more precisely, to please in order to instruct, then folklore is just as worthy of literary status as the ancient narratives. The point Lhéritier and Perrault seem to be making, then, is that the Ancients' insistence on both the imitation of classical models and the preeminence of the *plaire et instruire* ideal leads to a logical *aporia*. Classical literature does not have a privileged relationship to moral value. Rewritings of popular folklore are just as capable of fulfilling this function, and by extension, just as, if not more deserving of critical recognition as literature.

Lhéritier's and Perrault's manifestoes are strategic defenses of the "modernist" cause in another way as well. Both the "Lettre à Madame D.G**" and the *Préface* to the *Contes en vers* appeared in 1695, a year after Boileau and Perrault (the leaders of the Ancient and Modern camps respectively) had been publicly reconciled after many heated public disputes. Although this reconciliation was billed as the end of the Quarrel, Lhéritier's and Perrault's manifestoes, appearing when they did, continued the debate while bringing to it new material from which to make the "modernist" case. Subsequently, of course, both the *conteuse* and the *conteur* published still more tales as what might be considered practical applications of their theories. I would argue that the same might be said for the entire vogue of *contes de fées*. Apart from Lhéritier and Perrault, none of the fairy-tale writers make explicit allusions to the Quarrel. Yet, written and published in the polemical climate defined by Lhéritier and Perrault, the fairy tales published from 1696 on demonstrate, in a *de facto* manner, the recuperability of popular folklore and, thus, the "modernist" conception of literature. More decisive by far, the success of the vogue proved that there was wide-spread support for a resolutely modern literary form.

POPULAR STORYTELLING AND *MONDAIN* CULTURE

Folklore plays a paradoxical role in the first vogue of *contes de fées*. On the one hand, of course, folklore is, either directly or indirectly, the *sine qua non* of these and all literary fairy tales. On the other hand, the fairy tales distance themselves from the popular origins of folktales by recycling them for the literary consumption of an elite readership. This paradox is crucial to the genre's defense of "modernist" literature: folklore provides a strategic source of cultural renewal, yet that renewal is predicated on an effacement of the reality of popular story-telling. At the same time, the paradoxical role of folklore enables the genre to (re)affirm precise socio-cultural identities. As rewritings of folklore, the *contes de fées* posit, simultaneously, both a link and a distinction between the literate upper classes and the illiterate lower classes. Within the collective uncon-scious of the *mondain* public by and for whom the fairy tales were written, the popular (ie. lower class) tale-spinner becomes a model of sociable storytelling, which, in turn, (re)enunciates an elite socio-cultural ideal.[14] To understand why folklore and popular storytellers fulfilled this function, we must first consider the definition and status of *mondain* culture in the final years of the seventeenth century.

Not unlike current semantic usage, the adjective *mondain* in seventeenth-century France had ambiguous meanings. In reli-gious parlance, of course, it took on negative connotations and designated persons who are excessively attached to worldly (as opposed to spiritual) values. In the positive sense that I use here, this term could also refer to an elite sociological group and the ideal of sociability that exemplified it. It is from this perspective that Furetière designates one of the meanings of *le monde* as "des manières de vivre et de converser avec les hommes. Les gens qui hantent la Cour sont appelés les gens du *monde*, le beau *monde*, le *monde* poli" (ways of living and conversing with men. The people who live at court are called people of the *world*, the beautiful *world*, the polite *world*).[15] Referring to a similar semantic network, Richelet defines *le monde poli, le beau monde* as "les honnêtes gens et les gens de qualité, qui d'ordinaire sont propres, polis et bien mis" (*honnête* people and people of quality who are ordinarily clean, polite, and well dressed).[16] The adjective *mondain*, then, referred to an exclusive public recognizable by the elevated socio-economic station, outward appearance, and demeanor of its members, as well as their coveted social contacts. The *mondains* belonged to what Alain Viala has called the "intermediate stratum" of the three sociological groups of readers of seventeenth-century France.[17] Neither erudites in the limited sense nor "popular" consumers of pamphlets and chapbooks, this "intermediary" public, including both aristocrats and bourgeois, read and produced most of the literature of the period.

Throughout the seventeenth century, specific aspects of what might be broadly called *mondain* culture were repeatedly attacked by various conservative religious interests, including among others the Compagnie du Saint Sacrement and the Jansenists. Religious critics railed against everything from fashion to pastimes. These attacks were not always confined to verbal admonitions. As the famous controversies surrounding Molière's *Le Tartuffe* and *Dom Juan* attest, for instance, religious cabals could even exert pressure to have plays banned. However, the final years of the century witnessed an intensification of religious piety that translated into overt hostility toward *mondain* culture. What differentiated these attacks from the preceding ones was that the court at Versailles, following what was probably Madame de Maintenon's lead, had become an important center of this religious conservatism. The renowned bishop and orator Jacques-Bénigne Bossuet, for instance, argued vigorously against "worldly" pleasures. In 1694, he wrote two polemical pieces, *Traité de la concupiscence* and *Maximes et réflexions sur la comédie*, in which he staked out an uncompromising position *vis-à-vis* artistic and, particularly, literary endea-vors.[18] Not content to decry the secular *sciences*, Bossuet was one of a number of ecclesiastical authorities to press for increased regulation if not outright abolition of the theater in the 1690s. Even if public pressure prevented any drastic measures, officials of both Church and State increased their control over the theater. The atmosphere of suspicion and repression was endorsed, if only indirectly, by Louis XIV who, although an avid sponsor in his earlier years, appears to have totally abandoned the theater after 1692.[19] The most famous indica-tion of this hostility came in 1697 with the expulsion from France of the Comédiens italiens, probably for staging a play with satirical allusions to Madame de Maintenon (Adam, *Histoire*, 5: 257, n. 12). Considering this climate, Antoine Adam is most likely justified to conclude that during the final years of Louis XIV's reign, "the theater was ... subjected to a surveil-lance and regulations unknown in previous periods" (Adam, *Histoire*, 5: 258).

Opposition to the theater was only the more palpable of attacks against *mondain* culture in general. Compared to pre-ceding decades, the 1690s and 1700s witnessed the publication of far more "moralist" tracts and treatises aimed at reforming sociable conduct and denouncing the dangers of *divertissements* such as opera, theater, novels, and gambling.[20] It is possible that the mushrooming of such publications is at least in part attributable to an expansion of the reading public in this period and a corresponding (but paradoxical) desire to make the demands of sociable conduct more stringent. Jacques Revel has noted that during the last third of the seventeenth century, when civility became a common point of reference for a socially heterogeneous public, an aristocratic reaction developed against a code of civility perceived to be too accessible.[21] The insistence on the difficulty of "transparent" and "simple" politeness corresponds to this socio-historical interpretation. Whatever the motivation, the regularity with which *mondain* entertainments and activities are scrutinized is striking. They are most often denounced as impeding the authenticity of "vrai mérite" (true merit) and "honnêteté sans artifice" (nobility without artifice) essential to acquiring moral and thus social distinction.[22] Consistently undergirding these critiques is a religious discourse not unrelated to the Church's attacks on theater. Thus, when the Duchesse de Liancourt advises her granddaughter to shun novels, the reasons she gives involve piety: "le démon vous présentera aussi des romans qui auront de la vogue ... mais il y a un venin dans ces sortes de livres ... on se sent si froid pour la prière et pour la lecture spirituelle, et si fort en goût pour les folies du monde qu['] ... on demeure avec un cœur tout changé" (the devil will show you novels in vogue ... but there is a venom in that sort of books ... one feels so cold for prayer and spiritual readings, and so inclined for the follies of the world that ... one comes away with a completely changed heart.)[23] Just as significant as the reality of these attacks were the perceptions on the part of *mondains* themselves. In what amounted to the counterpart of religious denunciations of public immorality, many writers observed the oppressive piety of official circles. In 1696, for example, the Abbé du Bos wrote: "si Dieu ne nous assiste, on mettra bientôt la moitié de la ville en couvents, et la moitié des bibliothèques en livres de dévotion" (if God does not help us, half of the city will soon turn into convents and half of the libraries into devotional books [quoted in Adam, *Histoire*, 5: 8]). Perceptions such as these lead to more concrete reactions: after a highly public campaign by the Church against the theater in 1694, the numbers of play-goers increased dramatically.

If we consider that the vogue of *contes de fées* appeared against this backdrop of hostility to and reaction of the *mondain* sphere, then the cultural function of the genre comes into sharper focus. Although the vogue did not represent anything like a direct reply to the pietistic condemnations of polite society and its pastimes, it did appear as a revalorization and reenunciation of the sociable ideals of the *mondains* (including their literary tastes) at a time when they were drawing considerable criticism. In other words, the *contes de fées* were more of the order of a compensation for this criticism than a counterattack. Traces of this *mondain* response are perhaps visible when, at the end of "La Princesse Carpillon," d'Aulnoy decries the "*censeurs* odieux

/ Qui voulez qu'un héros résiste à la tendresse" (odious *critics* /
Who want a hero to resist the tenderness of love [NCF, 4: 307–
308; emphasis added]) and again at the end of "La Princesse
Belle-Etoile et le Prince Chéri" when she declares: "L'Amour,
n'en déplaise aux *censeurs*, / Est l'origine de la gloire" (Love, in
spite of its *critics*, / Is the origin of glory [NCF, 5: 266; emphasis
added]). But the clearest indication that the *conteurs* and *conteuses*
were conscious of the prevailing religious rigorism while writing
their tales is to be found in Lhéritier's "Lettre à Madame
D.G**," which announces the new vogue but also preempts
pietistic critics:

> Je sais, Madame, que le grand nombre de vos pieuses occupations ne
> vous empêche pas de vous divertir quelquefois par la lecture des
> ouvrages d'esprit, et que vous souhaitez d'être informée du caractère
> des nouveautés qu'il produit. Cette humeur chagrine qui paraît dans
> certaines personnes qu'on nomme pieuses, et qui les rend farouches,
> ne se trouve point en vous, quoique vous remplissiez tous les devoirs
> d'une piété profonde et solide. Ainsi je me fais un plaisir de vous
> annoncer aujourd'hui, qu'on est devenu depuis quelque temps du
> goût dont vous êtes. On voit de petites Histoires répandues dans le
> monde, dont tout le dessein est de prouver agréablement la solidité
> des Proverbes.

> I know, Madam, that your numerous pious activities do not prevent
> you from sometimes entertaining yourself by reading works of the
> mind and that you wish to be informed of the nature of the new works
> that it produces. That disgruntled mood which appears in certain
> persons who are called pious and which makes them inflexible is not
> to be found in you, even though you fulfill all the duties of a profound
> and solid piety. Thus it is a pleasure for me to announce to you today
> that people have come to be of your taste as of late. One sees little
> Stories told throughout polite society, the entire purpose of which is
> to prove agreeably the solidity of Proverbs. ("Lettre," 299–300)

If only implicitly, Lhéritier distinguishes between the authentic
piety of both her addressee as well as the "little stories told
throughout polite society" and the more questionable piety of
"certain persons." More than a counterattack on euphemisti-
cally designated individuals, Lhéritier's description defends the
moral integrity not only of the fairy-tale vogue but also of
mondain culture itself. Against the arguments of Bossuet and

others, the *conteuse* argues that piety and secular diversions are not inherently incompatible. To the contrary, the "petites Histoires," based on "the solidity of proverbs," serve as proof of their compatibility.

As I argued in chapter 2, the moral defense of the fairy-tale genre is most often an ironic pretext for saying something else. In the case of the above passage from the "Lettre à Madame D.G**," it is clear that Lhéritier is not only defending the moral function of the "petites Histoires" but also using it to legitimize the reading of secular "works of the mind" as well as the social context that receives them and makes them possible. Far from being unusual, the reaffirmation of *mondain* culture is central to the seventeenth-century *contes de fées*. Whether in the prefaces, frame-narratives, or the tales themselves, the ideals of polite society are the essential ideological framework. Paradoxically, however, these ideals are conveyed through gentrified folktales. But how can narratives associated with the lowest classes become a means of self-affirmation for a social and cultural elite?

Few of the *conteurs* and the *conteuses* make explicit reference to their tales' folkloric intertexts. Those who do, most notably Lhéritier and Perrault, trace these narratives to the storytelling of lower class women, namely nurses and governesses who spin tales for children. From all appearances, allusions to this type of storytelling reflect a widely held assumption on the part of the upper classes at the time.[24] If the *contes de fées* were predicated on an infantilizing pretext, it is because folktales were thought to be, above all, what women domestics told to the children of their masters and mistresses. More important, however, is the importance this storytelling scene assumes as the vogue's phantasmatic origin.

Historians of folklore have established that most folktales were recounted among adults, and by women *and* men.[25] Thus, the storytelling scene prevalent in the seventeenth-century elite imagination is a reductive recuperation of a more varied popular tradition. Nonetheless, this scene figures prominently in the theoretical discussions of both Perrault and Lhéritier. In

what is doubtless a strategic jibe at the Ancients, Perrault cites
the similar origins of the classical myth of "Psyche and Cupid"
and the folkloric "Peau d'Ane":

La Fable de Psyché écrite par Lucien et par Apulée est une fiction
toute pure et un conte de Vieille comme celui de Peau d'Ane. Aussi
voyons-nous qu'Apulée le fait raconter par une vieille femme à une
jeune fille que des voleurs avaient enlevée, de même que celui de
Peau d'Ane est conté tous les jours à des Enfants par leurs Gouvernantes, et par les Grands-mères.

The Fable of Psyche written by Lucian and by Apuleius is a pure
fiction, and an Old Woman's tale like that of Donkey-skin. Therefore
we see that Apuleius has it told by an old woman to a young woman
whom thieves had abducted, just as Donkey-skin is told every day to
Children by their Governesses, and by their Grandmothers. (50; 121)

In spite of her otherwise harsh judgment of popular storytelling,
Lhéritier affirms the pedagogical motivation of the women who
appropriated the *contes* of the troubadours: "la tradition nous a
conservé les Contes des Troubadours, et comme ils sont
ordinairement remplis de faits surprenants, et qu'ils enferment
une bonne morale, les Grands-mères et les Gouvernantes les
ont toujours racontés aux Enfants pour leur mettre dans l'esprit
la haine du vice et l'amour de la vertu" (tradition has preserved
for us the Tales of the Troubadours, and since they are
ordinarily filled with surprising details and include a good
moral, Grandmothers and Governesses have always told them
to Children in order to instill in their minds hatred of vice and
love of virtue ["Lettre," 305–306]).

But what is the purpose of evoking the transmission of
folklore by women of the popular classes? One answer can be
found in the inherent class configuration of this storytelling
scene. Be she *grand-mère*, *nourrice*, or *gouvernante*, the storyteller is a
lower-class woman given the responsibility of entertaining
children with traditional stories. Identifying with these children,
readers and writers of the *contes de fées* rely on the imaginary
storytelling of the surrogate mothers to reassert the values of
their own class. The mediation of this radical other (who is both
lower class and a woman) does not threaten the hegemonic
system since she is constructed as complicitous with it and since,

as Michèle Farrell has argued, she "functions symbolically as a symptom of the asymmetry of the class relationship obtaining between the aristocracy and the people..."[26] Given this ambivalence, she is at the very center of an outlook perhaps best described as "aristocratic romanticism,"[27] the elitist, idealized vision of peasant life enabling members of the upper classes to capitalize on the advantages of what Norbert Elias calls the "civilizing process" (such as a decrease in the amount of interpersonal violence) while simultaneously retreating from its constraints. In this sense, the figure of the "originary" *conteuse* is profoundly nostalgic. As an imagined point of origin in the earthly immanence of base materiality, she guarantees the authenticity of experience and identity for a group in need of such reassurance. Specifically, the popular female storyteller reaffirms the exclusive socio-economic boundaries of *mondain* culture at a time when censors were calling into question its moral legitimacy. She represents a nostalgic fixation on social hierarchy as a means of displacing and compensating for the ethical attacks on the elite group.[28] She is also significant as a maternal figure: she comes to resemble the primal mother of psychoanalytic theory since she is an object of longing that both resolves and bespeaks deep-seated anxieties.

Ultimately, of course, the storytelling of the real *conteuses* is effaced by the seventeenth-century fairy tales and is transformed into narratives that reflect the elevated social stature of their audience. As a result, the *contes de fées* endorse an ethic of sociability central to *mondain* culture. That is, the entire vogue (with the exception of Fénelon's tales) is an extension or recreation of salon storytelling and the ideal of social interaction it implied. The inscription of this particular ideal of sociability had itself been waning since the middle of the seventeenth century and is, thus, one of the central nostalgic characteristics of the genre.

In Durand's novel, *La Comtesse de Mortane*, which contains two *contes de fées*, the countess expresses her pleasure when her suitor offers to spin a tale for her assembled salon: "Ah! ... ne différez pas un moment, j'aime les contes comme si j'étais encore enfant..." (Ah! ... don't wait a moment longer, I love fairy tales as if I were still a child),[29] thus inscribing this infantilizing genre within the activities of the privileged space of seventeenth-century sociability. The little evidence that remains suggests that storytelling based on folktales was an activity of the salons and the court from at least the mid-century.[30] However, without more substantial information, it is impossible to know how wide-spread this practice was, what the nature was of the tales told, and even (as has been suggested) if the published tales replaced the oral practice.[31] It is somewhat helpful, then, that many of the seventeenth-century *contes de fées* appear in frame-narratives that feature salon settings.[32] Although these fictional accounts obviously cannot be taken as historical records, they do suggest something of the ideology of sociability that the oral and the written vogues exemplified. Robert concludes that the frame-narratives and the tales told therein uphold "the image of an exclusive social group arrogantly turned in on itself" (*Le Conte de fées*, 341). In this analysis, the effect of storytelling in the frame-narratives is no different from that of other representations of the salon in seventeenth-century literature.[33] To be sure, it is crucial to recognize the elitist prejudice that is conveyed by these representations of storytelling. But it is also crucial to examine the precise nature of the sociable ideals on which the genre is predicated, whether in the frame-narratives, the meta-commentaries on the genre, or the tales themselves.

It is not insignificant that the seventeenth-century fairy tales are often embedded in frame-narratives as a *jeu d'esprit*,[34] a salon game in which one player improvises according to certain rules while the others guess the meaning of the riddle-like piece (Baader, *Dames de lettres*, 49–52). For, like the other *jeux d'esprit*, *contes de fées* involve a recognition of (what is perceived to be) polite society's fundamental need for variety. Consequently, they are coded as a short-lived vogue, as the title of one of d'Aulnoy's *recueils*, *Contes nouveaux ou les Fées à la mode* (New Tales or Fairies in Fashion), makes explicit. The fairy-tale genre thus provides the spontaneous "give and take" of salon conversation, which is intended to stave off the boredom *les honnêtes gens* must never display (Stanton, *The Aristocrat as Art*, 100–101). In opposi-

tion to the trivialization of *divertissements* by a long line of
moralists,[35] the *conteurs* and *conteuses* follow the lead of writers
such as Madeleine de Scudéry in justifying the need for multiple
diversions: "depuis qu'on commence à parler jusqu'à ce qu'on
cesse de vivre, les plaisirs changent, et doivent changer" (from
the time one begins to speak until one stops living, diversions
change and must change), says the narrator in Madeleine de
Scudéry's *Les Ieux*;[36] "c'est proprement dans les plaisirs qu'il
faut de la variété et des intervalles, et que le cœur et l'esprit ont
besoin de se délasser" (it is especially in diversions that there
must be variety and change and that the heart and the mind
need to be able to relax ["Les Ieux," 16]).

Spinning, reading, or listening to tales is part of the
seventeenth-century *art de la conversation* – an esthetic enabling
interlocutors to interact poetically and to display the
"natural" superiority of the elite group.[37] Like sociable
conversation, *contes de fées* are to reflect an ease or naturalness
of expression – a stylistic trait that is consistently emphasized
in discussions of the genre.[38] The terms used to describe this
quality, such as *naïveté*, *simplicité*, and *engouement* (literally,
playfulness), all reflect the contemporary esthetic ideal of
négligence – a refinement designed to give the appearance of
being innate, effortless, and aristocratic. Not surprisingly, this
quality is dependent on an intuitive perception that is difficult
to achieve. As Lhéritier observes, "Il faut être très-éclairé
pour connaître les différences des styles et l'usage qu'on en
doit faire. La naïveté bien entendue, n'est pas connue de tout
le monde" (One must be very enlightened to know the
differences among styles and the use one must make of them.
Well-understood naïveté is not known to everyone ["Lettre,"
317]). Lhéritier further connects this stylistic simplicity with
the ethical purity she perceives in the purportedly original
medieval fairy tales: "il me paraît qu'on fait mieux de
retourner au style des Troubadours ... Ce qui serait à
souhaiter, est qu'en nous ramenant le goût de l'antiquité
Gauloise, on nous ramenât aussi cette belle simplicité de
mœurs, qu'on prétend avoir été si commune dans ces temps
heureux" (it seems to me that we are better off returning to

the style of the Troubadours ... What we could hope for is that by bringing back the taste for Gallic antiquity, that beautiful simplicity of morals which is supposed to have been so common in those happy times would be brought back to us as well ["Lettre," 309–310]). Through her own eccentric genealogy of fairy-tale storytelling, Lhéritier gives unique expression to the moralizing pretext of the entire genre: its elusive negligence calls forth the ethical purity of a golden age. The deceptively natural quality of *l'art de la conversation* communicates a profoundly nostalgic vision of society.

More important, however, is the fact that the sociable ideals in the telling of *contes de fées* are imbued with nostalgia. Just how nostalgic they are becomes apparent when they are contrasted with the growing emphasis on "sincerity" in epistolary writing at the end of the century. Whereas early letter manuals concentrate on models as the best way to learn the rhetoric of a "balanced verbal dialogue," after about 1670, writers such as Grimarest and La Fevrerie begin to valorize the frankness, personal attitudes and sentiment best exemplified in the *lettre d'amour* (love letter).[39] This particular change leads Elizabeth Goldsmith to conclude that by the end of the century the ideology of sociability was being replaced by an emphasis on "sincerity" (35). By contrast, the fairy-tale storytelling rejects this tendency toward individualism in favor of an earlier ideal of *honnêteté* in which the exclusivity of the group predominates. Like other forms of "aristocratic romanticism" and like nostalgia generally, the prescribed enunciation and reception of the *contes de fées* portray the present as a decline from an idealized past. This nostalgia for a disappearing form of sociability might also be a longing for a vanishing dynamic within the salons. It is possible, for instance, that the seventeenth-century fairy tales are an early form of the nostalgic allusions to the mid-seventeenth-century salons that are prevalent in certain eighteenth-century circles.[40] In any event, the entire vogue of fairy tales can be read as an inscription of *mondain* culture within a backward-looking vision of social interaction, the evocation of an idealized past.

FAIRY TALES AND NOVELS

In the *contes de fées*, folklore is subjected to a radical transformation. It is no longer conveyed in the dialect of the peasants or lower classes, nor can it be said to reflect their worldview. Rather, it is poured into the mold of the period's elite literary forms. Among these, the most important is the novel. Characters, motifs, plot situations, and other devices common in seventeenth-century novels (especially those of the mid-century *romans*) are prominent in most of the *contes de fées*.[41] These are far from being the only literary fairy tales in which folklore is melded with the topoi of novels.[42] In the case of the vogue, such features package unadulterated folktales for an elite audience. They allow *mondain* readers to recognize their own literary tastes in the folklore of the masses by effacing the disconcerting traces of popular storytelling.

The link between the *contes de fées* and the novel was perceived by seventeenth-century readers and, more importantly, by those hostile to such productions of polite society. For the acerbic Abbé de Villiers, the vogue of fairy tales is decisive proof of the indefensibility of *all* prose fiction: "Rien ne marque mieux qu'on a aimé les Romans par esprit de bagatelle que de voir qu'on leur compare des contes à dormir debout et que les femmes autrefois charmées de *la Princesse de Clèves* sont aujourd'hui entêtées de *Griselidis* et de *la Belle aux cheveux d'or*" (Nothing better proves the trivial nature of people who like novels than to see that they are compared to old wives' tales and that the women who used to be enchanted by the *Princesse de Clèves* are today stubbornly attached to *Griselidis* and *la Belle aux cheveux d'or*).[43] Implicit in this critic's statement is a widely articulated attack on the (supposed) implausibility of novels, and particularly the mid-century *romans*. An explicit example of this kind of critique can be found in Boileau's *Dialogue des héros de roman*. In the *Discours* that precedes this dialogue, Boileau insists on the puerility of the novels that appeared after d'Urfé's *L'Astrée*: "On vantait surtout ceux de Gomberville, de La Calprenède, de Desmarets, et de Scudéry. Mais ces Imitateurs, s'efforçant mal-à-propos d'enchérir sur

leur Original, et prétendant anoblir ses caractères, tombèrent,
à mon avis, dans une très grande puerilité" (Those of Gomberville, La Calprenède, Desmarets, and Scudéry were especially
praised. But these Imitators, inappropriately trying to exceed
their Original and claiming to make its characteristics noble,
slipped into a very great puerility in my opinion).[44] When we
remember the infantilizing pretext on which the first vogue is
predicated, Boileau's reference to implausibility as puerility
reveals an important link between seventeenth-century novels
and *contes de fées*: fairy tales are but a radical infantilization of
the *romans*. For *mondain* writers and readers of fairy tales,
though, this link shows the genre to be a strategic redeployment
of the attacks on the novel's purported *invraisemblance* and
puerility. The genre is a defiant illustration of such criticisms
and exposes itself to an irony which, as I suggested in chapter
2, critics seem unable or at least unwilling to perceive.

The use of novelistic devices by the *contes de fées* is also
noteworthy as a sign of nostalgia. Not only does the vogue
display features that go against the grain of narrative fiction of
the second half of the seventeenth century, in many respects it
also harks back to the earlier *romans*. So doing, the great
majority of fairy tales betray a longing for an idealized aristocratic identity.

During the second half of the century, the novel developed a
different relation to history than had previous forms. Whereas
the epic-length *romans*, published mostly before 1660, were set
in a remote past and presented idealized characters in complex
adventures, the *nouvelles* (novellas), which flourished during the
1660s and 1670s (Lafayette's masterpiece *La Princesse de Clèves*
among them), had more recent time-settings and presented
fewer characters in simpler plots. Both of these forms were
predicated on an ambiguity between historiography and
fiction.[45] In the *romans*, writers "appropriated history for those
[nobles] who were beginning to be excluded from it" (Harth,
Ideology and Culture, 141), resulting in "mock histories" and *romans
à clef*. In the *nouvelles*, novelists purported to present truth in the
form of "secret history" unrecorded by historians (Harth,

Ideology and Culture, 147). As discussed in chapter 1, these developments in narrative fiction reflect a change in the status of the
categories of the *vrai* and the *vraisemblable* in seventeenth-
century esthetics. While the romances claim to be plausible and
thus give a moral corrective to truth, the novellas favor truth
(understood as an objective view) over verisimilitude. Hence,
the *romans* and the *nouvelles* have diverging ideological founda-
tions. The romances "offered a class of people whose political
integrity was being threatened the image of historical and
ideological continuity with the golden age of French aristocracy" (DiPiero, *Dangerous Truths*, 90–91). The *nouvelles*, on the
contrary, "articulated the historical construction of images of
grandeur by reveling in the seamier sides of monarchic
splendor" (DiPiero, *Dangerous Truths*, 231).

Now, in the last years of the seventeenth century, the *nouvelles*
tended to portray ambivalent social and political stances so as
to appeal to both aristocratic and bourgeois readers.[46] From all
appearances, the fairy tales too enjoyed a wide readership
composed of both nobles and non-nobles, and yet the ideological position they endorse is unequivocally aristocratic.
Perhaps nowhere is this more apparent than in the similarities
the *contes de fées* share with the pastoral and heroic romances
that flourished in the early and mid-part of the century. Beyond
their complicated, extraordinary plots and non-linear exposi-
tion, many of the tales feature pastoral settings that bespeak a
nostalgic return to the romances and the ideological universe
they construct.[47] The pastoral topoi found in several of the
fairy tales recreate an elusive and exclusive location that
resembles d'Urfé's *L'Astrée*. In that novel, shepherds and shep-
herdesses, acting more like "nobles dressed up as if for an
amateur theatrical in a local château" (Harth, *Ideology and
Culture*, 39) than sheep-herders, are engaged in amorous intri-
gues against the backdrop of the beautiful rolling hills and
forests of fifth-century Forez (in southeastern France). As Erica
Harth has shown, this retreat to nature and peasant life had a
precise function in the context of early seventeenth-century
France. "The ambition of the noble in the real world is
replaced by love in the world of Forez ... Loss of social and

economic privilege is transmuted into a world-weary flight from the world" (*Ideology and Culture*, 47). The *contes de fées* offered a similar imaginary compensation. But I would argue that the pastoral topoi in particular reveal a nostalgia for the discursive realization of a (seemingly) lost or endangered aristocratic essence.

In d'Aulnoy's "La Princesse Belle-Etoile et le Prince Chéri," the pastoral topoi are used to highlight the characters' quest for identity. Involving the misfortunes of two generations, this tale depicts the refuge and, ultimately, the benefits afforded by a retreat to a simpler life. The story begins with an impoverished queen, along with her three daughters, leaving court to set up shop as a cook in the country. When they serve a crotchety old fairy with undeserved graciousness, the daughters are rewarded with marriages befitting their true social rank. Another round of misfortune befalls their offspring, who are banished by an evil queen-mother. But they are miraculously saved by a pirate couple who retire to a forest upon discovering that the children's hair produces jewels whenever it is combed. The pirates, inspired by innate goodness and an intuitive understanding of the children's high birth, give them a proper education. After unknowingly arriving at their birthplace, the children must endure a series of tests imposed by the queen-mother before their true identities are revealed to them. Finally, Chéri and Belle-Etoile are married, and the impoverished queen, their grandmother, returns to court.

This ending is evidence enough that the pastoral motifs in this tale reinstate a lost or obscured identity. During the pastoral "retreats" of both generations – when the queen and her daughters become cooks and when the children of these latter are raised as the pirates' offspring – their inborn nobility is always clearly in evidence. The queen's daughters grow out of childhood, "leur beauté n'aurait pas fait moins de bruit que les sauces de la Princesse [ie. the queen] si elle ne les aurait cachées dans une chambre ..." (their beauty would not have been any less appreciated than the Princess's sauces if she had not hidden them in a room.)[48] And later, the banished children of this queen's daughters "passaient pour être les leurs [les enfants des corsaires], quoiqu'ils marquassent, par toutes leurs actions, qu'ils sortaient d'un sang plus illustre" (passed as their own [the pirates' children], even though they displayed, by all their actions, that they descended from a more illustrious family [197–198]). Finally, the characters' pastoral retreat is a time for solidifying and proving the merit of their aristocratic existence.

The fact that the characters in this tale and the vast majority of the *contes de fées* are of noble birth and abide by heroic ideals demonstrates how similar they are to the heroes and heroines of the *romans*.[49] By contrast, the existence of protagonists in the *nouvelles* is anything but idealized; in fact, their world is often marked by the conflict between the real nature of the world and an ideal set of norms or expectations. The characters of the fairy tales inhabit a universe in which their aristocratic nature – their physical, emotional, and intellectual superiority – is destined to prevail. Rather than problematize this existence, these characters serve as a superlative model for noble conduct (Bannister, *Privileged Mortals*, 20–26). The adventures of the characters in "La Princesse Belle-Etoile et le Prince Chéri," for instance, are designed to show the validity of the maxim "un bienfait n'est jamais perdu" (a good deed is never lost), recalling the magnanimity of the queen and her daughters toward the old fairy, who then promised to grant their wishes. At the end of the tale, the fairy tells the queen how, out of gratitude for her initial act of kindness, she protected her children and grand-children. The inborn goodness of the queen and her daughter perpetuates itself and, ultimately, receives the recognition and power it deserves – regained social status. In the end, so the tale seems to say, aristocratic essence always wins out.

It is not implausible that the requirement of noble birth for the vast majority of fairy-tale heroes and heroines represents a reaction against the diminishing significance of the distinction between noble and non-noble in late seventeenth-century France.[50] The fairy tales' valorization of aristocratic class identity parallels the entrenchment at the end of Louis XIV's reign of *marques de noblesse* (chief among which was the require-ment of noble birth) as a means of compensating for the loss of socio-political recognition.[51] No less compensatory is the sumptuous wealth lavished upon protagonists throughout this corpus. As Raymonde Robert has shown, the *contes de fées* equate spectacular displays of wealth with authentic aristocratic superiority (*Le Conte de fées*, 362–363). And ultimately, noble birth is always recognized by the material trappings of a socio-economic elite.

Nostalgia, then, governs not only the fairy tales' rewriting of folklore but also their rewriting of early seventeenth-century romances; and between these two intertexts there is a mutual interdependence. The structures of an identifiable literary form legitimize the recourse to folkloric narratives. At the same time, since the *contes de fées* rely on folklore and the *merveilleux* associated with it, they give new life to an aristocratic ethos promulgated by the *romans* and make it a means of wish-fulfillment. In "La Princesse Belle-Etoile et le Prince Chéri," for example, the quest for aristocratic identity is woven into the folkloric tale-type AT707 (The Three Golden Sons), whose protagonists are non-nobles in most recorded oral versions.[52] A purportedly popular narrative is made to purvey a distinctively aristocratic worldview in a form that reflects elite literary tastes. Melding folkloric and novelistic features, the *contes de fées* reify the contingencies of *mondain* culture into the certainty of aristocratic essence. Culture, in this case, is tied to being. The nostalgic return to both the romances and popular storytelling provides an escape from the constraints on *mondain* culture as well as a reaffirmation of its validity.

GENDERED STORYTELLING AND THE *EMPIRE DE FÉERIE*

As a product of polite society that embodies the ideals of "modernist" culture and e(xc)lusive sociability, the vogue of fairy tales had strategic value for writers and readers of both sexes. It is nevertheless striking, especially in the context of seventeenth-century literary production, that so many women published so many of the *contes de fées* that appeared between 1690 and 1715. Accounting for nearly half of the writers of the vogue, the *conteuses* published two-thirds of all the fairy tales in this period. Significantly, the proportion of female-authored tales within the corpus is even higher than the comparatively large number of novels written by women in roughly the same period. The question we are led to ask, then, is why women were drawn to this genre in such numbers. What attraction did the fairy-tale form hold for the *conteuses*, distinct from the *conteurs*? To be sure, there are considerable differences among the female writers of the vogue, as indeed there are among the male writers. In spite of these, the fairy-tale form does have a strategic value for the *conteuses* as a group. It allows them to assert their role as women writers in the production of literary and, more specifically, *mondain* culture. In other words, the *conteuses* highlight their own *gendered* relation to the genre and the creation of cultural artifacts in general.

The vogue takes on clear tactical significance for the *conteuses* when we consider that the attacks on *mondain* culture during the last decade of the seventeenth century gave particular attention to women. Among the fiercest were those formulated by Madame de Maintenon, who founded and oversaw an orphanage for girls at Saint-Cyr, and Fénelon, who wrote a treatise on the education of women (*De l'éducation des filles*, 1687) and served for a time as secret advisor to Madame de Maintenon. Both saw in women the instrument by which the French aristocracy, having (in their view) fallen into moral and genealogical decline, could be renewed. If women of noble extraction were to assume the responsibilities of pious virtue, they argued, then the purity of French nobility would be restored and the social order reinstated. For women to perform this essential role, they would have to turn away from the pleasures of *mondain* life, including all forms of "worldly" *divertissements* and sociability, to take on instead the duties of domesticity. As Carolyn Lougee has argued, "the perception of the antithesis between domesticity and polite society was implicit in Maintenon's thought as in Fénelon's. The family, the source of both individual and social salvation, was, Maintenon felt, vulnerable to the temptations of *mondain* life. All was lost if girls were allowed to aim at the pleasures of *sociabilité*, acquiring 'the taste for wit and for conversations that they will not find within their families'" (*Le Paradis des femmes*, 190–191). Assailed by both of these reformers was what they called *bel esprit*, the mastery of verbal and intellectual skills that were an integral part of *l'art de la conversation* and, thus, prized by polite society. In its place, they promoted an ideal of femininity that privileged domesticity over sociability, submission over assertiveness, and silence over conversation. The result was women who, by respecting the proper limits of their own so-called capacities, eschewed the pitfalls of "worldly" women.

Although Maintenon and Fénelon are primarily concerned with education, they rely on many of the same arguments expounded by "moralist" critics concerning the moral dangers that novels, plays, operas, and gambling pose for women. Above all, they deemed the representation of love in these works to be pernicious to women, who are said to possess more vulnerable imaginations than men and who are, thus, more easily led into debauchery.[53] In the eyes of such censors, female sociability represented the most visible of the dangers produced by *mondain* culture. To restrict women's access to the cultural sphere, in their view, was to fight against a pervasive corruption of society. In the domain of literature, it was also to fight against the corruption of taste in the marketplace, for which women above all were responsible. "Les femmes n'ont-elles pas quand elles veulent le talent de donner du débit aux plus mauvaises choses?" (When women desire to do so, don't they have the talent to sell the worst things?), asks one of the speakers in the Abbé de Villiers's *Entretiens sur les contes de fées*. "Pour moi je croirais que de tous les moyens de faire valoir les Livres qui ne valent rien, le meilleur c'est d'engager les femmes à les prôner" (As for me, I would tend to think that of all the ways to promote Books that are worth nothing, the best is to get women to praise them.)[54] The other speaker affirms this opinion by explaining: "Tout ce qui demande un peu d'application les fatigue et les ennuie [les femmes]; elles s'amusent d'un Livre avec le même esprit dont elles s'occupent d'une mouche ou d'un ruban, êtes-vous étonné après cela que les Contes et les Historiettes aient du débit?" (Anything that requires a little effort tires and bores them [women]. They have the same mindset when amusing themselves with a Book as when attending to a mouche or a ribbon. Are you surprised then that *Contes* and *Historiettes* are a commercial success? [286]). Over and beyond a condemnation of women's frivolity if not to say bad taste, these statements testify to the fear that women's power as readers evoked in opponents of *mondain* culture. Arguably, the attacks on women promulgated by critics such as the Abbé de Villiers were in part a reaction against women's increased control of literary taste, if not the book trade itself, during the seventeenth century.[55] Whatever its causes, Villiers's attacks are similar to those of the moral reformers in their ultimate effects on women. For, all of these critics share a desire to make women the scapegoat for the perceived evils of polite society. All of them argue either explicitly or implicitly that the only way to reform the cultural public sphere is to exclude women from it.

Now it is particularly significant that the vogue of seventeenth-century *contes de fées*, dominated numerically by the *conteuses*, appeared at a time of such hostility to women's activity in *mondain* culture. By developing a genre that in many ways seems to confirm the attacks on women's frivolity, the *conteuses* openly defy such critiques. Even further, they develop a strategic affirmation of their own *mondain* literary activity as a group of women writers. So doing, they might be said to capitalize on the period's prevalent lexical association of folk- and fairy tales with women in such expressions as "*contes de quenouille*" (tales of the distaff), "*contes de vieille*" (old wives' tales), "*contes de ma Mère l'Oye*" (Mother Goose tales). Of course, before the advent of the vogue, this association had considerable negative connotations. Even in its midst, a hostile reader like the Abbé de Villiers uses the link between fairy tales and popular women storytellers to denounce the fairy-tale vogue as "ce ramas de contes qui nous assassinent depuis un an ou deux" (this heap of tales that has plagued us for a year or two [*Entretiens sur les contes de fées*, 69]). Finding in the *contes de fées* a lack of erudition that he attributes to the gender of their authors (regardless of their class), Villiers's Provincial speaker makes the perception of female attribution the reality of female authorship: "l'invention en est due à des Nourrices ignorantes;

et on a tellement regardé cela comme le partage des femmes,
que ce ne sont que des femmes qui ont composé ceux qui ont
paru depuis quelque temps en si grand nombre" (they were
originally created by ignorant Nurses, and they are considered
to be the domain of women, so much so that only women have
composed those [tales] that have recently appeared in such
great numbers [76–77]). The *Parisien*, Villiers's alter ego,
concurs with this assessment in further condemning the tales of
the *conteuses*:

> Ce n'est pas à dire que ces Contes ne pussent être bons. Il y a des
> femmes capables de quelque chose de meilleur encore; et si celles qui
> ont entrepris d'en composer, s'étaient souvenues que ces Contes n'ont
> été inventés que pour développer et rendre sensible quelque moralité
> importante, on ne les aurait point regardés comme le partage des
> ignorants et des femmes.

> This is not to say that these Tales could not be good. Some women
> are capable of something even better; and if those who endeavored to
> compose some had remembered that these Tales were only invented
> to develop an important moral and make it understandable, people
> would not have looked on them [the tales] as the domain of the
> ignorant and women. (77)

To the mind of the *Parisien*, the association of the *contes de fées*
with women is something that the *conteuses* should have
attempted to overcome by infusing their tales with moral
significance. In other words, they should have written so that
readers like Villiers would not be able to recall the tradition
of female authorship that produces folkloric narratives. The
Parisien is clearly appalled that this tradition continues unin-
terrupted.

By conjoining fairy tales, women, and ignorance, Villiers
attacks the legitimacy of the *conteuses* as women writers. Yet,
these same writers engage in a sexual/textual politics that
contradicts Villiers's phallocentrism by constructing a positive
collective identity, an emphasis on the interconnections
between themselves and their tales that is non-existent in the
texts of the *conteurs*. In her "Lettre à Madame D.G**," Lhéritier
evokes this identity when she reminds her addressee of a
conversation they had on fairy tales:

Je me souviens parfaitement combien vous vous étonniez qu'on ne s'avisât point de faire des Nouvelles, ou des Contes, qui roulassent sur [des] maximes antiques. On y est enfin venu, et je me suis hasardée à me mettre sur les rangs, pour marquer mon attachement à de charmantes Dames, dont vous connaissez les belles qualités. Les personnes de leur mérite et de leurs caractères, semblent nous ramener le temps des Fées, où l'on voyait tant de gens parfaits.

I remember perfectly well how astonished you were that no one had thought to write Novellas or Tales based on ancient maxims. People have finally gotten around to doing it, and I have attempted to place myself among their ranks in order to show my connection with some charming Ladies, whose beautiful qualities you are aware of. Persons of their merit and character seem to bring back the time of the Fairies, when so many perfect people could be seen. (302)[56]

Lhéritier's linkage of the "charmantes Dames" and fairies is repeated in several texts of the *conteuses*. In Murat's "Anguillette," for instance, the narrator makes an explicit intertextual reference to d'Aulnoy and her tale, "La Princesse Carpillon," when describing prince Atimir: "Le Prince qui alors régnait descendait en droite ligne de la célèbre Princesse Carpillon, et de son charmant époux, dont une Fée moderne, plus savante et plus polie que celles de l'antiquité, nous a si galamment conté les merveilles" (The Prince who reigned at that time descended directly from the famous Princess Carpillon and her charming husband, about whom a modern Fairy, more learned and polite than those of antiquity, has so gallantly told us the marvels [277–278]).[57] In fact, Murat develops this comparison at length in the dedication letter to the "Fées modernes" preceding her *Histoires sublimes et allégoriques*, in which the household chores and popular magic of peasant women storytellers are contrasted with the courtly refinement of the *conteuses* and their fairies. Dramatizing as it does the tensions between the recuperation of a gendered storytelling tradition and the investment of the vogue of *contes de fées* in "aristocratic romanticism," this passage is worth quoting at length:

Les anciennes Fées vos devancières ne passent plus que pour des badines auprès de vous. Leurs occupations étaient basses et puériles, ne s'amusant qu'aux Servantes et aux Nourrices. Tout leur soin consistait à bien balayer la maison, mettre le pot au feu, faire la lessive, remuer et endormir les enfants, traire les vaches, battre le beurre, et mille autres pauvretés de cette nature; et les effets les plus considérables de leur Art se terminaient à faire pleurer des perles et des diamants, moucher des émeraudes, et cracher des rubis. (unpaginated preface)

Your predecessors the ancient Fairies pass for little more than jesters next to you. Their activities were lowly and puerile, interesting only to Servants and Nurses. Their only cares were to sweep the house well, put the pot on the fire, do the laundry, rock the children and put them to sleep, milk cows, churn butter, and a thousand other miserable things of that sort. And the most important effects of their Art consisted of making people cry pearls and diamonds, sneeze emeralds, and spit rubies. (unpaginated preface)

She then contrasts these "ancient" fairies with her *dédicataires*, the "Fées modernes":

Mais pour vous, MESDAMES, vous avez bien pris une autre route: Vous ne vous occupez que de grandes choses, dont les moindres sont de donner de l'esprit à ceux et celles qui n'en ont point, de la beauté aux laides, de l'éloquence aux ignorants, des richesses aux pauvres, et de l'éclat aux choses les plus obscures ... Pour prévenir toutes les marques de reconnaissance que chacun s'efforcera de vous donner, je vous offre quelques Contes de ma façon, qui tous faibles et peu corrects qu'ils sont, ne laisseront pas de vous persuader qu'il n'y a personne dans l'Empire de Féerie qui soit plus véritablement à vous que LA COMTESSE D***.

But as for you, MESDAMES, you have taken a very different path: You are only concerned with great things, the least of which are giving wit to those men and women who have none, beauty to ugly women, eloquence to the ignorant, riches to the poor, and clarity to obscure things ... To anticipate all the marks of gratitude that everyone will attempt to give you, I offer you a few Tales in my own style which, however feeble and incorrect they are, will nonetheless convince you that there is no one in the Empire of Fairy Magic who is more truly devoted to you than THE COUNTESS OF ***. (unpaginated preface)

Ostensibly a comparison of "ancient" and "modern" fairies as they appear in folktales and *contes de fées*, this letter is also (and not without a little ambiguity) a comparison of the "ancient" and "modern" *conteuses*. Beyond the fact that Murat's authorial voice identifies herself as belonging to the *Empire de féerie*, the title "*Fée*," as we have already seen, was a conceit given to many salon women in the seventeenth century.[58] Consequently, the *fées* referred to in this letter can be read as both fairies who performed the deeds mentioned themselves, and storytellers who perform them in their tales. The description of the *fées modernes* given here is both a flattering portrait *of* the *conteuses* and an attribution of the powers of fairies *to* the *conteuses* – a wish-fulfillment for discursive powers. Yet, these are opposed to, if not derived from, the more lowly ones of the "ancient" fairies/*conteuses*. On one level, of course, these "popular" fairies/women storytellers are mentioned *in order to* be rejected. But the *fées modernes* and the *conteuses* can only ever be a refinement of the traditions they seemingly negate. While distancing themselves from the "originary" storytellers, the *conteuses* nonetheless appropriate to their own ends the over-determined genderedness of these women's folkloric talespinning. And so doing, they idealize the figure of the learned *conteuse* who demonstrates the refinements of the salon setting and the importance of women within it.[59]

Besides asserting and illustrating women's activity in *mondain* culture, the fairy tales of the *conteuses* also reveal their affinities, as women writers, with the "modernist" side of the Quarrel of the Ancients and the Moderns. For the most part, the connections between the *conteuses* and the Moderns are implicit rather than explicit, and therefore somewhat difficult to assess. If the seventeenth-century *contes de fées* are a demonstration of the Moderns' arguments, though, at the very least the *conteuses* are indirectly linked to their side of the Quarrel. Nonetheless, it is a widely held assumption that women, and especially women writers, generally supported and had a vested interest in the "modernist" arguments of the quarrel.[60] The vast majority of literate women were denied direct access to formal education – especially to the classical learning vaunted by the Ancients – and women writers excelled in genres, such as the novel and the letter, that lacked recognized classical models. To date, however, scarely any work has been devoted to just which women might be classified as Moderns, and the complex interests they might have had in adopting this viewpoint are unclear.

It is not my aim here to resolve this problem, but rather to examine the evidence for a link between the *conteuses* and the "modernist" cause in order to further understand the large numbers and strategic functions of the tales written by women.

This link is all the more convincing when we consider that the majority of the *contes de fées* appeared in the wake of one of the most heated confrontations of the Quarrel, namely the controversy surrounding the publication in 1694 of Boileau's *Satire X* (often called "Contre les femmes" [Against Women]). In this vicious text reminiscent of an earlier tradition of *gauloiserie*, a thoroughly misogynistic narrator dialogues with a nephew who has just announced his imminent marriage. Attempting to curtail the nephew's optimism, the uncle argues that wives are almost always unvirtuous and husbands miserable as a result. Infidelity is rampant among wives, declares the narrator, and women are prone to a multitude of vices. Among other things, this text proclaims that they are likely to become coquettes, spendthrifts, gamblers, misers, hypochondriacs, pedants, and religious hypocrites. As much as it was an assault on women, this satire was a direct attack on Perrault (who was mentioned by name in the original version) and the Moderns in general. Perrault immediately fired back with his *Apologie des femmes*, and numerous other responses were published by partisans of the Moderns.[61] For them, Boileau's denigration of women was tantamount to an offensive against polite society, the most receptive public for "modernist" literature and culture.[62] The father in Perrault's *L'Apologie des femmes* makes this clear when arguing against his son's misogyny: "Peux-tu ne savoir pas que la Civilité / Chez les Femmes naquit avec l'Honnêteté? / Que chez elles se prend la fine politesse, / Le bon air, le bon goût, et la délicatesse? (Can you not know that Civility / In the company of Women is born with *Honnêteté*? / That in their company is acquired refined politeness, / Good demeanor, good taste, and refinement?)[63] To understand how Boileau's satire could be interpreted as an assault on the Moderns and, further, how the *conteuses* are connected with their cause, we must briefly consider the role of women in "modernist" esthetics.

Among the Moderns and, more generally, the polite society of seventeenth-century France, women's language was considered to display a naturalness and ease of expression that served as a model for men, who were otherwise confined to the strictures of rhetorical exercise. Moreover, women's judgment of artistic taste was taken to be more immediate and thus more reliable than men's, which depended on erudite standards of taste. Underlying all of these qualities, according to the Moderns and polite society, was the fact that women were deemed to incarnate the "negligent" (seemingly effortless and refined) esthetic ideal of *naïveté*. Speaking of women, the "modernist" abbé in Perrault's *Parallèle des anciens et des modernes* declares: "on sait la justesse de leur discernement pour les choses fines et délicates, la sensibilité qu'elles ont pour ce qui est clair, vif, naturel et de bon sens, et le dégoût subit qu'elles témoignent à l'abord de tout ce qui est obscur, languissant, contraint et embarrassé" (we know the precision of their discernment for fine and delicate things, the sensitivity they have for that which is clear, lively, natural and of good sense, and the sudden disgust they show when approaching all that is obscure, languorous, forced and awkward).[64] The models that women furnished regarding polite discourse and artistic judgment provided a middle ground between erudite and polite, but non-erudite publics. This indigenous cultural domain, which Marc Fumaroli has termed the *mémoire parallèle* (parallel memory), was a common point of reference for these two groups, enabling the "*sçavans*" and the "*ignorans*" to counterbalance each other. As Fumaroli has put it:

Between the culture of the small elite of *sçavans* and the "mémoire parallèle" that the vast and heterogeneous community of *ignorans* conveys in the vernacular tongue, one must introduce a mediation – *mondain* culture – which should not be confused with "learned culture." For, this mediation ... sketches out an unstable compromise between two extremes – the Latin and erudite memory and the collective French memory.[65]

The compromise of the *mémoire parallèle* was accessible to polite society, but even more significantly, offered an esthetic model of simplicity and grace grounded on indigenous or "natural" sources. As Fumaroli goes on to show, it was women who best incarnated the common ground shared by both the learned and the polite ("Les Enchantements de l'éloquence," 158). It was women who held together an otherwise disparate cultural community.

Ultimately, however, women's "innate" qualities were appropriated by men to enhance their own position in the Quarrel of the Ancients and the Moderns as well as the polite society of the salons.[66] Indeed, concerned above all to answer Boileau's vendetta, Perrault, in *L'Apologie des femmes*, lauds above all the ideals of feminine domesticity and subservience.[67] Therefore, by exploiting and developing the fairy tale, the *conteuses* might be said to reappropriate their mediating agency and their relation to language. Implicitly, at least, their rewriting of a genre associated with the *naïveté* of peasant women italicizes the role of women in "modernist" and *mondain* circles. However, many of the tales by the *conteuses* inscribe this reappropriation in more overt ways, not least of which is a foregrounding of women's speech as innate and stylistically perfect.

Such a link between women and "modernist" culture is dramatically illustrated in Lhéritier's "Les Enchantements de l'éloquence." From the very beginning of this tale, the heroine, Blanche, is a model of natural and captivating eloquence; indeed, her adventures repeatedly demonstrate the tale's moral: "Doux et courtois langage / Vaut mieux que riche héritage" (Sweet and courtly speech / Is more valuable than a wealthy inheritance). Blanche's speech enchants a prince and causes two fairies with names evoking the prized qualities of the heroine – Dulcicula and Eloquentia nativa – to bestow her with the gifts of being "toujours plus que jamais douce, aimable, bienfaisante, et d'avoir la plus belle voix du monde" (always more than ever sweet, nice, doing good and having the most beautiful voice in the world [258]) and having spew from her mouth "des perles, des diamants, des rubis et des émeraudes chaque fois qu'elle ferait un sens fini en parlant" (pearls, diamonds, rubies, and emeralds every time she spoke concisely [260]). As Fumaroli has demonstrated,[68] the descriptions of Blanche's speech

are reminiscent of seventeenth-century rhetorical ideals, as are
the names of the fairies: "Dulcicula" evoking *douceur*, and thus
the ideals of *suavitas* and *effeminatio*, and "Eloquentia nativa"
reminiscent of *neglegentia diligens*. Yet, Blanche's eloquence is not
the result of learning, but a gift of the fairies, who are anxious
to embellish her pleasing way with words. Blanche, then, is the
innate demonstration of rhetorical eloquence, the natural and
effortless incarnation of what could (usually) only be learned
with great effort. The importance of Blanche's speech does not
stop here, however, for, at the end of the tale, it is used by the
narrator to assert the superiority of modern over ancient, but
also female over male eloquence. Before leaving home to join
her husband-to-be, Blanche attracts a crowd with her oratorical
gifts:

Les choses brillantes qui sortaient de sa bouche attiraient encore plus
de monde que celles qui sortent de la bouche de Mr. de ******, toutes
belles qu'elles sont. Ce peuple avait raison: n'était-il pas bien plus
agréable de voir sortir des pierres précieuses d'une belle petite bouche
comme celle de Blanche qu'il ne l'était de voir sortir des éclairs de la
grande bouche de cet orateur tonnant qui était cependant si couru
des Athéniens.

The brilliant things that came from her mouth attracted still more
people than those that come from the mouth of Mr. de ******, as
beautiful as they are. These people were right: wasn't it much more
agreeable to see precious stones come from a beautiful little mouth
like Blanche's than it was to see lightening bolts come from the big
mouth of that thundering orator who was, however, so appreciated by
the Athenians. (264)

While it is unclear exactly to whom Lhéritier is referring in this
passage, the male figures represent erudite and ancient models
of rhetoric to which Blanche's speech is compared. In the final
paragraph of the tale, the narrator connects Blanche's example
to "modernist" ideals even more explicitly:

[Ce conte] ne me paraît pas plus incroyable que beaucoup d'histoires
que nous a faites l'ancienne Grèce; et j'aime autant dire qu'il sortait
des perles et des rubis de la bouche de Blanche, pour désigner les
effets de l'éloquence, que de dire qu'il sortait des éclairs de celle de
Périclès. Contes pour contes, il me paraît que ceux de l'antiquité
gauloise valent bien à peu près ceux de l'antiquité grecque; et les fées

ne sont pas moins en droit de faire des prodiges que les dieux de la Fable.

To me, [this tale] does not seem to be any more unbelievable than many of the stories that ancient Greece handed down to us; and I am just as disposed to say that pearls and rubies came out of the mouth of Blanche, in order to indicate the effects of eloquence, as to say that lightning came out of Pericles'. Tales for tales, it seems to me that those of Gallic antiquity are more or less comparable to those of Grecian antiquity; and fairies are no less able to perform miracles than the gods of mythology. (265)

Blanche is the representative of this "modern" genre, but she is also an example of the link the literary fairy tale allows the *conteuses* to forge between themselves and the "modernist" cause. She is the expression and realization of Lhéritier's utopian desire for discursive powers that resist the recuperation and subordination of women by the Moderns.

Both nostalgic and utopian impulses are at work in the appropriation of folklore by the *conteuses*. On the one hand, these writers posit an idealized narrative tradition of an unspecified past as the origin for their own writing. On the other, they affirm through their intertextual and interpersonal allusions a group consciousness that contrasts with or even defies the attacks on women's activities in polite society. They might even be contributing to the "invention" of a female literary and cultural tradition occurring at this time through eulogies of French women writers published by Lhéritier and Vertron, among others.[69] However fleetingly, the *conte de fées* also afforded women writers the opportunity to recapture the mediating agency of women in "modernist" esthetics. All in all, the *conteuses* use the fairy-tale form to create a counter-ideology in which women assert their own abilities and desires to participate in cultural and, especially, literary production. Not unlike the tensions in the Moderns' recuperation of folklore, so too are there profound ambiguities in the story-telling of the *conteuses*. The nostalgic return to folklore makes possible the creation of a utopian counter-ideology. By the same token, the utopian function of this storytelling is insepar-able from the nostalgic reification of the real popular women storytellers. The *Empire de Féerie* is indeed a liberatory space, but not for everyone.[70]

The marvelous offered the *conteuses* the possibility of presenting a strategic (re)inscription of women's literary activity. But it mediated many other desires as well. In a genre recognized but also dismissed as collective daydreaming, the *merveilleux* made it possible for writers and readers to reiterate and/or reimagine what is taken to be plausible and real. Moreover, the ironic distance provided by the infantilizing and moralizing pretexts was a cover through which a sophisticated public could find wish-fulfillment in an otherwise lowly literary form. The vogue of fairy tales conveyed longings that varied according to the particular notions of plausibility or reality perceived as most crucial by three distinct but potentially interdependent groups – the Moderns, polite society, and women writers and readers. For all of these, the marvelous allowed a retreat from the strictures of an oppressive present, a refuge in an idealized past and/or a partially imagined future. It mediated the conflicting nostalgic and utopian desires inherent in a period of cultural crisis and transition.

PART II

Marvelous desires

CHAPTER 4

Quests for love: visions of sexuality

One would be hard pressed to think of more stereotypical representations of love than fairy tales. Common motifs such as love at first sight, its power to conquer all obstacles, and marriage as "happiness ever after" are central features of our culture's most popular fairy tales.[1] These motifs are also, of course, among the most abiding myths of Western romantic love. Why is it, then, that these myths have become so closely linked with the fairy-tale genre in our popular imagination? To begin to answer this question, we might consider colloquial expressions such as "fairy-tale romance" and "fairy-tale marriage." As a non-ironic adjective, the word "fairy-tale" in these expressions recognizes a romantic ideal and, simultaneously, the near impossibility of its realization. The logic of these expressions would seem to hold that fairy tales are imaginary, unbelievable narratives, but that they also embody a fundamental truth to which everyone should aspire. Our culture seems convinced that the love portrayed in fairy tales is only rarely encountered in real life, but that "true" love is not fundamentally different from what stories like "Cinderella" or "Sleeping Beauty" tell us it is.

What precisely is the "truth" about love that so many fairy tales seem to represent? It is that heterosexual love, in its ideal form, presupposes the mutual satisfaction of masculine and feminine desires. It is, further, that such mutual satisfaction occurs as a "natural" if not "predestined" result of a purported "sexual relation," an understanding of the "difference between the sexes in terms of pre-given male or female entities which complete and satisfy each other."[2] It is, finally, that a man and a woman "in love" complement each other sexually, emotionally, and socially. Thus, like so many other literary and cultural forms that pay homage to the ideology of Western romantic love, our culture's most popular fairy tales elaborate what might be called a myth of heterosexual complementarity, in which the romantic couple finds perfect happiness because of a purportedly inevitable bond between men and women.

It goes without saying that this "truth" is hardly unequivocal, even if it remains firmly embedded in the popular imagination of our own and many other cultures. Of course, the attempts to deconstruct the myth of heterosexual complementarity are probably as old as the myth itself, dating back as far as the Middle Ages. In more recent times, however, feminist scholarship has challenged it from a wide variety of perspectives,[3] exposing how the supposed complementarity between the sexes in fact legitimizes and perpetuates a radical disparity between the status of men and women in society. This myth masks the unsavory truth of repression and inequality. It is women who lose and, contrariwise, men who gain in the varieties of romantic love that have dominated Western cultures. The myth of heterosexual complementarity confers on women a subjectivity and activity that patriarchal society has long endeavored to deny them. From this contradiction, we might conclude that discourses of romantic love palliate masculinist society's consciousness that it in fact dominates and possesses women.

Several feminist studies have demonstrated how folk- and fairy tales have been used to perpetuate patriarchal gender roles. Karen E. Rowe, for instance, has noted that "fairy tales are ... powerful transmitters of romantic myths which encourage women to internalize only aspirations deemed appropriate to our 'real' sexual functions within a patriarchy."[4] Repeatedly, she shows, our "classic" fairy tales display the rewards for women who submit to marriage and accept traditional feminine "virtues" such as passivity, dependency, and self-sacrifice. Besides the prince, they very often find wealth, not to mention the vague promise of "happiness ever after." Finally, then, "fairy tale portrayals of matrimony as a woman's *only* option limit female visions to the arena of hearth and cradle, thereby perpetuating a patriarchal *status quo* ... Fairy tales require [women's] *imaginative* assent to the proposition that marriage is the best of all possible worlds. Hence, the comic endings call upon young females to value communal stability over individual needs, because their conformity is the cornerstone for all higher social unities ..." (221).

As a recognition of how the genre socializes highly conservative gender roles, perspectives such as Rowe's are of course crucial. They demonstrate that fairy tales are not the trivial and innocent narratives for which they have often been taken, but are profoundly influential tools for reproducing patriarchal constructions of identity. However, since this work is, for the most part, based on currently popular fairy tales taken from a wide variety of traditions, the conclusions drawn are most applicable to the contemporary American reception of the genre as children's literature. To determine the effects of the literary fairy tale over time requires that we examine the treatment of romantic love in specific groups of tales, taking into account the literary and cultural contexts in which they appeared. To be sure, work on the Grimms' *Kinder und Hausmärchen*,[5] but also tales by Basile and Perrault,[6] has begun to explore the variable ways that sexuality and gender are treated. Given its influence on subsequent literary fairy tales, the vogue deserves to be scrutinized more closely in this regard, especially since it displays an ambivalence that is not characteristic of the "classic" fairy tales by the Grimms and Andersen, among others.[7]

THE QUEST FOR CLOSURE

In an overwhelming majority of the *contes de fées*, a love story is either the sole focus or a significant part of the plot, and two narrative features, the romantic quest and the final marriage, are of particular importance. Although neither of these is specific to the fairy-tale genre, both are stereotypical characteristics of our best-known fairy tales. It follows, then, that the quest and the marriage closure are key to exploring the various ways that the *contes de fées* treat the myth of heterosexual complementarity. Enhanced by marvelous settings, these features are used both to reinforce and resist the traditional understanding of romantic love as the mutual satisfaction of masculine and feminine heterosexuality. They also become objects of cultural desire. That is, the quest and the marriage closure convey both nostalgic and utopian longings that attempt to redefine, in antithetical ways, the cultural boundaries of sexuality.

What I will be calling the quest takes a variety of forms throughout this corpus and, indeed, all of folklore. In structuralist terms, the quest might be defined as the chain of plot events set into motion by the initial lack or misfortune that befalls the narrative's protagonist(s). In the first case, the protagonist(s) embark on a search and, in the second, they receive outside help or themselves set out to rectify their plight. Even more generally, we might follow Claude Brémond, who has characterized the narrative structure of fairy tales as the movement from degradation to amelioration of the protagonists' fate. Says Brémond, "the supreme law [of folk- and fairy tales], almost never violated, requires that good individuals be rewarded and evil ones be punished in the *dénouement*."[8] The quest is the protagonists' progression toward "amelioration" – by their own means, that of other (often supernatural) beings, or both at the same time.[9] Contrary to what the word commonly evokes, the quest (as I am using it here) does not necessarily presuppose resolute activity on the part of the protagonists. Rather, it indicates the predictable narrative trajectory assigned to fairy-tale heroes and heroines, the obstacle-strewn path to a better fate. Finally, heroes and heroines can be the subjects of the quest, objects of the quest, or both.

In its most common form, the quest involves the adventures of the heroic couple on their way toward sexual union, usually in marriage. Folk- and fairy tales are, of course, replete with quests that do not lead to the sexual union of male and female protagonists; however, only a small number of the *contes de fées*, by *conteurs*, can be classified thus.[10] The romantic quest can encompass other objectives in addition to marriage. As I suggested in chapter 3, d'Aulnoy's "La Princesse Belle-Etoile et le Prince Chéri" features a quest with two objectives. The protagonists set out first of all to find their biological parents, and thus their own identity. When they discover that they are not siblings but cousins, they acknowledge their mutual attraction and are married. In this and other tales that include a love plot, the sexual bond between the hero and the heroine is the most important objective, to which all other goals are hierarchically subordinate. Accordingly, Belle-Etoile's and Chéri's quest for individual identity becomes, finally, a quest for sexual union.

The romantic quest also provides concrete, physical proof of the heroic couple's sexual complementarity. In this sense, the romantic quest is indicative of a general fairy-tale feature whereby psychological traits are portrayed not by narrative description *per se*, but rather by characters' physical presence and their actions in the plot. As Maria Tatar puts it, "the physical descriptions and outer events of the tale serve not only to further the plot, but also to fashion ciphers of psychological realities" (*The Hard Facts*, 79). Although psychological description *is* present in the *contes de fées* (in contrast to most other folk- and fairy tales),[11] the hero's and heroine's mutual desire, compatibility, and fidelity (among other things) are tested and represented above all through diegesis and physical detail. Since internal processes and states of mind are externalized, especially by means of the quest, it is hardly surprising that the physical reality and actions within fairy tales have so often been interpreted as sexually symbolic. It might even be argued that it is the externalization and displacement of sexual impulses that have made folk- and fairy tales so attractive to listeners and readers. Paradoxically camouflaged and concretized, sexual desire supports multiple interpretations and identifications. The romantic quest enables the protagonists to affirm their sexual identity and to reestablish the familial and social order disrupted at the outset of the narrative.

Murat's tale "Le Parfait Amour" provides a clear (if not hyperbolic) example of the ways that sexual desire is externalized and concretized in the fairy-tale quest. This *conte de fées* relates the adventures of Parcin Parcinet, a prince, and Irolite, a princess, who overcome the evil intentions of the fairy Danamo in order to marry. As if the title weren't indication enough, symmetrical constructions, common to many folk- and fairy tales, make it obvious that the protagonists' romantic quest is the union of two ideally suited lovers. Parcin Parcinet and Irolite are, first of all, mirror images of each other. They are, respectively, Danamo's nephew and niece, whose parents' kingdoms were usurped by the same; they are both attended by faithful servants throughout the tale; and before the final *dénouement* they are both tormented by Danamo's (false) assertions that the other is unfaithful. The couple's predestined union is put into even greater relief by their symmetrical difference from the antagonists. At the beginning of the tale, Parcin Parcinet is promised to the ugly Azire, and Irolite to the equally unattractive Ormond. In the end, as we might expect, the protagonists undo the mismatched alliances planned by Danamo and see to it that Azire and Ormond are married to each other.

Beyond symmetrical relationships, the mutual desire of the hero and heroine is also indicated by physical objects and actions. To flee Danamo's court, Parcin Parcinet receives from the fairy Favorable a magic ring, which he uses to protect Irolite and himself from Ormond, sent by the evil fairy to capture them. Three times he invokes the ring's powers, and each time the inhabitants of three elements (earth, water, and fire) stave off Danamo's envoy and receive the couple into their kingdom.[12] The gnomes, water nymphs, and salamanders in turn lavish on Parcin Parcinet and Irolite magnificent feasts, entertainment, and praise in recognition of their superlative love. These festive receptions are not only a glorification of the couple's passion, but also a projection of their mutual desire onto the supernatural reality of the tale. Emanating from three of the four most basic elements of the natural world, the pleasures and praise they enjoy externalize and reify (quite literally) the internal sexual impulses that unite the protagonists in their flight from Danamo and, finally, their triumphant marriage.

No less significant is the importance Murat's tale places on the marriage closure. By definition, the quest has as its objective either the marriage of the hero and heroine or, in cases of a mid-plot marriage, the reunion of the couple or family (eg. Perrault's "La Belle au bois dormant" or d'Aulnoy's "Le Serpentin vert"). Yet, an overwhelming number of the *contes de fées* do feature a final marriage and, thus, conform to what is perhaps the most stereotypical of fairy-tale structures. Rather than dismiss this feature as a widely used convention, we need to consider the significance of the marriage closure within the narrative logic of these fairy tales.

Eleazar Meletinsky has concluded that marriage is "the highest of fairy-tale values."[13] It is the protagonists' ultimate reward for overcoming the obstacles that are part of their quest. At the end of "Le Parfait Amour," for instance, the fairy Favorable defeats Danamo, reunites the heroic couple, and then endows them with gifts that enhance their life together. "Favorable ... les doua d'une longue vie et d'un bonheur constant..." (Favorable ... granted them a long life and unending happiness [NCF, 2: 247]). However, marriage is also significant as the resolution of social and familial conflicts (Meletinsky, "Marriage," 68). In "Le Parfait Amour," the marriage of Parcin Parcinet and Irolite provokes Danamo's suicide and the repossession of the lands that rightfully belong to the protagonists. As if to highlight the return of virtue in this conclusion, the narrative points out that "Parcin Parcinet, aussi généreux que fidèle, ne voulut reprendre que le royaume de son père et laissa Azire dans ceux de Danamo" (Parcin Parcinet, being as generous as he was faithful, only wanted to reclaim his father's kingdom, and allowed Azire to stay in Danamo's [NCF, 2: 248]). Marriage is the "amelioration" of individual, familial, and societal existence.

As the culminating moment of the romantic quest, marriage is obviously fundamental to the representation of sexuality in fairy tales (and many other genres, for that matter). In its best-known form, the marriage closure establishes once and for all the "sexual relation" – the state of perfect understanding and interaction – between the hero and heroine. And this is certainly conveyed through the concluding sentence of "Le

Parfait Amour": "La noce du prince et de la divine Irolite se fit avec une magnificence infinie ... [et] le prince et l'aimable Irolite jouirent du rare bonheur de brûler toujours d'un amour aussi tendre et aussi constant dans une fortune tranquille que pendant leurs malheurs il avait été ardent et fidèle" (The wedding of the prince and the divine Irolite was performed with an infinite magnificence ... [and] the prince and the lovely Irolite enjoyed the rare happiness of always possessing a love as tender and constant in tranquility as it had been ardent and faithful during their misfortune [NCF, 2: 248]). Marriage is a perfectly static moment that defies any linear development. To describe this satisfaction further would require a "degradation" followed by yet another attempt to restore emotional and social order.[14] Only a narcissistic recoiling onto the protagonists' past existence is possible. This circular, tautological description refers us back to the supernatural events and powers that proved their compatibility and guaranteed their triumph. Within this self-enclosed and self-sufficient universe, the fairy-tale marriage is unhampered by the future, unknowable except as what preceded it.

In "Le Parfait Amour," as in all fairy tales, the self-reflexive circularity of the final marriage can be interpreted as a defensive posture. From a psychoanalytic perspective, the fairy-tale marriage closure involves the denial of two of the most significant features of human subjectivity. First, it obscures the recognition that (sexual) desire is, in fact, defined by lack. Lacanian psychoanalysis has taught us that to desire something is to experience it as lack, and in this sense the fairy tale's marriage closure is in fact a myth since satisfaction is fundamentally impossible. Second, the marriage closure denies the impossibility of the sexual relation. It is a basic tenet of psychoanalytic theory that (to quote Juliet Mitchell) "sexual difference can only be the consequence of a division; without this division it would cease to exist" (*Feminine Sexuality*, 6). As it appears in fairy-tale marriages, the sexual relation is a mirage that disavows this division, that covers over the fundamental non-complementarity between the sexes and among human subjects generally.

Through the final marriage, fairy tales depict complete and irrevocable satisfaction of the hero's and heroine's desire for sexual union. Sexuality is no longer the disruptive force that necessitated the protagonists' quest in the first place. Rather, it is expressed as the state of perfect equilibrium between man and woman, husband and wife, the moment at which the harmonious existence of family and society at large is restored. Yet, the fulfillment provided by the marriage closure must necessarily refer back to the marvelous setting. Defined by reference to itself and not to empirical laws, the marvelous puts the final marriage out of the reach of the uncertainty and instability of reality. It allows satisfaction to transcend the lack at the heart of desire and the psychic division among human subjects. To do so, however, the marvelous always takes culturally specific forms.

AMOROUS LONGINGS

Although the psychoanalytic model of sexuality is valid for literary fairy tales from a variety of historical and national traditions, it does not in and of itself account for the differing cultural functions that are served by the portrayals of love. Even if the quest and final marriage are remarkably consistent traits of literary fairy tales and, more broadly, of romance literature, their far-reaching appeal indicates just how adaptable the myth of Western romantic love was to different historical and cultural contexts. Against the norms of late seventeenth-century French literature, these features stand out as decidedly nostalgic. They are often signs of a shared longing for obsolete discourses of love, if not what was perceived to have been an earlier and more perfect state of heterosexual relations. What distinguishes the *contes de fées* from other manifestations of this nostalgia is the role the marvelous plays in recycling and remotivating out-of-fashion literary motifs and topoi, giving new life to outdated or time-worn commonplaces about love.

Throughout the vogue, the quest bears close resemblance to the adventures of chivalric romances that were more typical of early than of late seventeenth-century literary tastes, a fact that is perhaps most evident in the development of the novel. Chivalric romances such as Matteo Boiardo's *Orlando Inna-morato*, Niccolò Ariosto's *Orlando Furioso*, and especially the continuations of *Amadis de Gaule* were enormously popular in the early decades of the century. Just as important is the influence they wielded on the production of novels. Throughout the 1620s, 1630s, and 1640s, the dominant model for narrative fiction involved an intricately complex plot featuring the extra-ordinary adventures of incomparably faithful lovers.[15] Begin-ning in the late 1650s, however, this action-based model went into sharp decline. With some of the mid-century *romans héroïques* and even more so with the *nouvelles* and *histoires* that dominated the second half of the century, concentration on heroic adventures was replaced by an attention to extended verbal interchange and the psychological analysis it made possible.[16] As Joan DeJean concludes, "this deferred, deflected perspective on action is a vision that, while fatal to romance, generates what can be seen as the great French tradition of the novel" (*Tender Geographies*, 55). In light of these general trends, the *contes de fées* (especially those that are not directly based on folkloric tale-types) appear as a throwback to the romances of the first half of the century, in which the extraordinary adventures of superlative protagonists constitute the central focus of the plot.

The vogue of fairy tales was not alone in reviving motifs from chivalric romances in this period. Operas, notably *Amadis* (1684), *Roland* (1685), and *Armide* (1686) by Quinault/Lully, plays, and even *carrousels, courses de têtes*, and *combats fictifs* staged by the court reflect a nostalgia, in some quarters at least, for past ideals of heroism and love.[17] Exoticism, extraordinary adventures, and happy endings are distinctive traits of novels by d'Aulnoy, La Force, Le Noble, and Lesconvel (among others), although they also include features typical of the *nouvelles* from the second half of the century, such as recent historical settings.[18] Nevertheless, it is arguably in the *contes de fées* that the nostalgic longing for chivalric romance acquires its most intense form. Those tales that make use of conventions from romance do so with great predictability. In fact, the very repetition of these structures suggests a profound but ultimately elusive desire to revive an earlier literary discourse. The fairy tales' romantic quest is simultaneously a quest for the chivalric romances of the past.

This nostalgia comes into clearer focus when we consider that the quest also demonstrates the protagonists' elite class identity. To the requirement of noble birth are added the idealized (and stereotypical) traits that resemble those of heroes and heroines in chivalric romances and early seventeenth-century novels: heroes and heroines are consistently graced with superlative beauty and demonstrate undying fidelity to each other.[19] The supernatural obstacles they overcome in order to be united only further legitimize the superiority of their class. In contrast to the "realism" that was increasingly characteristic of novels in this same period (and that included the serious portrayal of bourgeois and other non-aristocrats, for example),[20] the recourse to a genre with idealized characters is archaic.

Ultimately, however, this type of characterization is inseparable from the romantic quest. Most tales provide external signs or proof of the couple's social compatibility. In some, however, appearances prove to be deceiving and expose just how inseparable the requirements of sexual and social compatibility really are. Murat's "Le Père et ses quatre fils" (The Father and his Four Sons), for example, includes the story of the princess Isaline who is taken by a dragon to a deserted island. In what turns out to be a sublime pastoral retreat, Isaline is courted by a simple fisherman with the tell-tale name of Delsirio, whom she eventually agrees to marry. Recounting her adventures later to a confidante, Isaline repeatedly attempts to justify her love for a socially inferior husband:

Le métier qu'il exerçait ne me donnait aucun mépris pour lui: quel prince lui pourrait disputer l'avantage de la beauté, des grâces et de l'esprit? (The trade he practiced did not make me scorn him. What prince could rival his beauty, grace, and intelligence?)[21]

Je connus bientôt après que l'amour tire ses coups juste par tout, qu'il n'est point de désert impénétrable à ses traits, et que la différence des conditions n'est qu'un faible obstacle quand on aime véritablement (I knew soon thereafter that love fires its shots accurately everywhere, that there is no retreat safe from its arrows, and that the difference of social background is but a weak obstacle when one is truly in love.) (93)

Je n'avais d'autre vue que celle de m'établir dans l'île. La condition de Delsirio était ce qui s'y opposait; mais à la fin tâchant de me défaire des préjugés, je conclus que je pouvais bien donner la main à qui j'avais donné mon cœur (I had no other goal than to establish myself on the island. Delisiro's social background was what prevented this; but in the end, attempting to undo my preconceptions, I concluded that I could just as well give my hand to the one whom I had given my heart to.) (94)

At the very moment that Delsirio and Isaline marry, the heroine feels obligated to rationalize her choice once again: "Et que m'importe après tout ... du jugement des hommes quand ils sauront mon choix? De tout l'univers je ne veux que vous" (And what difference after all ... does the judgment of men make when they find out my choice? In the whole universe, I want only you [95]). When she is rescued from the island and taken home against her will, Isaline tells her father of the fisherman who brought joy to her captivity. "Ce fut un coup de foudre pour ce père infortuné: il ne douta pas que sa fille n'eût laissé surprendre son cœur à un indigne amour ..." (This was a terrible blow for this unfortunate father: he did not doubt that his daughter had let her heart be surprised by an unjust love [88]). But the next day, when Delsirio arrives and reveals that he is actually the son of King Papindara, Isaline's "naturally" good (ie. noble) instincts are reaffirmed. In this tale, then, the quest for social compatibility, which Isaline paradoxically acknowledges by denial, is an extension of the quest for sexual union.

Compared to the greater flexibility in both literary and "real" matrimonial arrangements throughout the seventeenth century,[22] the insistence on royal marriages in the *contes de fées* is striking. It is also anomalous in the context of most other literary fairy tales, in which hypergamy (eg. paupers marrying royalty) is common. How are we to interpret this feature? One explanation, intimated by several critics, is that the vogue was produced and read primarily by aristocrats, for whom these heroes and heroines are an idealized self-image.[23] This, however, is highly misleading. Many of the *conteurs* and *conteuses* were bourgeois as were many of those who were likely the most avid readers of fairy tales.[24] For these readers and writers, the aristocratic protagonists are less figures of identification than figures of ideological wish-fulfillment. The powers of royalty were more often than not the stuff of an unrealizable dream, but they were also the largely uncontested ideal of political and cultural supremacy. What better way of imagining absolute perfection for fairy-tale characters than to model them on those officially designated as the rulers anointed by divine will? What better way of underscoring the total satisfaction and complementarity of the marriage closure than to make it the moment at which a hero and a heroine, both of royal lineage, are united and not infrequently given the task of ruling their own kingdom? These idealized protagonists demonstrate that the *contes de fées* share with romance literature as a whole a longing for authenticity, as multifarious and elusive as it inevitably is.[25] The requirement of royal birth transforms the romantic quest into the "truth" of social and sexual ideology.

Beyond literary models and characterization, nostalgia also pervades the dominant conceptions of love in the vogue. The last quarter of the seventeenth century is marked by a profound uncertainty as to how love should be represented.[26] During the middle decades of the century, two antithetical discourses dominated the literary scene. On the one hand was a discourse, derived from the early seventeenth-century neo-Platonic romances such as *L'Astrée*, called tender love that "continue[d] to take seriously and to the letter the traditional teachings on the perfection of love" (Pelous, *Amour précieux*, 38, n. 2). On the other hand was an antithetical discourse, *galant* love, which valorized a playful and even ironic subversion of the lofty ideals of tender love. Whereas the tender perspective proclaimed that love was compatible with virtue and thus led to individual and social happiness, *galant* love, in its most extreme form, expressed skepticism about the optimism of the tender discourse and sought pleasure in fleeting liaisons.[27] Even if the two theories were not necessarily adversarial (many writers play them off each other in an attempt to reconcile them [Pelous, *Amour précieux*, 30]), *galant* eventually overtook tender love and, in the end, cast doubt on the very possibility of knowledge about this passion. Pelous, for instance, concludes that *galanterie* eventually led to the recognition that "it was impossible to speak about love without lying or exaggerating" – there were no longer any criteria for distinguishing truth from artifice (*Amour précieux*, 286). Just as the adjective *galant* was used more and more often as a synonym for "insincere," the *galant* conception of love likewise lost its earlier popularity. Throughout the 1680s and 1690s, there were signs of a wide-spread desire for the earlier representations based on sincerity and fidelity. Thus, as Pelous has suggested, it is not unlikely that the revival of interest in heroic and chivalric themes was in part motivated by a desire to resurrect tender love as a viable representational model (*Amour précieux*, 460). At the same time, *galant* discourses did not entirely die out; indeed several writers at the end of the century, including several of the fairy-tale writers, attempted to breathe new life into this literary tradition. But in spite of these efforts, love ceased to be the central preoccupation it had been in the sociable circles of the mid-seventeenth century (Pelous, *Amour précieux*, 476). Here again, however, the *contes de fées* represent a countervailing trend.

The fairy-tale form proved a particularly apt medium for reviving the discourses of both tender and *galant* love. As the externalization of the hero's and heroine's passion in the extraordinary adventures of the plot, the romantic quest is a means of reframing these familiar (if not passé) discourses. Often, this is accomplished through the marvelous settings, which have the effect of reifying figurative commonplaces about love. One of the most extreme examples of this effect can be found in La Force's "La Puissance d'Amour" (The Power of Love). Beginning with the title, which plays on "Amour" as both "love" and "Cupid," this tale signals its self-conscious literalization of literary discourses on love. Throughout most of this story, it is Amour/Cupid, the personification of love, who controls the action by inspiring the magician Panpan with desire for Lantine, the Princesse de l'Arabie heureuse. Amour is also the central figure around whom the text actualizes textual commonplaces about love. In a scene that inaugurates the text's *mise en abyme* of textuality and its transposition onto diegesis, the god of love appears to Panpan as he reads the description of this passion/god by Anacreon. Further underscoring the self-reflexivity of this moment, the hero reacts with disbelief: "Est-ce que je lis encore, ou vois-je en effet ce que je lisais? Tu vois ton maître, lui dit l'Amour, tu vois le seigneur de toute la nature ..." (Am I still reading or do I really see what I was reading? You see your master, Cupid said to him, you see the lord of all nature ...).[28] During his quest to rescue Lantine from the clutches of the fairy Absolue and the Seigneur du roc affreux, Panpan is of course constantly served by Cupid. On one particular occasion, the hero is separated from his beloved by a burning lake. But when he decides to throw himself into the fire, rather than being incinerated, he is envelopped by pleasurable sensations as he muses about his mistress. Moments later, a similar adventure befalls Lantine. Engrossed in reverie next to a fireplace, she watches first in horror and then with great delight as sparks and flames bounce off her clothes and body and then metamorphose into an old man, who identifies himself as Cupid and announces his plans to unite the couple. For contemporary readers, these particular adventures would have constituted an obvious play on *flamme* (flame) as a metaphor for love. Literal flames turn out to be not harmful but pleasurable, not flames at all but Cupid himself.

In the end, this tale constitutes a curious mixture of *galant* and tender love. A *galant* perspective is apparent in the play on specific commonplaces throughout the tale. Through repeated allusions to the textuality of the protagonists' love, the tale posits itself as more real and more concrete than its intertexts, a stance that is undercut by the very unreality of the fairy-tale setting. In the passages cited above, for instance, the humorous clash of mixed metaphors (love as both Cupid *and* flames) calls attention to the implausibility of the text. At the same time, the marvelous setting encodes the hero's and heroine's passion for each other as tender love. In the face of various evil spells, Panpan's and Lantine's adventures prove their perfect fidelity toward each other and lead to their final marriage, which Cupid celebrates with supernatural splendor at the end of the tale. If the romantic quest exemplifies both *galant* and tender love, its marvelous setting attempts to amalgamate two incompatible discourses.

Of all the *conteurs* and *conteuses*, La Force along with Mailly and Perrault are the most prone to overtly playful or ironic *galanterie* in their tales. Like "La Puissance d'Amour," however, almost all of the *contes de fées* construct an idealized vision of past discourses of love as a counter-reality for the present. The supernatural adventures of the quest make it possible to return through nostalgia to a discursive past. Why this is so desirable is perhaps best explained by La Force's hero Panpan who, upon finding himself engulfed by the magical flames, declares: "bien souvent les plaisirs de l'imagination valent mieux que les plaisirs réels" (very often the pleasures of the imagination are better than real pleasures [152]). In most all of the *contes de fées*, the marvelous setting revives outmoded commonplaces about love not in their original state but in the "real" space of the imagination. Love experienced as an imaginary pleasure from the past is equivalent if not preferable to immediate pleasure in the present.

Further solidifying the vogue's nostalgic recontextualization of tender and *galant* discourses is the (nearly) inevitable marriage closure. Although hardly unusual in the larger body of literary fairy tales, this feature has particular significance in the literary context of late seventeenth-century France. Perhaps most striking is the contrast between the overwhelmingly positive view of marriage in the fairy tales and its negative portrayal in a large number of the period's novels and memoirs. Indeed, one of the most important traits of the novel during the second half of the seventeenth century, especially as it was developed by prominent women writers such as Scudéry, Lafayette, and Villedieu, is the rejection of marriage.[29] No longer the perfect resolution of individual and social struggles, love and, by

extension, marriage were now their principal cause. In Lafayette's *La Princesse de Clèves* and Villedieu's *Les Désordres de l'amour*,
to cite the best known of these novels, sexual alliances become
the secret sources of public intrigue and turmoil. Moreover,
marriage was also viewed with suspicion by the adherents of
galant love, if not by some advocates of tender love. From the
perspective of *galanterie*, whose very premise is the pursuit of
fleeting pleasure, marriage constituted the end of desire. And in
some versions of *amour tendre* (most notably Scudéry's), the lovers
preserve the constancy and virtue of their passion by forestalling
or excluding marriage.[30]

That the vast majority of the *contes de fées* portray the
protagonists' marriage as the crowning moment of their happiness is a sign of the nostalgia that dominates this corpus. This is
perhaps nowhere clearer than in the final lines of the moral to
d'Aulnoy's "La Grenouille bienfaisante" (The Beneficent Frog):

> Des époux si constants, des amis si sincères,
> Etaient du vieux temps de nos pères,
> Ils ne sont plus de ce temps-ci:
> Le siècle de féerie en a toute la gloire.
> Par le trait que je cite ici,
> De l'époque de mon histoire
> On peut être assez éclairci.

Spouses so faithful, friends so sincere, / Were of the olden days of our
fathers, / They no longer belong to our time: / The age of fairy
magic can alone boast their glory. / By what I cite here, / You can be
sure enough / About the epoch of my story.[31]

In denouncing the decadent present and deferring to the
perfection of the past, these verses underscore the fictive nature
of the tale itself. In it, the "vieux temps de nos pères" is melded
with the "siècle de féerie" as if to thwart any efforts to identify
a specific historical moment outside of the text, as if to promote
the "histoire" as the sole means of recovering an imprecise
past. The final marriage that prompts these verses is, therefore,
self-consciously fictive. And yet, in this tale as in many of the
contes de fées, this ficticity does nothing to diminish the wish-
fulfillment made possible by the narrative. On the contrary, it is

the implausible marvelous settings that invest both the romantic quest and the marriage closure with longings for a vision of love that is irretrievably lost. Through the fairy tales, readers rediscover a sexual union so perfect in its complementarity that it exceeds the past and becomes a blueprint for the future. So doing, this moral points beyond an exclusively nostalgic vision and, implicitly at least, expresses a desire for spouses and friends different from those encountered in reality. This moral reminds us, then, that the vogue conveys utopian along with nostalgic visions of love and sexuality.

SEXUAL EXCESS

In the vast majority of the *contes de fées* – as in much of seventeenth-century French literature – love is depicted in psychological and not physical terms. Explicit descriptions of sexuality are consistently avoided, if not to say prohibited. Indeed, the oft-cited *bienséances* that were codified by many seventeenth-century estheticians and writers generally suppressed the concrete and physical in favor of the abstract and the psychological.[32] And the fairy tales too observe the dominant literary discourse that associated descriptions of physical sexuality with base reality and, as such, proscribed them from representation.

Nonetheless, a few tales by d'Aulnoy, La Force, and Mailly especially contain what might be called sexually suggestive (as opposed to erotic) descriptions or allusions.[33] In relation to the period's governing *bienséances*, such descriptions represent an "excess" that is transgressive in theory but in practice is much less so. As a literary appropriation of folklore, the *conte de fées* was hardly expected to conform to the lofty abstraction of tragedy, for instance, and could thus incorporate descriptions not tolerated in other genres. An "*avis*" that precedes La Force's tale "L'Enchanteur" (The Sorcerer) explains that the author followed a medieval text from which "on ... a retranché beaucoup de choses qui n'étaient pas suivant nos mœurs" (were omitted many things that were not acceptable to our morals [NCF, 7: 48]). Following this (disingenuous?) proviso, the scenes of adultery that open the tale might be considered an integral part of the archaic intertext and a strategy to violate literary taste or decorum. Moreover, sexual suggestion sometimes occasions a humorous subversion of the fairy-tale form itself. In Perrault's "La Belle au bois dormant," for instance, it is the naïveté of the storyline that is underscored when, after describing how the prince had awakened Sleeping Beauty and immediately married her, the narrator states: "ils dormirent peu, la Princesse n'en avait pas grand besoin ..." (they slept little, the Princess didn't have a great need to ... [136]). In tales with more extended allusions, the physical expressions of sexuality occur very often as a result of metamorphosis or some other disguise, which obscures somewhat the erotic reality of the situation. In d'Aulnoy's "Le Dauphin" (The Dolphin), for instance, the hero, despised by the heroine, changes himself into a canary in order to win her affection and to penetrate her private space. When she falls asleep, he changes back into human form and joins her in bed, only to become a canary once again at daylight. When the heroine becomes pregnant, the fact that the canary is her favorite pet by day softens the impact of the canary/hero's real intentions. Like all the instances of sexual suggestion in the *contes de fées*, this example nonetheless exceeds the overwhelmingly psychological representation of love in the vogue as a whole. We might ask, then, what these suggestive descriptions reveal about the sexual ideologies that inform so many of the tales in this corpus.

With only a few exceptions (which I will discuss later), sexually explicit allusions depict scenes of masculine desire. Most often, these descriptions are (not so) veiled scenes of sexual aggression against the heroines. Hence, it is hardly coincidental that metamorphosis, metempsychosis, and other disguises are a pivotal part of these scenes and, even more important, that heroes are transformed decisively more often than heroines. Metamorphosis states aggressive male sexuality in a indirect way so that it can be attributed to the implausible marvelous setting and be more easily overcome in the course of the tale. Accordingly, in d'Aulnoy's "Le Prince Marcassin" (The Young Boar) and Murat's "Le Roy Porc" (The Pig King) the hero's aggression (outright violence in d'Aulnoy's tale) comes to an end when he regains his human form. Whatever harm the heroes commit in the first part of the tales is the result of their metamorphoses, their altered physical and psychological states. Yet, even female metamorphosis can be used to express male sexual aggression. In d'Aulnoy's "La Biche au bois" (The Doe in the Woods), for instance, it is the heroine who is transformed, and then hunted down, shot, and fondled by a king enraptured with the doe's beauty. In contrast to its indirect expression through metamorphosis, sexual aggression is represented even more overtly through metempsychosis and other magical disguises (invisibility being the most frequent). Of all the fairy-tale writers, it is Mailly who exhibits the most distinct predilection for these devices. In four of his tales ("Fortunio," "Le Prince Roger," "Le Bienfaisant, ou Quiribirini" [The Kind Man or Quiribirini] and "Le Roi magicien" [The Magician King]), metempsychosis or invisibility allows male characters to violate the heroines' private space and then occasions sexually suggestive allusions. These disguises give added freedom to male desires. Whereas metamorphosis is usually an enchantment that is imposed on an unwilling character and, as such, is a ready-made alibi for acts of sexual aggression, metempsychosis and invisibility are not since they are always magical powers at the service of the character's own desires.

In Mailly's "Le Prince Roger," invisibility is a crucial element of the hero's adventures. A king wants his son to travel so as to become "plus honnête homme, et d'être instruit à son retour de plusieurs choses qu'il avait curiosité de savoir ..." (more of an *honnête homme*, and to learn on his return about several things he was curious to know...)[34] To protect him against all dangers, the king finds the secrets of Mélusine's fairy magic – rings that make the wearer invisible and a magic wand that transforms everything it touches into whatever the user wants – and gives them to his son. Rather than protect himself, however, Roger uses the rings to slip unnoticed into women's bedrooms. On what happened in the bedroom of the first woman, "une dame pour qui il avait une forte inclination" (a lady for whom he had a strong attraction [33]), the narrator comments:

Comme le jeune cavalier n'aimait pas à dire les particularités de ses aventures, on ne sait pas ce qui se passa entre lui et la dame. Ce qu'on sait, est qu'il sortit le matin avec son écuyer, fort satisfait apparemment de la nuit, et d'avoir éprouvé le pouvoir de ses anneaux. Il retourna au plus vite à l'hôtellerie où il avait laissé ses chevaux ... On jugea dans ce lieu-là qu'il venait de passer la nuit en bonne fortune, et on le jugea d'autant plus qu'il se coucha en arrivant et dormit quelques heures.

As the young knight did not like to tell the specifics about his adventures, we don't know what happened between him and the lady. What we know is that he left in the morning with his squire apparently very satisfied because of the night and because of having experienced the power of his rings. He returned as fast as he could to the hotel where he had left his horses ... People there surmised that he had spent the night well, and they surmised this all the more so because he went to bed on his arrival and slept for several hours. (33–34)

More than a humorous sexual innuendo, this adventure is the first in a series during Prince Roger's trip. Upon arriving in Barcelona, he is attracted to a princess who is about to enter a loveless marriage. Unable to stop the wedding, he decides to humiliate the bridegroom by preventing him from consummating the marriage. The first several nights, Roger becomes invisible, touches the groom with his magic wand and makes him fall asleep immediately upon climbing into bed. Revelling in the disgrace he has brought to his rival, Roger turns his attention to another woman. But when he tries to approach her bed, she is frightened and denounces him as a sorcerer. At this point, Roger is forced to flee the city and head homeward. On the way, he meets Princess Tullie of Angoulême, falls in love with her, renounces the use of magic, and marries.

On one level, this tale charts the hero's passage from *galant* to tender love. The sexually suggestive adventures finally give way to the birth of Roger's "véritable passion" (true passion [45]), followed by the obligatory marriage closure. Throughout most of the narrative, however, the hero's adventures demonstrate, if anything, his *galanterie*, which would make him unsuited for marriage. And yet, the text indicates that Roger's "quest" prepares him for matrimony, that sowing one's wild oats is not incompatible with ideal love. It was his father, after all, who had encouraged him to travel and who had given him the magical implements that satisfy his appetite for (sexual) mischief. What begins as an exercise in character-building, according to the father at least, turns out to be a demonstration of his seductive powers, which the text repeatedly emphasizes. "Etant beau comme l'amour, il n'était pas possible qu'il ne fût désiré" (Being as beautiful as Cupid, it was not possible for him not to be desired [34]); "Il était ... continuellement à la cour, où il faisait les désirs de plusieurs personnes, car il était véritablement fait à peindre, et poli dans la dernière perfection..." (He was ... constantly at court where he came to be desired by several persons, for he was truly as handsome as a picture and courteous to perfection [41]). It is as if his physical appearance predestines him to his "adventures" in the women's bedrooms. Since he is irresistibly handsome, so the textual logic would seem to go, why shouldn't he force himself on women fortunate enough to attract him? We might conclude that Roger's avid pursuit of pleasure is not a departure from, but a fulfillment of the intended purpose of his trip. In the end, the final marriage is a retrospective justification for the hero's sexual exploits. What in most of the *contes de fées* is the supreme reward for the couple's mutual love is in Mailly's tale a defense of phallic desire. Sexual union and its mythic complementarity are replaced by sexual innuendo at the expense of women.

What the excess of Prince Roger's adventures reveals, finally, is that the ideology of romantic love prevalent in the *contes de fées* can be manipulated to fuel phantasms of (male) sexual aggression. However, in two other tales, d'Aulnoy's "L'Oranger et l'abeille" (The Orange Tree and the Bee) and La Force's "Vert et Bleu" (Green and Blue), sexual allusions (attempt to) redefine the sexual relation. In both tales, magical disguises play a central role since they accord the heroines a measure of control over their sexuality.

In "L'Oranger et l'abeille," metamorphosis not only allows the heroine and the hero to overcome a series of obstacles, but also to express their physical desire for each other. Aimée, the heroine, and, later, Aimé, the hero, are captured by a family of ogres. To escape from them, Aimée steals a magic wand with the power to metamorphose the bearer into whatever he or she wishes. Aimée uses it three times to hide from the furious ogres. The third time Aimée becomes a bee and Aimé an orange tree, and it is this metamorphosis that becomes the most important (as the title of this tale suggests). Before Aimée can reproduce their human form, some travelers take the wand, and the lovers are forced to resign themselves to their non-human forms. Far from impeding their love, their metamorphoses allow them to express their mutual attraction both verbally and physically. Fearing that she will be attracted by other trees, Aimé invites Aimée to enjoy his flowers: "Vous trouverez sur mes fleurs une agréable rosée et une liqueur plus douce que le miel: vous pourrez vous en nourrir. Mes feuilles vous serviront de lit de repos, où vous n'aurez rien à craindre de la malice des araignées" (You will find on my flowers a pleasant dew and a liqueur sweeter than honey. You will be able to nourish yourself with them. My leaves will serve as a couch where you will have nothing to fear from the malice of spiders). To this, Aimée responds by reaffirming her loyalty: "vous me verrez sans cesse voltiger autour de vous, et vous connaîtrez que l'Oranger n'est pas moins cher à l'Abeille que le prince Aimé l'était à la princesse Aimée" (you will see me buzz around you incessantly, and you will know that the Orange Tree is no less dear to the Bee than Prince Aimé was to Princess Aimée). When Aimée accepts her lover's invitation and encloses herself in one of his flowers, the text interprets this act as an expression of love and, by means of metamorphosis, "tenderness" takes the most physical of forms: "en effet, elle s'enferma dans une des plus grosses fleurs comme dans un palais; et la véritable tendresse qui trouve des ressources par tout, ne laissait pas d'avoir les siennes dans cette union" (indeed, she enclosed herself in one of the largest flowers as if in a palace. And true tenderness which finds satisfaction everywhere did not fail to have its own in this union).[35]

In contrast to "Le Prince Roger," then, this particular tale represents the sexual pleasure not only of the hero but also – and especially – of the heroine. The text emphasizes her active role in the sexual relation even further by inverting the courtly love model whereby a knight pledges his fidelity and service to a lady. In "L'Oranger et l'abeille," it is Aimée who reassures Aimé of her love and who defends him with chivalric-like prowess. When a princess attempts to pick some of Aimé's flowers, "la vigilante Abeille sor[t], bourdonnant dessous les feuilles où elle se tenait en sentinelle, et piqu[e] la princesse d'une telle force, qu'elle pens[e] s'évanouir" (the vigilant Bee flies out, buzzing under the leaves where she kept guard, and stings the princess so hard that she thought she would faint [344]). Later, when Aimé asks his bee-lover why she attacked the princess, she answers: "n'êtes-vous pas assez délicat pour comprendre que vous ne devez avoir des douceurs que pour moi, que tout ce qui est vous m'appartient, et que je défends mon bien, quand je défends vos fleurs?" (are you not sensitive enough to understand that you must only pay attention to me, that everything you are belongs to me, and that I defend my property when I defend your flowers? [345]). Aimée, then, further subverts the courtly love model; for instead of submitting to her lover's will, she exerts her own. The tale's final moral even generalizes her actions as an example to all women:

> Avec un tendre amant, seule au milieu des bois,
> Aimée eut en tout temps une extrême sagesse;
> Toujours de la raison elle écouta la voix,
> Et sut de son amant conserver la tendresse.
> Beautés, ne croyez pas, pour captiver les cœurs,
> 　　Que les plaisirs soient nécessaires;
> L'Amour souvent s'éteint au milieu des douceurs.
> 　　Soyez fières, soyez sévères,
> Et vous inspirerez d'éternelles ardeurs.

With a tender lover, alone in the middle of the woods, / Aimée always possessed a profound wisdom; / Always she listened to the voice of reason, / And knew how to keep the tenderness of her lover. / Beauties, do not believe that to capture hearts, / Pleasure is necessary; / Love is often extinguished amid sweetness. / Be proud, be severe, / And you will inspire eternal flames. (352)

Both the moral and the tale suggest that it is not by suppressing feminine desire but by asserting and by carefully managing it that men will remain constant.[36] In this light, the sexually suggestive scene between Aimée and Aimé (or rather the bee and the orange tree) demonstrates the satisfaction the heroine will continue to enjoy so long as she is an active partner. It is significant that this encounter is described from the bee's/ Aimée's perspective (Aimé tells her of the many pleasures his flowers can afford *her*) and that it is the heroine who is the active partner (*she* enters one of Aimé's flowers). To be sure, Aimée's and Aimé's metamorphoses (and, consequently, their respective activity and passivity) can be found in several versions of the tale-type AT313 (The Magic Flight). However, the end of "L'Oranger et l'abeille," in which Aimée assumes her resolutely active stance, differs from all other known versions of this tale-type.[37] It can be argued, then, that d'Aulnoy adapted the folkloric tradition so as to give a vision of feminine sexuality that exceeds not only the bounds of courtly love, but also the passivity to which so many other heroines are condemned.

Like d'Aulnoy's tale, La Force's "Vert et Bleu" also highlights feminine sexuality. Unlike "L'Oranger et l'abeille," however, this tale does not attempt to veil or displace erotic descriptions, but rather to capitalize on them. Although sexual allusions in several of La Force's tales are the most explicit of the entire vogue,[38] "Vert et Bleu" is arguably her most pronounced attempt to depict female eroticism and, more generally, her most explicit transgression of the period's literary *bienséances* proscribing representation of physical passion.

In this tale, eroticism is part of a more general insistence on vision as both an obstacle to and a catalyst for love. Indeed, the entire narrative is built around a visual conceit. This story opens with the fairy Sublime's prediction that the heroine Bleu (who is so named for the color of her eyes) would only be happy "lorsqu'elle s'unirait à quelqu'un d'aimable, mais qui lui serait entièrement opposé" (when she would be united with someone lovely but completely opposite her).[39] When, at the end of the tale, Princess Bleu is about to marry Prince Vert (named for the greenery with which his father, King Printemps, graces the world), the necessary impediment between them continues to be a mystery, until the fairy explains that the colors green and blue clash. To literalize the union of contrasting names, however, the fairy presents the couple with enchanted wedding clothes made of fine grass and blue hyacinths. Thus, what was incompatible becomes, in this symbolic and supernatural form, complementary.

Beyond this general thematization, vision plays a decisive role in the birth and expression of Vert's and Bleu's love. Observing a topos of this period that recurs frequently in the *contes de fées*, it is the first glimpse they catch of each other that inspires their love. Yet, Princess Bleu exerts ultimate control over men's gazes by means of the *voile d'Illusion* (veil of Illusion), given to her by the fairy Sublime. Intended to protect her astonishing beauty from unworthy eyes, the veil allows Bleu to appear to be whatever object she desires. Thus, when she first spies Vert, she "becomes" a statue. As the latter-day Pygmalion laments that the statue is but stone, the princess herself takes extreme pleasure in observing him. Their passion is born.

Perhaps the most significant and certainly the most sexually explicit moment in this tale occurs a little while later when Bleu, bathing in a fountain, catches sight of Vert and decides not to use her veil. Showing that this scene is one of mutual passion, this passage is worth quoting at length.

Elle se baignait, et son beau corps n'était couvert que d'un linge transparent ... Mais quelle joie et quelle surprise lorsque se jouant avec ses compagnes, elle l'aperçut tout d'un coup appuyé contre un arbre qui la considérait avec des yeux tout remplis d'amour.

C'était le prince Vert: quel autre au monde pouvait être fait comme lui? Le hasard l'avait conduit là, et son ravissement était extrême de trouver le merveilleux original de la belle statue qu'il avait vue et qu'il avait toujours depuis dans l'imagination. Il était charmé de voir qu'il y eut une fille au monde faite comme celle qu'il voyait. Il se flattait qu'elle ne serait pas insensible à tout l'amour qu'il ressentait ... Dans cette pensée, il considérait avidement tant de merveilles qu'il avait devant les yeux quand la princesse l'aperçut. Elle était plongée dans l'eau. Elle se leva inconsidérément, sans savoir ce qu'elle faisait, et par là elle offrit de nouvelles beautés aux regards du prince amoureux. La proportion et les grâces de cette divine figure lui causèrent un si tendre transport qu'il ne put s'empêcher de lui dire avec impétuosité tout ce qu'il ressentait. Bleu ne pouvait se cacher, elle n'avait plus le voile d'Illusion, il était à terre avec ses habits. Et à dire le vrai, elle n'en fut pas fâchée, et trouva quelque plaisir à l'effet que produisait sa beauté. Il y avait même tant d'esprit à ce que le prince lui disait, et ses sentiments paraissaient si nobles et si naturels, que la princesse, par un instinct qui est presque toujours sûr, ne douta pas qu'il ne fut celui que le ciel avait fait naître pour son bonheur.

She was bathing and her beautiful body was covered with only a transparent cloth ... But what joy and what surprise when, playing with her friends, she suddenly noticed him leaning against a tree watching her with eyes filled with love.

It was Prince Vert. What other man could be built as he? Coincidence had led him there, and his delight was extreme to find the marvelous original of the beautiful statue he had seen and kept since in his imagination. He was charmed to see that there was indeed a girl who looked like the one he saw. He hoped that she would not be insensitive to all the love he felt ... In this frame of mind, he was avidly gazing upon the many marvels he had before his eyes when the princess noticed him. She was immersed in the water. She stood up without thinking, without knowing what she was doing and thereby offered new beauties to the gaze of the amorous prince. The proportion and the graces of this divine figure caused a surge of such tender feelings in him that he could not keep himself from impetuously telling her everything he felt. Bleu could not hide herself, she no longer had the veil of Illusion. It was on the ground with her clothes. To tell the truth, she was not upset about it and found a certain pleasure in the effect that her beauty produced. There was even so much wit in what the prince told her and his feelings seemed so noble and so natural that the princess, through an instinct that is almost always right, did not doubt that he was the one the heavens had predestined for her happiness. (114–115)

The shifts in narrative point of view suggest that this scene is more than an instance of male voyeuristic pleasure. Describing first Bleu's gaze, the narrator next adopts Vert's perspective, only to shift back to Bleu's, then to Vert's, and finally to Bleu's one last time. Such a back-and-forth movement demonstrates the mutual desire between the couple. It underscores the fact that the princess not only accepts but enjoys the prince's erotic gaze ("[elle] trouva quelque plaisir à l'effet que produisait sa beauté"). This two-sided narrative perspective puts into relief

what turn out to be Vert's and Bleu's involuntary declarations
of love for each other. After contemplating the grace of Bleu's
perfectly proportioned body, Vert "ne put s'empêcher de lui
dire avec impétuosité tout ce qu'il ressentait" (could not keep
himself from impetuously saying everything he felt [115]).
Although Bleu is no less certain of her feelings for Vert, she also
declares her love by psychological denial: "elle voulut lui
répondre avec fierté, mais elle n'eut que de la modestie. En le
priant de la laisser, elle le retenait par une action passionnée.
Elle voulait qu'il ne lui parlât plus d'amour, et ses regards lui
faisaient voir que son cœur en était tout rempli" (she wanted to
answer him sharply, but she showed only modesty. Asking him
to leave her, she held him back with an impassioned act. She
did not want him to speak to her about love any more, and yet
her eyes showed him that her heart was filled with it [115]).
Through these declarations, the exchange of gazes leads to a
mutual certainty.[40] And finally, this erotically charged scene
pushes Bleu to the conclusion that "il ... fût celui que le ciel
avait fait naître pour son bonheur" (he ... was the one destiny
had created for her happiness) and Vert sees in the princess's
eyes that "son cœur ... était tout rempli [d'amour]" (her heart
was filled with love [115]). Eliciting rather than repressing the
erotic within the sexual relation, this passage simultaneously
accentuates mutual pleasure and activity. To be sure, Vert's
point of view is discussed at greater length than Bleu's. But if
not entirely equal, the hero and heroine are at least both willing
participants in this erotic field of vision.

Although a utopian vision of feminine sexuality is somewhat
clearer in "Vert et Bleu" than in "L'Oranger et l'abeille," in
the end neither tale questions the mythic sexual relation.
Moreover, both of these *contes de fées* express in only a muted
way an eroticism that gives pleasure to both partners. In
d'Aulnoy's tale, metamorphosis provides a veil of ambiguity
that strategically blurs any transgressive connotations. While
Bleu's *voile d'Illusion*, in La Force's tale, is more of a tease than
a protective cover, the second half of the narrative effectively
attenuates the eroticism of the fountain scene by focusing on
the couple's (obligatory) misfortunes and (equally obligatory)

final reunion and marriage. Yet, in spite of these limitations, both "L'Oranger et l'abeille" and "Vert et Bleu" envision what in most of the *contes de fées* and indeed most of seventeenth-century literature is inconceivable – the deliberate expression of a woman's physical desire. As tentative and nuanced as they are, then, the sexually suggestive passages in these tales are longings for an eroticism that is not the sole province of male voyeurism, for a literary discourse that envisions the "excess" of feminine sexuality.

BEYOND THE ENDING

A happy ending is perhaps the most predictable of all narrative features throughout the *contes de fées*. More than often, this convention takes the form of the marriage closure, even when love is not a primary focus of the plot (such as in Perrault's "Le Chat botté" or Le Noble's "L'Apprenti magicien"). However, a small group of tales by four of the *conteuses* (d'Aulnoy, d'Auneuil, Bernard, and Murat), which I will call dysphoric tales, defy these conventional endings. Concluding with the death of one or both of the protagonists[41] or a rejection of love and/or marriage,[42] these texts do not resolve the "degradation" of the protagonists' fate at the beginning of the story with a final "amelioration." Rather, they constitute, inherently at least, a critical perspective on the representation of love that dominates the vast majority of the *contes de fées*. By displaying the failure of the marvelous to ensure a happy ending, these texts have the potential to cast doubt on the newly-weds' mutual and everlasting satisfaction, their perfect complementarity, and, in some cases, the very possibility of the sexual relation.

The endings in the dysphoric tales closely resemble those in a strain of late seventeenth-century novels, authored mostly by women, that depict the turbulence and ultimate failure of love.[43] From this perspective, then, these *contes de fées* do not represent anything original or new, but are a continuation of a pre-existent literary tradition. And yet, over and against the highly predictable happy endings of the corpus as a whole, these tales stand out in stark relief. In them, the marvelous, which ordinarily enables the protagonists to overcome even the most overwhelming of obstacles, is of no avail. Love resists the reestablishment of order that usually occurs in the supernatural setting. These unhappy endings clearly do not provide a nostalgic wish-fulfillment for a by-gone vision of love, as do the happy endings in most of the other *contes de fées*. How, then, might we interpret these tales, especially against the backdrop of the larger corpus?

Many of them might be classified as what folklorists call "warning tales," in which the unhappy ending serves an explicitly stated didactic purpose, usually in the form of a negative example.[44] Most often, a final versed moral or, failing this, maxims interspersed throughout the tale make it clear that the dysphoric end is intended to have a precise meaning for readers, and particularly to impart some general knowledge about human existence. In d'Aulnoy's "L'Isle de la félicité" (The Island of Happiness) – the inaugural tale of the vogue, one of the two dysphoric tales based explicitly on folkloric tale-types, and the only one with an unhappy ending in its folkloric versions[45] – the story is said to have made people conclude that "le temps vient à bout de tout et qu'il n'est point de félicité parfaite" (time catches up with everything and that there is no perfect happiness).[46] Ultimately, however, not all of the tales with unhappy endings can be classified as "warning tales." And while this folkloric category explains how the comparatively unconventional closure could be justified, it does not necessarily explain why it might have been attractive to writers and, presumably, readers. To do so, I would suggest, requires that we consider the extent to which these tales critique love and/or marriage.

In d'Aulnoy's "Le Nain jaune," the ending does not question the existence of the sexual relation. This tale tempers its tragic ending, in which both the hero and the heroine expire, when their "good" siren intervenes to have their bodies metamorphosed into two palm trees. "Ces deux corps si parfaits devinrent deux beaux arbres. Conservant toujours un amour fidèle l'un pour l'autre, ils se carressent de leurs branches

entrelacées et immortalisent leurs feux par leur tendre union"
(These two bodies, so perfect, became two beautiful trees.
Conserving forever a faithful love for each other, they caress
one another with their interwoven branches and immortalize
their flame through their tender union.)[47] Far from rejecting
love and marriage, this closure simply transposes them onto the
marvelous setting. Resurrected as trees, the lovers replace the
dangers and unpredictability of their human existence with the
stability and immortality of their metamorphosis. What was a
tragedy becomes, apparently, a fate even happier than a final
marriage. For, the protagonists' love acquires an irreversible,
physical form.

By comparison, the other dysphoric *contes de fées* adopt a
much more critical view of love and marriage. In them, the
final outcome is the result of the inconstancy of desire itself,
rather than the imperfection of the protagonists' supernatural
powers (as in "Le Nain jaune") or the result of fate (as in
d'Aulnoy's "L'Isle de la félicité" and "Le Mouton").[48] It is
Bernard and Murat who most clearly demystify the idealized
vision of love that appears in the rest of the vogue. Specifically
linking the dysphoria of the conclusion to the impermanence of
desire, these *conteuses* subvert the very possibility of a final
marriage as the means to happiness. At the end of Bernard's
"Le Prince Rosier," for instance, the hero and heroine are
married only to find that life together falls far short of fairy-tale
expectations: "le mariage, selon la coûtume, finit tous les
agréments de leur vie. Heureux s'ils en étaient demeurés à une
honnête indifférence, mais les gens accoûtumes à aimer ne sont
pas si raisonnables que les autres et ne sont guère l'exemple des
bons ménages" (marriage, as usual, ended all the pleasures of
their life. They would have been happy had they retained a
polite indifference, but people accustomed to loving are not as
reasonable as others and are hardly the example of good
couples.)[49] Likewise, at the end of Murat's "Le Palais de la
vengeance," the evil magician Pagan encloses the lovers in a
crystal palace where they cannot escape each other's sight.
After a few years, the narrator explains, the couple wanted
nothing else than to find an end to "des enchantements

agréables" (pleasurable enchantments).[50] This tale's "lesson" is summarized in the final moral:

> Avant ce temps fatal, les amants trop heureux
> Brûlaient toujours des mêmes feux,
> Rien ne troublait le cours de leur bonheur extrême;
> Pagan leur fit trouver le secret malheureux,
> De s'ennuyer du bonheur même.

Before that fateful time, the happy lovers / Always burned with the same flame, / Nothing troubled the course of their extreme happiness; / Pagan made them find the unfortunate secret, / Of becoming bored with happiness itself. (367)

The assurances of other fairy tales to the contrary, this tale proves that love is not eternal, that the satisfaction of desire spells its own end, and that the sexual relation is a mirage. The transparency of the crystal palace in which the lovers are imprisoned allows them to see through each other, so to speak, and thereby, to see through the myth of eternal love.

Perhaps the most sustained demystification of desire in this corpus occurs in Murat's "Anguillette." Although the end of this tale closely resembles the end of "Le Nain jaune" – the bodies of the deceased lovers are transformed into trees – Murat's take on love is considerably more pessimistic than d'Aulnoy's. In fact, the final metamorphosis is not the perpetuation of love beyond death, as in "Le Nain jaune," but rather a simple memorial to the lovers' appearance in life. "[Les restes] se changèrent en deux arbres d'une beauté parfaite. La fée les nomma CHARMES, pour conserver à jamais la mémoire de ceux qu'on avait vu briller dans ces malheureux amants" ([The remains] were changed into two trees of perfect beauty. The fairy named them CHARMES to preserve forever the memory of those that had been seen to shine in these unfortunate lovers.)[51] In contrast to the celebratory tone of d'Aulnoy's ending, Murat's has a funereal reserve. Yet, this somber ending is carefully prepared from the very beginning of "Anguillette." After rewarding the heroine, Hébé, with intelligence (*esprit*), beauty, and riches for her kindness, the fairy Anguillette warns her young charge that she has no power over the heart and that she is incapable of ending love once it is born. Hébé disregards her fairy's admonition and allows herself to be wooed by Prince Atimir. Throughout their courtship and the ensuing events, the narrative adopts a highly critical posture, with imagery and even plot elements reminiscent of *La Princesse de Clèves*. Both Madame de Chartres in Lafayette's novel and the fairy Anguill-ette warn the heroines about the dangers of love. The *conte de fées* describes Hébé's passion in terms similar to those used for the Princesse de Clèves: love is labelled a "poison" that makes Hébé lose her "tranquillité."[52] The most decisive parallel between the two texts is that both heroines are wed to men they do *not* love and are pursued by men they *do* love.[53] To regain control over her emotions – to regain her "tranquillité" – Hébé retreats from court, as does Madame de Clèves. I evoke these similarities not so much to argue that Murat rewrote Lafayette's masterpiece (although the similarities are striking) but rather that "Anguillette" transposes a very similar vision of love onto a marvelous setting. The result, however, is even more pro-foundly pessimistic. That even a heroine, like Hébé, with seemingly limitless supernatural resources at her disposal, is unable to escape the suffering of love makes happiness all the more elusive. And, whereas Madame de Clèves dies only after overcoming her love for the Duc de Nemours, Hébé succumbs once again to her passion for Atimir and dies of grief when he is killed at the end of the tale.

I would argue that the pessimism in "Anguillette" and all the dysphoric *contes de fées* (with the possible exception of "Le Nain jaune") serves a utopian function. The unhappy ending in these tales is not only a negation of received conceptions of love and sexuality but also – thereby – a yearning for different ones.[54] In "Anguillette," this utopian longing is figured in the miraculous Isle Paisible (Peaceful Island). It is to this island that Hébé retires, with her fairy's help, when her suitor Atimir abandons her for another woman. After swearing to Anguillette that she will never again set eyes on Atimir, Hébé lands on the island and immediately feels that her heart is "tranquille" (277), a sentiment that is reinforced by her marriage to the Prince de l'Isle Paisible, whom she respects but does not love. When, against Anguillette's orders, she leaves the island to return to court, Hébé sees Atimir and discovers that the passion between them has been rekindled. Finally, at the end of the tale, the Prince de l'Isle Paisible returns to his island-kingdom after killing his rival in a duel and witnessing his wife die of grief. Once there, he finds consolation on his loss and eventually forgets his love for Hébé. The island is the material wish-fulfillment for a solution to amorous misfortune. "La fée Anguillette ... avait attaché [à l'Isle Paisible], depuis deux mille ans, l'heureux don de guérir les passions malheureuses: l'on assure même que ce don y dure encore; mais la difficulté est de pouvoir aborder dans cette île" (The fairy Anguillette ... had granted to [the Isle Paisible], for two thousand years, the felicitous power to heal unfortunate passions: it is even claimed that this power still exists there; but it is difficult to reach this island [277]). By claiming that this island really exists, the narrative externalizes the desire for refuge from the suffering of love. The fact that this island is difficult to reach and cannot prevent Hébé's tragic end is a sign of the incomplete nature of this utopian longing. Ultimately, the Isle Paisible plays a paradoxical role within this tale. On the one hand, it amplifies the conclusion's negation of the mythic happiness of love. In spite of their potential, neither the island nor its prince is able to completely satisfy Hébé, nor can her retreat banish her fateful desires. On the other hand, it offers, if nothing else, limited hope for a solution to the suffering that this tale equates with love. The Isle Paisible is the longing for something other than the inevitable failure of the sexual relation, something other than the impossible complementarity of masculine and feminine desires. Neither the Isle Paisible nor the dysphoric *contes de fées* (with one notable exception, as we will see below) describe what this "something other" might be. They do, however, go beyond the endings of the rest of the corpus by replacing the tautological certainty of the marriage closure or the reunion of husband and wife with the unpredictability of fate and desire.

In "Peine Perdue" (Lost Effort), one of her manuscript tales, Murat again evokes a geographical refuge from the suffering caused by love. In this story, however, we catch a more precise glimpse of what might lie beyond the unhappy ending. Unsuccessful in her attempts to court Prince Isabel, Peine Perdue (whose name of course prefigures her failure) is led by her mother, a fairy, to the "pays des injustices de l'amour" (the country of the injustices of love). This country is inhabited by "ceux ... qui étaient dans la douleur, mais une douleur qui n'avait rien d'emporté" (those ... who were in sadness, but a sadness that had nothing extreme about it).[55] By contenting themselves with a natural simplicity, the inhabitants find a relative peace that escapes the constraints of worldly interaction: "les habits étaient simples, on ne connaissait point la magnificence dans ce royaume; nulle recherche dans l'ajustement parce qu'il n'y avait plus de désirs de plaire. On n'y logeait que dans de petites cabanes. La nature seule sans aucuns ornements faisait toute la beauté des promenades" (the clothes were simple, magnificence was unknown in this kingdom; there was no affectation in fashion because there were no longer any desires to please. Only small cabins were used for lodging. Nature alone, without any decoration, constituted the entire beauty of the walks [135]). Proving the adage that "misery enjoys company," Peine Perdue finds if not happiness then at least solace in a land whose very existence is based on a negation of love: "Peine Perdue trouva, ainsi que la fée le lui avait fait espérer, quelque adoucissement à ses maux en voyant qu'elle n'était pas seule à plaindre. Elle demeura volontiers dans ce pays et elle ne voulut même jamais le quitter, s'étant fait une douce habitude de vivre avec des personnes tendres, malheureuses et fidèles" (Peine Perdue found, just as the fairy had promised her, a slight alleviation of her pain by seeing that she was not the only one to be pitied. She agreed to stay in this country and she never even wanted to leave it, having accustomed herself to living with people who were tender, unhappy, and faithful [135]). In the end, then, Peine Perdue resigns herself to masochistic contentment. What makes this land of refuge desirable, we might surmise, is that its inhabitants, in spite of their unhappiness, are tender and faithful, among the most prized traits in seventeenth-century amorous discourse.[56] Devoid of desire, the inhabitants still retain the qualities necessary for the highest form of friendship. These inhabitants move beyond the failure of love by making it into something concrete, something other than negativity or death. Sexuality is suppressed and replaced by friendship, which assumes the affective and ethical components of love. With this tale, then, Murat takes the dysphoric *conte de fées* beyond the unhappy ending. She demonstrates, explicitly and in geographical terms, how the failure of love can become a place of refuge. She sketches in perhaps the clearest terms how the quest for love, especially by a heroine, can be rewritten to utopian ends.

Taken as a group, the *contes de fées* do not convey a single or univocal vision of love and sexuality. And in its multiple and conflicting representations, the vogue seems to suggest a cultural malaise or even anxiety about the place of sexuality in society. If we recall that it was primarily during the seventeenth century that sexuality was relegated (by Church and State) to the confines of the family unit, then the presence of opposing nostalgic and utopian desires within this corpus can be understood as attempts to come to terms with this situation. The nostalgic glorification of romantic love, ending almost invariably with an eternally blissful marriage, accepts the dominant codification of sexuality and obscures the repression of women within this ideology. Fueled by the marvelous, nostalgia offers an alternative vision of the real that accepts but mystifies its basic tenets. At the other extreme, as we have seen, are indications of utopian resistance to the strictures placed on sexuality by the idealized family unit. The *contes de fées* attempt to redefine the increasingly strictly controlled domain of male–female relations within the (albeit highly relative) freedom of imaginary worlds. In another sense, however, the diverging and in some instances contradictory forms taken by these utopian longings offer a more radical insight, namely, that there can be no one, single vision of sexuality. Both mystifying and rejecting the myth of the sexual relation, both adopting and rewriting folkloric and literary tradition, the vogue as a whole and even the *conteurs* and *conteuses* taken individually expose the tensions among competing discourses of sexuality. Of course, accepting the multiplicity of human sexuality, far beyond that outlined in the *contes de fées*, is a utopian project for the real worlds of our own time.

CHAPTER 5

(De)mystifications of masculinity: fictions of transcendence

Compared to other literary forms, characters in fairy tales occupy a world apart. Perhaps most obvious are the super-human powers of some and the extraordinary adventures of all characters in this genre. Just as salient as supernatural traits, however, is the predictable, repetitious quality of fairy-tale characterization. In fact, part of what distinguishes fairy tales is that they draw on a set of stock characters – fairies, ogres, tricksters, princes, princesses, and the like – who perform similar (nearly identical) tasks from text to text. So predictable and so repetitious are they that critics have often noted the one-dimensionality of fairy-tale characters.[1] Usually devoid of individuating psychological traits, protagonists and antagonists alike highlight specific narrative and ideological functions. In other words, they are first and foremost incarnations of cultural values. They purvey the norms of the community and reject those of the individual.

Ideologically speaking, the repetition of characters from fairy tale to fairy tale is, in and of itself, highly significant, for it is through repetition that the meanings embodied by characters become self-evident. Susan Stewart has observed that repetition is only truly possible outside of everyday life, and most notably in fiction. "Repetition can only take place in a domain where context is folded into text, where the text can control all variations in context by presenting an illusion of timelessness."[2] Operating within the controlled time and space of textuality, repetition has a generative power. "What is repeated is what is, a parameter defined in spite of time ... If repetition in fictions is an aid to our sense of closure, giving us a sense of return to a beginning, it is because repetition is always involved in giving integrity to what is repeated" (*Nonsense*, 121). Of course, fairy tales make a point of insulating themselves from the everyday world of their readers. So doing, they ensure the conditions necessary for a limited cast of characters to be used time and again in a set and predictable number of situations. The recurrence of these characters and their narrative functions create the assurance of fixity, the illusion that the mutable is immutable.

Not surprisingly, the repetitive use of characters in fairy tales is crucial to their representations of gender. On the whole, the strictly codified traits that distinguish protagonists from antagonists are equally strict in differentiating male from female characters. Thus, heroes are not granted the same qualities as heroines, and evil sorcerers are distinct from wicked fairies. Moreover, by (re)using set character-types, fairy tales (re)enact specific gender identities. Since they are usually devoid of individuating traits, fairy-tale characters might be said to highlight their gender and sexual identities as do few if any other literary personages. Generally speaking, protagonists incarnate – stand for – a culture's positive gender traits as antagonists do for the negative ones. The fact that these character-types as gender stereotypes recur over and over suggests (at least implicitly) that one of the most prominent functions of fairy tales is to give the appearance that gender differences are fixed, "natural" entities. As if to guard against the erosion of what a culture considers to be the irrevocable "truth" of masculinity and femininity, fairy tales state and restate, often with tiresome predictability, just what that "truth" is.

Why is it that fairy tales are so bent on representing the same restricted set of characters, the same set of masculine and feminine norms? To answer these questions, it may be helpful to consider these representations as performances, as social figurations that give the appearance of being real or natural and are capable of being enacted indefinitely. Judith Butler has used the notion of performance to theorize the social construction of gender. For her, performance and performativity enable us to understand that "the gendered body ... has no ontological status apart from the various acts which constitute its reality" (*Gender Trouble*, 136). In this perspective, gender identities are repetitions of fabricated roles that are contrived to make sense of the instability of social reality. Considering gender as performative suggests the instability of the very norms it specifies within a given culture. If gender is a matter of imitating and repeating conventional norms (rather than of recognizing and bringing to the fore a biological essence), then the risk of deviation is always at hand. More specifically, gender identities like performances are temporary, contingent on repetition. Their performance is an unending process that reacts to a culture's regulatory norms. Because the enforcement of such norms is never complete – because they are norms – performance is a cultural imperative, the stability of which is always at least potentially at risk.

What this means for fairy tales is that the repetition of highly codified characters with predictable gender traits is as many performances designed to reinforce and to "naturalize" a particular "sex/gender system." Paradoxically, it also means that fairy tales, like other texts, have the capacity to manipulate gender representations in ways not prescribed by cultural norms. For, as Butler has concluded, "the possibilities of gender transformation are to be found precisely in the arbitrary relation between such [performative] acts, in the possibility of a failure to repeat, a de-formity, or a parodic repetition that exposes the phantasmatic effect of abiding identity as a politically tenuous construction" (*Gender Trouble*, 141). Generally speaking, however, fairy tales in our culture (the best known at any rate) have been used far less to alter gender identities than to reinforce them. And yet, close examination of specific, lesser known literary fairy tales suggests that this is an oversimplification. The first vogue of *contes de fées* repeats highly codified and highly conventionalized gender performances, but in certain cases it also deviates from them. The two chapters that follow examine the range of gender performances that appear throughout the *contes de fées*. Normative structures of masculinity and femininity in this corpus are reified through repetition but also disrupted. As we will see, both the repetition and the ambivalence of these fairy-tale representations reflect a moment of transition and crisis in larger cultural understandings about the boundaries of gendered subjectivity.

In the Western literary heritage, romance literature has served overwhelmingly to mystify patriarchal dominance. The quest and love plots so central to this tradition regularly subjugate women to male authority and then glorify this inequality. Women are not only willing participants but often the crucial objects of the romantic plot, short of which the masculine quest is meaningless. But this centrality does not mean that women are granted a subjectivity of their own. Indeed, as Leslie Rabine has put it, "the dominant masculine voice of the traditional romantic narrative imposes a totalizing structure on romantic narrative and represses an independent feminine other. Reducing the heroine to a reflection of himself, the hero makes of her an 'intermediary,' as Simone de Beauvoir says, through whom he can realize his desire to return to a mythical union with himself."[3] In its most prevalent forms, then, romance literature has privileged masculine subjectivity and, through it, a patriarchal social order. Romance literature is an effect of a cultural romance with masculinity – a desire if not a compulsion to direct attention away from the weaknesses of the masculine subject.

This chapter examines the constructions of masculinity in the *contes de fées*, which like many fairy tales are perhaps the most extreme form of romance literature. By taking masculinity as an object of study here, I intend first of all to deconstruct the textual/narrative mechanisms by which this corpus perpetuates patriarchal power on the level of characterization and then to explore the ways that many of these fairy tales question or even offer alternatives to such dominant models. To focus on the representations of masculinity, however, is not to slight femininity and, thus, unwittingly reproduce the marginalization of women so characteristic of patriarchal relations. Rather, it is to re-examine the radical interdependence of masculinity and femininity as psychic and social entities, to analyze how these interactions are legitimated and/or disrupted.

(DE)MYSTIFYING LACK

The notion of lack is central to both psychoanalytic discussions of human subjectivity and structuralist theories of narrative. For psychoanalysis (especially in its Lacanian inflection), all human subjects are defined by lack. An individual enters into the symbolic register that allows a sense of self and a recognition of others by subordinating itself to "a discursive order which pre-exists, exceeds, and substantially 'speaks' it" (Silverman, *Masculinity*, 35). The subject does not possess existential being nor is it "in possession" of itself or of language. Rather, through the workings of fantasy, the subject is granted the illusion of reality, of self, of other, and of wholeness. To exist, the subject covers over the reality of lack with the illusion of being.

Implicitly or explicitly, lack is also given a central place in structuralist accounts of narrative. For Propp, for instance, it is either the lack of an object, person, or status or an act of villainy creating a situation of lack that typifies all narratives. Similarly, for Brémond, an initial degradation of the protagonist's fate generates the subsequent narrative sequences. For both Propp and Brémond (among others), narrative – and above all folkloric narrative – is predicated on lack and its "liquidation" (to use Propp's term). Narrative cannot exist without lack, nor can it exist without the drive to eliminate it.

Now this parallel is not as arbitrary as it may seem, for subjectivity and narrative criss-cross and are interdependent. The psychic trajectory of the human subject is unknowable except as narrative, as a figurative story with beginning, middle, and end. Contrariwise, narratives concern nothing other than the dilemmas faced by human beings as they come to terms with psychic and cultural patterns of existence. Moreover, both subjectivity and narrative share a number of characteristics. Both require lack in order to come into existence. Both attempt to displace or suppress lack. And in the end, both are in a situation in which lack can never be eliminated. Struggle as he or she may, the human subject can never master the symbolic register that defines him or her. Even if the classic fairy-tale narrative ends by providing satisfaction or rectifying the initial misdeed, it can never get away from lack. Its suppression in any particular story is always temporary and unstable, something to be rehearsed again and again in countless other stories.

The notion of lack is also crucial to understanding the ways that Western culture has differentiated between masculinity and femininity. According to Lacanian psychoanalytic theories, "normative" masculinity precludes the recognition of lack or symbolic castration that defines all human subjects. At the same time, femininity is said to assume or embody it. Needless to say, the denial of lack within masculinity and its displacement onto femininity buttress the cultural edifice of masculine privilege. To deny lack and, thus, to maintain its hegemony, the normative masculine subject must conflate anatomical difference and sexual difference (the penis and the phallus) as well as the biological father and the symbolic father (or the Law of the Father). Thus, dominant masculinity is predicated on both a figuration and a reduction of this figuration to visibility. While the penis is in fact equated with the phallus (the arbiter of symbolic meaning) and the father with the Law (the symbolic register itself), the penis and the father are denied a status as cultural/psychic metaphors and are granted the authority of the phallus and the Law.

In its dominant cultural form, then, masculinity transcends its own lack of being and the figurative equivalence founding its dominance. This transcendence – or rather, this appearance of transcendence – requires collusion from every side. Women, especially, are called upon to disavow reality. Indeed, femininity becomes the objectification of lack, of (symbolic and sexual) castration, even as it becomes the complementary supplement to heterosexual masculinity. Thus, transcendence is not transcendence at all, but disavowal and displacement. Transcendence is a fiction, but a fiction upon which dominant masculinity is grounded and which our culture presents as truth.

It is not surprising, then, that much narrative is concerned with proving the truth of (what is actually the fiction of) male transcendence. The repetitive and predictable gender performances of romance literature privilege narrative schemata in which heroes strive for and succeed in obtaining a satisfying wholeness that obliterates the specter of lack, most often at the expense of the heroine. As Rabine has put it, "the hero is the quintessentially phallocentric subject, and the heroine figures as the lack which promises his plenitude ... He projects onto her both his own lack and also the guarantee of its transcendence" (*Reading the Romantic Heroine*, 10). If this dominant narrative model stipulates that, when all is said and done, the hero will enjoy the benefits of self-mastery, of unimpeded subjectivity, at the same time "the heroine is everything but the subject of her own autonomous language, of her own desire, and of her own history" (Rabine, *Reading the Romantic Heroine*, 12).

Murat's tale "Le Prince des Feuilles" (The Leaf Prince) provides an emphatic but also ambiguous example of how the *contes de fées* go about ensuring that masculinity will escape lack unscathed. The title notwithstanding, the beginning of this tale concentrates not on the hero, but the heroine, the incredibly beautiful Ravissante (meaning "ravishing" or "delightful"). She is raised by a fairy who takes her to an enchanted island in hopes of sparking a romance between the heroine and her nephew Ariston. It is at this point that the Prince des Feuilles enters the scene and becomes the center of narrative attention. From the very first, the Prince des Feuilles is quite literally a spectacular presence. He washes ashore in a barrel propelled by a multitude of winged fish. As we might expect, as soon as he and Ravissante cast eyes on one another, they are instantly overcome with passion. The hero's spectacular debut, so to speak, is followed by numerous displays of his supernatural powers. He gives Ravissante a pair of anthropomorphic butter-flies who, acting as couriers, escape the surveillance of the fairy and Ariston. From them, Ravissante learns of the adventures of the magical Prince des Papillons (the Prince of Butterflies), who is a close friend of the Prince des Feuilles. She also discovers that the adventures of the two princes mirror each other. Not only have they both fallen in love with a princess imprisoned by a fairy, but they also must rely on each other. The Prince des Papillons can only communicate with his beloved through the

Prince des Feuilles, who cannot rescue Ravissante without his butterfly friend.

Ensuring as it does the successful conclusion to the heroes' parallel love stories, the bond of friendship (re)doubles the powers of heroic masculinity in the tale. It could be argued that this homosocial bond rivals the heterosexual bonds between the princes and their princesses. For, the tale turns out to be as much a story about the two heroes as a story about their quests for love. The Prince des Papillons emerges from a tale within the tale to complement the powers of the Prince des Feuilles. Through this complementarity, the hero's magical presence is in effect doubled and his deficiencies overcome twice as it were, which makes the triumph of the heroic couple even more inevitable. Banished from this tale, then, would seem to be the very possibility of doubting the success of masculine heroism.

Yet, to transcend the threat of lack, the hero must be recognized as the superlative being who confronts and resolves the narrative's central dilemma. And, it is Ravissante who most clearly fulfills this role. By expressing her amazement at the Prince des Feuilles and his powers, Ravissante becomes the measure of just how much the hero transcends the existence of ordinary heroes. When the prince makes his grand entrance by sea, the princess's own surprise is reflected back onto her. Through his attention, she is made the object of this spectacle of heroic love

Ce bel inconnu éprouva un étonnement pareil à celui qu'il causait. La beauté de Ravissante ne lui laissa pas la liberté de s'amuser à regarder le reste du spectacle, dont l'éclat l'avait attiré d'assez loin jusques à ce rocher. Il s'approcha de la princesse avec une grâce qu'elle n'avait jamais vue qu'en elle-même. Je suis si surpris, lui dit-il, de ce que je trouve sur ces bords que j'ai perdu même la liberté de pouvoir exprimer mon étonnement. Est-il possible, continua-t-il, qu'une déesse comme vous n'ait pas des temples par tout l'univers? Par quels charmes, par quels prodiges êtes-vous encore inconnue aux mortels?

This beautiful stranger felt an astonishment similar to the one he caused. Ravissante's beauty did not give him the liberty of amusing himself by watching the rest of the spectacle, the splendor of which had led to this rock from far away. He approached the princess with a grace that she had only seen in herself. I am so surprised, he told her, by what I find on these shores that I have lost even the ability to express my astonishment. Is it possible, he continued, that a goddess like you does not have temples throughout the universe? By what enchantment, by what miracle are you still unknown to mortals? (377)

I have already suggested that throughout the *contes de fées* the expression of amazement at the marvelous emphasizes the transcendence of the real and the ordinary.[4] In this particular scene, however, a superhuman hero praises the human heroine in terms that liken her to himself. Albeit conventional, the prince's praise works a magic on Ravissante. The spectacle of the prince encompasses the heroine in a self-irradiating glow of astonishment. The heroine reflects back onto him the mystery and power of his being.

If the hero emerges bolstered from his spectacular appearance before Ravissante, she on the contrary is reduced in status. More precisely, she assumes for herself the lack deflected from the hero. Responding to the prince's lofty praise of her beauty, the heroine insists on the lowliness of her real situation: "Je ne suis point une déesse, dit Ravissante en rougissant. Je suis une princesse infortunée..." (I am not a goddess, said Ravissante blushing. I am an unfortunate princess ... [377]). Similarly, when the butterflies given to her by the Prince des Feuilles begin to speak, the heroine is taken aback in spite of the hero's warning that "les papillons ne sont pas seulement ce qu'ils ... paraissent" (the butterflies are not only what they ... appear to be [383]). The textual emphasis on Ravissante's surprise has a dual effect, at once indicating the superhuman powers of all that comes from the hero and subtly reminding us of the ordinary position occupied by the heroine. If the prince alludes to the supernatural state of the butterflies while giving them to her, it is above all to remind her of his own powers. She exists to demonstrate these superlative psychic and physical powers. She is the necessary object through which these powers manifest themselves. In and of herself and in spite of her remarkable beauty, Ravissante is the embodiment of lack.

Despite all the textual resources guaranteeing the hero's

success, Murat's tale nonetheless suggests how fragile masculinity really is. In fact, if "Le Prince des Feuilles" seems so preoccupied with the signs of masculine transcendence, it is perhaps most of all because the hero's gendered identity must overcome several threats. Perhaps the most direct is the brief suggestion of sexual rivalry between the Prince des Feuilles and the Prince des Papillons. When his butterfly form prevents him from declaring his love to the Princesse des Linottes, the Prince des Papillons refuses to ask his princely equal for help, fearing he will usurp what he judges to be his rightful place. Only the intervention of Cupid, who inclines the hero's heart toward Ravissante, diffuses this potential disruption of the homosocial bond. The very mention of jealousy between the two protagonists – highly unusual in the *contes de fées* or fairy tales generally – draws all the more attention to the tale's depiction of heroic male friendship. But it also exposes a more insidious truth. As the work of René Girard and, especially, Eve Kosovsky Sedgwick has shown, homosociality is predicated on antagonism between men.[5] Summarizing Girard, Sedgwick observes that "in any erotic rivalry, the bond that links either of the rivals is as intense and potent as the bond that links either of the rivals to the beloved: that the bonds of 'rivalry' and 'love,' differently as they are experienced, are equally powerful and in many senses equivalent ... [In many instances] the choice of the beloved is determined in the first place, not by the qualities of the beloved, but by the beloved's already being the choice of the person who has been chosen as a rival" (Sedgwick, *Between Men*, 21). Far from exemplifying the purity of courtly love and the "authentic" desire of the two heroes, then, the matrimonial triumph at the end of "Le Prince des Feuilles" is actually born of rivalry. The eruption of jealousy reminds us that masculine identity is structured mimetically, and that desire, premised on lack, is central to heroic transcendence.

Yet, the extent to which the heroes actually attain and maintain self-mastery is called into question in the tale's final moral, which laments the fictiveness of Ravissante's happiness:

> Qu'on doit porter envie au sort de Ravissante!
> Par une ardeur vive et constante,

> L'amour lui prodigua ses trésors précieux;
> Pour en pouvoir jouir comme elle,
> Hélas! que l'on serait heureux,
> S'il suffisait d'être fidèle!

How we should envy Ravissante's fate! / With firm and constant ardor, / Love poured out its precious treasures upon her; / To be able to enjoy them as she does, / Alas! how happy we would be, / If it were sufficient to be faithful! (400)

These concluding verses contrast sharply with the story's insistence on the happiness that follows faithfulness in love. At the very beginning, for instance, the fairy predicts that Ravissante will only be happy if "son cœur fût toujours fidèle aux premières impressions qu'il recevrait de l'amour" (her heart were always faithful to the first inklings it would feel of love [369]). To promote the heroine's *constance*, the fairy takes her to an island of sky-blue rock. Not surprisingly, Ravissante's propensity for fidelity is immediately evident. Fidelity is exemplified even more directly and more concretely by the Prince des Papillons. Ruler of subjects whom Cupid has metamorphosed into butterflies as punishment for inconstancy, the prince is the paragon of constancy and, accordingly, becomes a blue butterfly since "cette couleur ... signifie la fidélité" (this color ... signifies fidelity [390]). By the time one reads the final lines of the story, the *dénouement* is a foregone conclusion, to say the least: "le Prince des Feuilles et la belle Ravissante régnèrent avec toute la félicité imaginable et furent toujours heureux, parce qu'ils ne cessèrent jamais d'être amoureux et fidèles" (the Prince des Feuilles and the beautiful Ravissante reigned with all the felicity imaginable and were always happy because they never ceased being in love and being faithful [400]).

How striking it is, then, that the final moral insists on the *insufficiency* of faithfulness to ensure happiness. But whose happiness? At first glance, the initial exclamation ("Comme on doit porter envie au sort de Ravissante") seems to suggest a universal address. On closer examination, however, it is from the heroine's perspective that the final moral comments upon the tale. In the rereading of the narrative that is suggested here, Ravissante's fictive happiness becomes the privileged point of view ("Pour en pouvoir jouir *comme elle*, / Hélas! que l'on serait heureux, / S'il suffisait d'être fidèle!"). The heroine is the point of comparison between the idealized emotions of the fairy tale and the unstable/unpredictable emotions of the readers. Implicit in the final moral, then, is a comparison between fictional and real males. If fairy-tale heroes are always faithful, so the logic would seem to go, real men are much less so. Through the moral, the transcendent virtue of the Prince des Feuilles and the Prince des Papillons becomes an object of discursive wish-fulfillment from Ravissante's point of view. Although only indirectly, the fairy-tale heroes point out the lack that typifies "real" masculinity. How readers are to interpret this contrast is highly ambiguous at best. By directing attention back to the narrative, the final moral clears the way for two possible readings. Either we demystify the heroes' purported exemplarity or we take comfort in their fictionality. "Le Prince des Feuilles" stands at the crossroads of desires – between two contradictory visions of masculinity. Lack is banished, but it is also exposed.

OF KNIGHTS AND CHIVALRY

Nostalgia is doubtless among the preferred means of disavowing the lack within masculinity. Since time immemorial, in literature and the collective imaginary, the freely embellished stories about men of old are the epitome of what a culture interprets to be manhood. Veterans' war stories are perhaps the most vivid example of a nostalgia that works to dispel lack and to set up a norm to which all males are presumed to aspire. Of course, it is hardly coincidental that nostalgia has been a premier ideological tool in defense of normative masculinity. Nostalgic desires arise from a realization that the present is in and of itself inadequate and lacking. They are an escape to an illusory world of plenitude. And as such, they are well suited to the never-ending task of shoring up masculinity.

A large proportion of the heroes in the *contes de fées* are distinctively nostalgic. Measured against literary and cultural norms of late seventeenth-century France, many of these heroes embody archaic ideals, foremost among which are the traits of heroes in chivalric or knightly romances. Indeed, with the exception of Perrault's heroes, a large number of the other fairy-tale writers' heroes correspond to this type.[6] Deriving from the vogue's intertextual debt to romances such as *Amadis de Gaule* and the early seventeenth-century heroic novels,[7] the chivalric hero of the *contes de fées* had relatively few counterparts at the time.

The heroes of fairy tales and romance literature share many traits. In the most general sense, both character-types are adventurers, who leave the comforts of home and undertake seemingly impossible tasks that prove their innate superiority. In some cases, such as d'Auneuil's "La Princesse Léonice," the hero is turned out of his homeland; in others, as in d'Aulnoy's "La Belle aux cheveux d'or" or Choisy's "Histoire de la Princesse Aimonette," he sets out willingly, often on a mission of some sort. As scholars have often noted, this rupture in the hero's familiar existence is vital to proving his superiority, his difference from ordinary humanity.[8] The hero's superiority is demonstrated through his superhuman feats, which often take the form of armed struggle. When confronted with his tasks, the chivalric hero of the *contes de fées* almost always has at his disposal supernatural means that only further enhance his already extraordinary courage. Thus, when Choisy's hero Lohier battles his rival, the contest is described as a "combat fort inégal" (extremely unequal battle);[9] and later while fighting lions who guard his kidnapped beloved, he refuses the help of a friendly sorcerer until the very last moment (he receives a flaming sword that destroys everything in its path). Of course, the feats of heroes such as Choisy's are more than physical exploits, they show that the hero truly possesses the innate *vertu* (derived from the *virtù* of Italian theorists of sociability) of the most distinguished of nobles. Such is the case of Avenant in d'Aulnoy's "La Belle aux cheveux d'or." He sets out to gain the Princess Belle's hand in marriage for his lord. Besides the obvious onomastics ("avenant" means "pleasing" or "welcoming"), the tale repeatedly underscores Avenant's selflessness as he endures three life-threatening tests imposed on him by

Belle. Not surprisingly, in the end, he himself wins Belle's affections as well as the narrator's praise for his innate "virtue": "quand à son bonheur il paraît plus d'obstacle, / Le ciel lui devait un miracle, / Qu'à la vertu jamais le ciel n'a refusé" (when there appear so many obstacles to his happiness, / Destiny owed him a miracle, / That destiny has never refused virtue).[10]

What differentiates the fairy-tale heroes from many of their counterparts in romance literature is the prominence of the marvelous setting. Many tales include fairies who become central characters alongside the hero by carrying out his tasks for him. Thus, in "La Belle aux cheveux d'or," it is not Avenant but three fairies he befriended who complete the tests imposed by Belle; and in d'Auneuil's "La Princesse Léonice," the hero's final triumph is overshadowed by the fairy Levrette's narrative about her own kingdom, which he has unwittingly helped to disenchant (albeit with magical weapons provided by Levrette herself). Throughout the *contes de fées*, the marvelous setting plays a decisive role in guaranteeing the chivalric hero's superiority. Without it, his quest is doomed to failure and his being to the fate of ordinary mortals. With it, he is assured of overcoming otherwise impossible odds to transcend the lack besetting masculinity and subjectivity generally.

Just how important the marvelous backdrop is to the hero's identity can be discerned by referring to other cultural forms that feature this heroic type. In Quinault/Lully operas that include knights appearing against the backdrop of marvelous settings, superhuman powers are used sparingly – usually only once, in the *dénouement*.[11] For example, the fairy Logistille in *Roland* (first performed in 1685) makes her solo appearance in the final scene of the last act in order to calm Roland's fury. Moreover, in spite of the omnipresence of supernatural effects in seventeenth-century French opera (most often to incorporate ballet, machines, and musical interludes), human characters only use the marvelous as a last resort.[12] The hero's superior identity does not depend on the marvelous. Quinault/Lully's *Amadis*, *Roland*, and *Armide* (in keeping with operatic norms) use chivalric ideals as a backdrop to display their heroes' emotional turmoil rather than their feats of physical valor. By contrast, the *contes de fées* rely less on psychological description in favor of action, which virtually always necessitates supernatural powers or events. As a fundamental part of plot structure, the marvelous is the very fabric of the heroes' (as well as other characters') narrative identity. It underscores the hero's physicality and, so doing, enables the fairy tales to feature heroes with a more precise chivalric cast than their more eclectic counterparts in seventeenth-century opera.

Just as significant, the use of the chivalric hero is distinctively archaic. Just how much so can be understood by contrast with the literary and social ideal of the *honnête homme* that dominated throughout much of the seventeenth century. Although it would be misleading to claim that the chivalric hero (or the closely related feudal warrior) and the *honnête homme* are diametrically opposed – they are both norms of civility promulgated as codes of behavior for the masculine elite – *honnêteté* in many important respects is predicated on a rejection of feudal chivalry. Contrary to the chivalric hero, physical and especially military activity is not the *sine qua non* of the *honnête homme*. If, as Domna Stanton has shown, theoreticians of *honnêteté* assimilated (by sublimation) the discourse of military conquest into their own writings (*The Aristocrat as Art*, 63–64), the *honnête homme* is nonetheless promoted as an incomparable refinement of the feudal warrior because of his contact with sociable society and the self-restraint it promotes (in conversation, for instance). By rejecting the physical qualifications of the feudal noble, *honnêteté* simultaneously eschews socio-political utility as a sign of its ideological superiority. Indeed, it is commonplace to assert that the shift away from these traditional feudal values (in *honnêteté* but also in Louis XIV's strategic agenda) provoked an identity crisis of sorts in the seventeenth-century *noblesse d'épée*. A specific manifestation of this crisis that has been aptly analyzed by Michael Nerlich concerns the change in the conception of individual spatial movement. No longer called upon to embark on military missions and sequestered at court, the high aristocracy began to valorize stasis over mobility.[13] The aristocratic "ideology of adventure" (as Nerlich calls the ethos of chivalry) that involved "movement into a distance that was theoretically unlimited" (Nerlich, *Ideology of Adventure*, 304) became obsolete as the nobles' utilitarian mobility was recuperated by the *noblesse de robe* and the commercial bourgeoisie. The *honnête homme* was impervious to the errant existence of the knightly adventurer, or at least sublimated it. In another important sense, however, both ideals resemble each other. At first sight, the code of courtly love would appear to function identically in both feudal chivalry and *honnêteté:* in both systems, men are to serve and, thereby, please their lady. And yet, there is a difference between these two, for the *honnête homme* does not slavishly submit to his beloved (as does the courtly lover) but rather uses his courtship skills to display his artistry. "In this highly eclectic version of the courtly code, love represents an indispensable stage in the construction of the self-as-art, and woman an instrumentality of competence in the *art de plaire*" (Stanton, *The Aristocrat as Art*, 139). There are, then, two versions of courtly love: the chivalric hero devotes his energies to his beloved while the *honnête homme*, to the contrary, concentrates ultimately on himself.

It is not difficult to see that the vast majority of fairy-tale heroes have more in common with the heroes of chivalric romance than the *honnête homme*. In the *contes de fées*, where characters' actions and not their dialogue take center stage, true heroic superiority is found in physical far more than conversational dexterity. The hero's physical feats serve not only to win the right to his loved one's hand, but also to restore order to the socio-political realm of the fairy-tale world. Thus, in both d'Aulnoy's "La Belle aux cheveux d'or" and d'Auneuil's "La Princesse Léonice," the hero is able to take the throne from an evil king virtually at the same moment that he marries the heroine. Unlike the *honnête homme*, socio-political utility, although usually confined to the background, is the very basis of the fairy-tale hero's identity. Due to the importance of physical heroism and political service, movement through space is hardly surprising. Indeed, it is a given of folkloric and fairy-tale narrative wherein the psychological is transposed onto concrete physical or topographical reality. More precisely, scholars have repeatedly observed the high frequency with which the heroes (and less often heroines) of folklore are required to leave home before establishing their own individual identities,[14] and the chivalric hero of the *contes de fées* is simply a variant of this general feature. Less common in folkloric narratives but more specific to the romance tradition is the courtly code that guides the fairy-tale hero's adventures on behalf of the heroine. Over and against the example of the *honnête homme*, this hero's amorous conduct appears as a re-instrumentalization and re-sexualization of courtly love.

On the whole, then, the fairy-tale hero represents an alternative to *honnêteté* that would have been desirable to two very different groups of late seventeenth-century readers. For reactionary aristocrats, it can be hypothesized, the chivalric/knightly hero offered nostalgic compensation for the loss of social exclusivity that occurred through the wide-spread diffusion of civility norms. As Jacques Revel has stressed, the last third of the seventeenth century witnessed a hostile aristocratic reaction to the universalization of civility. Nobles increasingly derided what they considered to be the "excesses" of bourgeois sociability ("The Uses of Civility," 201). What they were no doubt reacting to was the declining status of civility as a marker of social distinction. By the mid-eighteenth century, as Revel points out, the very word "*civilité*" was synonymous with superficial politeness, a general norm accessible to nearly everyone ("The Uses of Civility," 204). In this context, the fairy-tale hero offered an imaginary foreclosure of the loss of prestige that *honnêteté* potentially caused through its blurring of class boundaries. By restricting heroism to superlative inborn qualities and then endowing these with supernatural powers, the *contes de fées* created an exclusive masculinity to which aristocrats could no longer aspire as a personal or a cultural identity except as the figment of the most far-flung fiction.

The chivalric hero was a potentially much more ambivalent figure for bourgeois readers. At the end of the seventeenth century a bourgeois class consciousness was at best only beginning to take shape and the aristocratic worldview was still the dominant ideological model.[15] Hence, the fairy-tale hero could have provided readers with an imaginary compensation for aristocratic status and privileges. The hero's imaginary quest stands for the bourgeois's real quest for respectability. But the enterprising bourgeois reader may well have seen more in this fairy-tale hero than just a nostalgia for aristocratic identity. As Michael Nerlich has shown, the errant knight is the direct ancestor of the commercial adventurer, promoted by the likes of Colbert and of course opposed by the traditional aristocracy (*Ideology of Adventure*, 326). From the mid-seventeenth century on, a new type, the *commerçant–honnête homme*, entered the popular imaginary and both supplanted and superceded the feudal courtier:

He needs skills that are completely unknown to the courtier but which would relativize the courtier's self-importance if he had them. He has to have physical qualities that the courtly nobility no longer need. He has to know foreign languages, while the courtly nobility understands only French. He has to ... open himself to the world and conquer it ... At the same time ... the nobility and the noble bourgeoisie ... strive to get to court, to Versailles or close to it, and to remain there. (Nerlich, *Ideology of Adventure*, 326)

The knightly hero of the *contes de fées*, while a stranger to trade, nonetheless incarnates many of the ideals put forth for the *commerçant–honnête homme*. Thus, the confidence with which Avenant (in d'Aulnoy's "La Belle aux cheveux d'or") embarks on his mission to win Belle's hand in marriage for the king, foreshadowing the adventuresome spirit of the proto-capitalist entrepreneur, reaps benefits beyond his wildest imagination, and above all for himself (the king's throne and the heroine). The implicit lesson of the bourgeois "ideology of adventure" gives new meaning to the chivalric quest of the *contes de fées*. To be sure, only very rarely does anything resembling explicit mercantile exchange surface in this entire corpus,[16] for wealth is assured, often by magical means, to those who innately deserve it. Unlike the capitalist adventurer, then, the knightly hero usually does not seek to enrich himself. However, the fairy-tale hero embodied qualities antithetical to the *honnête* ideal, which was itself inimical to the entrepreneurial spirit. And thus, he could be rather easily assimilated into the evolving bourgeois character-type, which in any event was a heterogeneous amalgamation (as the designation *commerçant–honnête homme* makes clear). It is as if the fairy-tale hero provided a mythic link to the past, a means of integrating the bourgeois adventurer into the monarchic and feudal order without disrupting it.

PATERNAL (DIS)ORDER

Either directly or indirectly, an overwhelming number of folk- and fairy-tale heroes aspire to fatherhood. Even if they do not have children during the story itself, the marriage and ascension to a throne at the end of so many tales signify a succession of powers and the promise of yet other successions to come. Heroes, in this scheme, are fathers in the making. It might seem surprising, then, that most fathers play only a marginal role at best in the *contes de fées*. More often than not, they appear at the beginning of the tale when the hero/heroine embarks on his/her adventure and/or at the end. In spite of a few notorious fathers (eg. those in Perrault's "Griselidis" and "Peau d'Ane"), mothers and stepmothers are more prominent in this corpus.

Yet, the marginality and, even, absence of fathers is in sharp contrast, and perhaps inversely proportional to their symbolic importance. In the majority of *contes de fées*, they incarnate stable order. Fathers are most frequently mentioned at the birth of their children (the beginning of the tale). This formulaic appearance traces the hero's or heroine's identity back to the parents and anchors it in the stable order from which the fairy-tale plot, for a time, will deviate. If fathers are spoken of again at the end of the tale, it is to mark the reestablishment of this order and the hero's or heroine's place in it. In theoretical terms, then, such fathers are the biological representatives of familial and political order, the surrogates of the symbolic father/Law upon which society and subjectivity depend. Again in theoretical terms, these fathers' presence defines all the subjects who come within its purview. The title of king, which is held by a large proportion of the fairy-tale fathers, suggests the kind of absolute power they possess, even if only potentially. In the fusion of familial and social realms that typifies folk- and fairy tales, these ideal fathers reign over their families and their kingdoms at one and the same time, embodying and imparting the "natural" order of both realms.

At first glance, the fairy-tale fathers would seem to share remarkable similarities with the *paterfamilias* of the *ancien régime*, whose "power over ... his wife and children, and in practice also over his servants [increased] as the seventeenth and eighteenth centuries advanced."[17] However, it is difficult to draw any close parallels between the fathers of the *contes de fées* and the evolving cultural representations of fatherhood in late seventeenth-century France. Throughout various historical and geographical traditions, folk- and fairy-tale fathers have remarkably consistent functions, which reappear in this corpus. The situation is even further complicated by the conventional literary portrayals of fathers (from comedies and novels, for instance) that are incorporated into the vogue. Nonetheless, several aspects of the contemporary valorization of fatherhood illuminate the tales with prominent fathers.

Historians have characterized the seventeenth century as a period of rising "paternalism."[18] What might be termed the ideology of fatherhood was given, if not an entirely new formulation, then at least a newly emphatic expression. In both religious and political discourse, the *paterfamilias* was included in a continuum of authority that stretched to the king and, ultimately, God. The individual father was to be master of his family as the king was master of his kingdom and God was master of the universe. This pyramid of paternal authority was a topos frequently used during this period to justify fatherly hegemony in the emerging bourgeois nuclear family. Although paternal benevolence was a common refrain in political and religious texts, images of the "père terrible" were a no less frequent means of driving home the authority of fathers. Several political theorists went to great lengths to prove the necessity of paternal violence in many circumstances of family life.[19] In the end, this renewed valorization of paternal authority exceeded the bounds of textual images; in fact, it was likely an integral part of the concentration of the powers of fathers and husbands in matrimonial, inheritance, and artisanal practices at this time.[20]

Consistent with this "absolutist" vision of paternal power, the fairy-tale fathers who intervene in the plot beyond a summary appearance at the beginning and/or end almost always take one of two diametrically opposed forms. Either they are weak and thus responsible for the disorder that arises in the tale, which demonstrates the exigency of strong fathers. Or they are excessively and unreasonably strong (usually expressed by imposing unwanted marriage partners) which, if nothing else, at least reinforces the images of paternal violence and the "père terrible" that permeated the French seventeenth-century cultural imaginary. In both instances, fathers disrupt the order that they are ordinarily called upon to enforce and symbolize. The plots of *contes de fées* with either of these types of father usually concern the return to the equilibrium and paternal order that are emblematic of a patriarchal universe. Of these two types, however, weak fathers are the more marginal, and in their case, fatherhood is readily restored to its rightful position. Either the father attains a strong presence or the hero himself becomes a real or potential father at the end of the tale (as in Perrault's "Cendrillon"), thus replacing the initial, weak father.[21]

By contrast, the presence of strong fathers is much more likely to underscore the disruption of narrative order they cause and, in extreme cases, to expose the arbitrariness of paternal authority. The actions of these fathers fall into one of two forms – commands and prohibitions – either of which becomes the basis of the protagonist's (and thus the tale's) adventures. Although there are a few instances in which commands or prohibitions do not disrupt narrative order,[22] this is usually not the case. Paternal commands ordinarily involve undesirable marriage partners. Thus, Murat's "Le Sauvage" begins with a father's demand that his magnificently beautiful daughter wed a horribly deformed prince; the princess then flees her father's court and is drawn into a series of adventures. Paternal prohibitions are more frequent by far, however, and take several forms. As in comedy, fathers often put up obstacles to their children's choice of marriage partner. The hero's father in d'Auneuil's "La Princesse Léonice" refuses to allow his son to marry the heroine and decides to disinherit him when he opposes his plans. Another type of prohibition obtains in Lhéritier's "L'Adroite Princesse" in which a father commands that his three daughters not "manquent à leur devoir" (fail to do their duty), an imperative with explicitly sexual connotations. As one would expect, only the heroine (the adroit princess) has what it takes to resist the seductive powers of the treacherous Riche-cautèle and to save her sisters from their father's wrath. If, as Flahault argues, folktales are structured around rules that are made to be broken,[23] then it is not at all unusual that even supposedly legitimate prohibitions, such as this one, lead to their infraction. Nor is it unusual that even "good" fathers disrupt the order of the plot.

Whether weak or strong, fathers who appear in the course of the plot are decidedly different from their maternal counterparts. Throughout the *contes de fées*, "bad" fathers are much less frequent than "bad" mothers (usually stepmothers). More significant still, fathers are less frequently split into "good" and "bad" personae not only in this corpus but in folk-and fairy tales generally. Mothers, on the contrary, are regularly doubled in this way. While this phenomenon has been explained in various ways,[24] its effect is always to draw a radical distinction between fairy-tale fathers and mothers. Wayward fathers come around in the end whereas "evil" stepmothers can never be redeemed (in fact, they are often killed off). The larger significance of this fact can be gleaned through Bettelheim's suggestion that the "evil" alter-father figure in fairy tales is often personified in ogres, monsters, or dragons, who are outside the family unit (*The Uses of Enchantment*, 114). From this perspective, then, "evil" fathers are generally less disruptive than stepmothers, who represent a threat from within. By changing "bad" into "good" fathers, the *contes de fées* eclipse the risk that fatherhood will be interpreted as threatening the stability of the family and thus society.

In d'Aulnoy's "Le Mouton" (The Sheep), La Force's "L'Enchanteur" (The Sorcerer), Mailly's "Le Roi magicien" (The

Magician King), and Perrault's "Peau d'Ane" (Donkey-skin), conflict between fathers and their children takes center stage. Rather than attenuate the fathers' role in the disruption of patriarchal and narrative order, these tales expose and even magnify it. At the same time, they throw new light onto the hero's/heroine's quest for identity and particularly his/her gendered identity within the family unit. By foregrounding paternal conflict, then, these tales emphasize the central role of fathers and aggression in the protagonists' quest.

However, even among these four tales, paternal conflict takes several different forms. Perhaps the most obvious distinction is between tales that oppose fathers and sons (La Force, "L'Enchanteur"; Mailly, "Le Roi magicien") and those that pit fathers against daughters (d'Aulnoy, "Le Mouton"; Perrault, "Peau d'Ane"). On a superficial level, both La Force's and Mailly's heroes struggle aggressively and physically with their fathers. La Force's hero, Carados, is drawn into a duel with a stranger who turns out to be none other than his own father. Mailly's hero comes to the aid of the beautiful princess whom his father has kidnapped by confronting the giant eagle his father has become. By contrast, both d'Aulnoy's and Perrault's heroines avoid outright confrontation and, in fact, are emotionally distraught about opposing their father's will. D'Aulnoy's Merveilleuse, the youngest and favorite of her father's three daughters, inadvertently offends him by relating a dream in which he washes her feet. When he orders that she be killed in the woods and that her tongue and heart be brought back to him, the princess is overcome with despair. The object of her father's incestuous desires, Peau d'Ane suffers no less than Merveilleuse, but her internal conflict is brought into clearer focus than her counterpart's. Even in the midst of their victimization, daughters are bound to the absolute obedience due to fathers. Sons, on the contrary, seem to make a heroic virtue out of *dis*obedience.

Now, the classic interpretation of this difference between father–daughter and father–son conflict is the Freudian one (elaborated most notably by Bettelheim). When Carados (in La Force's tale) duels with his real father and then rejects his mother, he enacts the classic male Oedipal struggle. Although complicated somewhat, the Freudian scenario also obtains in Mailly's tale with the paternal prohibition (the father forbids his son to go near the princess he has kidnapped), the son's transgression (he finds her portrait and falls in love with her), and resolution of her struggle (he wins over her affection and, finally, marries her). For both Merveilleuse and Peau d'Ane – as for the little girl in the Oedipal model – fathers are potential seducers, a phenomenon Freud explains as a projection of the girl's own desire for her father. The advances of Peau d'Ane's father are, of course, a central feature of Perrault's tale. Although much less prominent, incest also obtains in d'Aulnoy's tale: when Merveilleuse returns incognito from exile to attend her sisters' weddings, the text insists on his attraction to her. The first time: "Le roi . . . brûlait de la connaître" (The king . . . burned with desire to know her [442]); and the second time: "Le roi se sentit charmé de la revoir. Il n'ôta les yeux de sur elle que pour ordonner que l'on fermât bien toutes les portes pour la retenir" (The king felt overjoyed to see her again. He did not lift his eyes from her except to order that all the doors be tightly closed to keep her [443]). Ultimately, in both tales, the fathers' incestuous leanings fold almost effortlessly into legitimate parental love, which Freud might attribute to the *dénouement* of the girl's Oedipal conflict. From this perspective, Peau d'Ane's ambiguous fear/love for her father is transposed onto the ambiguity between the father's incestuous and legitimate love at the end of the tale. "Il en avait banni [de son âme] tout désir criminel / Et de cette odieuse flamme / Le peu qui restait dans son âme / N'en rendait que plus vif son amour paternel" (He had banished from his soul all criminal desire / And of this odious flame / The little that remained in his soul / Only made his paternal love stronger [114]). The "désir criminel"-turned-"amour paternel" not only projects the heroine's ambivalent feelings toward her father, it also places paternal conflict squarely within the realm of Peau d'Ane's internal psychic drama. If incest rekindles the fires of fatherly love, at least according to Freud, it is because these two passions spring, transformed, from the heroine's own evolving psycho-sexual identity.

In La Force's and Perrault's tales, the Freudian model of Oedipal conflict (and resolution) dramatizes a rite of passage through which one assumes a place not only within the normative family, but also within the larger socio-political world. By struggling with their fathers, the embodiment of authority, Carados and Peau d'Ane are in fact struggling to define themselves both within and beyond the patriarchal family unit. Ultimately, the upheaval of paternal conflict enhances its own peaceful resolution. As estrangement gives way to mutual love, both La Force's and Perrault's protagonists return to the world of paternal order that reigned before the outbreak of conflict. Their homecoming bespeaks a longing for stability through the repetition or re-establishment of paternal authority at the end of the tale.

However, in d'Aulnoy's "Le Mouton" and Mailly's "Le Roi magicien," paternal conflict has a much more ambiguous outcome. Rather than establish the protagonist's identity, these tales impede the harmonious construction of patriarchal order by exposing the dysfunction and instability of the father's rule. Both tales begin with the predictable irruption of disequilibrium into an initial state of equilibrium. "Le Roi magicien" tells the story of a magician–king's son whose mother has him secretly endowed with gifts of supernatural powers and raised by fairies (her husband's rivals). When the queen dies, the magician–king searches far and wide until he finds a beautiful princess, whom he kidnaps. Meanwhile, the young prince, seeking adventure, comes upon the family of the kidnapped princess and vows to recover her, unaware that his rival is his own father. In "Le Mouton," the heroine must flee her father's kingdom after inadvertently offending him. As the plot develops, tension arises between her loyalty to her father and sisters and the budding love she feels for the lover she discovers in sheep guise.

Although one might readily imagine a happy ending for both tales (namely, the reconciliation of father and son/daughter along with the establishment of a new family unit), neither follows the model of so many other *contes de fées*. In "Le Roi magicien," equilibrium is restored at the expense of the king–

magician–father: with the help of his fairy godmother, the prince delivers the princess (his father's fiancée) whom he is then able to marry while his father is reduced to powerlessness. What this predictable narrative structure obscures, however, is the fairly unpredictable role of the king–magician–father. That he is the opponent (in actantial terms) is hardly unusual. That he is explicitly repudiated at the end of the story, however, is unique among the *contes de fées*. The other examples of conflictual fathers in the vogue evolve from opposing/disrupting order to, in the end, (re)embodying it. From the very beginning to the very end of "Le Roi magicien," the father is cast as the excluded other, the (paternal) nemesis. As a sorcerer, the tale explains, the powers of the magician–king are inherently inimical to those of the fairies who raise his son. Thus, the conflict between father and son is inevitable. The outcome, however, is anything but predictable. Structurally speaking, the hero should fill the void of legitimate paternal authority; yet this never quite happens. After the king flees his kingdom never to return, there is no explicit mention of the prince/hero inheriting his throne. In fact, the end of this tale tends to reaffirm a vague female authority as much as or even more than the prince's own position. Not only do the newly-wed prince and princess settle in the princess's kingdom, they also invite the prince's fairy god-mother to live with them. From this point on, the fairy occupies center stage: "l'on ne songea plus dans cette cour qu'à rendre à la généreuse fée la reconnaissance qu'on lui devait de tant d'obligations et à jouir de la félicité parfaite où elle avait mis toute la famille royale" (all that the court thought about was paying the homage due to the fairy for so many good deeds and enjoying the perfect happiness she had made possible for the royal family [29]). Even if the last sentence affirms that "le prince et la princesse passèrent ensemble une longue vie très heureuse" (the prince and the princess had a long and very happy life together [29]), their debt to the fairy is clear. Given her links to the prince's mother (who on her deathbed entrusted the fairy with her newborn son), the fairy symbolizes in part a maternal authority that overshadows the patriarchal structure of this "famille royale."

Both the vagueness of the prince's role and the precision of the fairy's in this closure point toward a vision of familial order where male and female authority coexist.

In d'Aulnoy's "Le Mouton," the father–daughter conflict is resolved only to provoke a tragic *dénouement*. Instead of transferring the daughter's love from father to male love object (as the Freudian model prescribes), this tale dramatizes a situation of fatal competition. After meeting and falling in love with Mouton, a king-turned-sheep by the evil fairy Ragotte, Merveilleuse returns to her father's kingdom and is reconciled with him. Fearing that his daughter will leave him once again, the subjects of the father–king refuse to let Mouton enter his palace. And in despair, Mouton commits suicide. Obviously, then, the father–daughter conflict is not so much resolved, but rather replaced/displaced by a rivalry between the two kings. By exacerbating this rivalry, d'Aulnoy rejects the happy ending common to most other versions of this tale-type (AT425 The Search for the Lost Husband), thus inscribing a critical distance from both the folkloric tradition and the patriarchal order.

This dysphoric ending is the subject of the final moral, which deplores the irony of fate as a sign of the decadence of "[les] hommes d'aujourd'hui" ([the] men of today [447]):

> Souvent les plus beaux dons des cieux
> Ne servent qu'à notre ruine:
> Le mérite éclatant que l'on demande aux Dieux
> Quelquefois de nos maux est la triste origine.
>   Le roi mouton eût moins souffert,
> S'il n'eût point allumé cette flamme fatale
> Que Ragotte vengea sur lui, sur sa rivale:
>   C'est son mérite qui le perd.
> Il devait éprouver un destin plus propice.
> Ragotte et ses présents ne purent rien sur lui;
> Il haïssait sans feinte, aimait sans artifice,
> Et ne ressemblait pas aux hommes d'aujourd'hui.
> Sa fin même pourra nous paraître fort rare,
>   Et ne convient qu'au roi Mouton.
>   On n'en voit point dans ce canton
>   Mourir quand leur brebis s'égare.

Often the most beautiful gifts from the heavens / Only bring about
our ruin: / The splendid merit we ask of the Gods / Sometimes is the
sad origin of our ills. / The sheep king would have suffered less, / If
he had not ignited that fatal flame / For which Ragotte sought
revenge on him and his rival: / His merit fails him. / He should have
experienced a more favorable destiny. / Ragotte and her presents
had no effect on him; / He hated without pretense and loved without
artifice, / And did not resemble the men of today. / Even his end can
seem very unusual to us, / And suitable only for the Sheep king. / We
don't see any in this region / Die when their lamb gets lost. (447)

The fact that even the hero's "merit" (one of the most prized
virtues of seventeenth-century sociability) does not spare him
final tragedy indicates all the more forcefully the instability of
this fairy-tale universe. For, uncertainty threatens the repetitive
regularity of the patriarchal order, even if it is founded upon
the (usually) triumphant fairy-tale marvelous. Neither father
nor lover can be certain of his dominance in the long run,
because merit does not ensure happiness. If this patriarchy is in
crisis, it is because of its own moral dissolution, its inability to
recognize and reward *true* merit. (Doing so, of course, would
have meant installing Mouton on the father's throne, making
Merveilleuse's powers secondary at best.) The dramatic failure
of this tale's conclusion allows the final moral to idealize
Mouton and to express through his example a longing for a
masculinity that defies the standards of the day. What specific
forms this utopian longing might take are difficult to divine
from the tale or its moral. Even more elusive is what newly
defined role fathers might assume (the heroine's father fades
from view at the end of the tale and is never mentioned in the
moral). Yet, paternal conflict in "Le Mouton" becomes a
means of interrogating the patriarchal order. And, in this sense,
d'Aulnoy, of all the *conteuses* and *conteurs*, goes the farthest in
exploring the darkest sides of paternal authority.

PORTRAITS OF LACK

Among the many features the *contes de fées* import from the
seventeenth-century novel is the portrait that enables the hero

and heroine to fall in love and, eventually, be married. Although they are hardly ever described at length, these portraits are nonetheless *mises en abymes*, miniature representations of existing characters. As such, they invite reflection on the multiple effects of representation *on* characters *within* a fictional universe. Who uses portraits? and to what end? are but two of the questions that might be asked. To be sure, the use of portraits in seventeenth-century narrative fiction was widespread and highly conventional, but their appearance in the marvelous settings of the *contes de fées* draws particular attention to the evolving sexual union between the protagonists. As material representations of one of the lovers offered to the other, they demonstrate the control, or lack of control, they have over their gendered and sexual destinies.

The role of *painted* portraits in seventeenth-century fiction is closely tied to the mid-century literary vogue of *written* portraits. Emanating from the salons, literary portraits became especially popular through Madeleine de Scudéry's *Artamène ou le Grand Cyrus* (1649–1653) and Montpensier's *Divers portraits* (1659). Common to this vogue, as Erica Harth has concluded, is a desire to make the imaginary real. Literary portraits share with the painted portraits of this period a propensity for idealized representations of the "real" subject. If the genre of the literary portrait flourished in this period, as Harth further notes, it is because of the nostalgic wish-fulfillment it offered. At a time when the real social status of the nobility was in decline or at least under scrutiny, literary portraits, which always foregrounded a putative accuracy, recognized individual worth through a group identity from a mythic golden past. Almost simultaneously and through the end of the century, however, both literary portraits and their derivatives were put to decidedly counter-nostalgic uses by writers such as Bussy, La Bruyère, Retz, and Saint-Simon. These moralists and memorialists used "accurate" representation to tell the unflattering "truth" about their subjects. Indeed, by the time of the vogue of fairy tales, most of the literary portraits produced were of this latter category.[25]

Although difficult to confirm, it is possible that the reference to painted portraits in the *contes de fées* is a nostalgic rewriting of the earlier vogue of idealized literary portraits. Of course, a large proportion of the protagonists in these tales are themselves based on the idealized heroic characters of early seventeenth-century fiction. More pertinent, however: the fact that the vogue's heroes and heroines sometimes resort to portraits in order to communicate their passion is itself a desire to realize an imaginary ideal. These portraits seem well suited to the fictional universes that have as their most basic principle imaginary wish-fulfillment. In order for them to transform the ideal into the real, however, the painted portraits of the *contes de fées*, like their literary cousins, must purport absolute fidelity to their subjects. In the end, they operate on a representational principle analogous to that of the fairy tales. By transforming the unreal into the real, they are a *mise en abyme* of the vogue's claim to uncover the ethically and socially "natural" through the marvelous.

The portraits are also a *mise en abyme* of transcendent masculinity, which is confirmed by the fact that most of them are of men.[26] In mythic masculinity, what Lacan would call the Symbolic order is the framework within which subjectivity can assert its claim to self-mastery. Representation is an extension of the masculine subject and especially of his self-knowledge and self-control. Such at least is the ideal proclaimed by the portrait that the fairy-tale hero gives to his beloved. Even if the painted image does not replace the hero's ontological presence, it nonetheless guarantees the physical and spiritual perfection of the original. It thus aims to evoke the heroine's unconditional desire, even before the first encounter. In this scheme, the portrait is an external physical sign of an internal psychological process. The heroine's desire for the hero is symbolized, but especially elicited, through this representation.[27]

And yet, however much the portrait appears to belong to the heroine, its most significant effect is reserved for the hero himself. For, the image of his perfection – his transcendence – depends on the heroine's recognition of it as such. The hero's portrait *is* what the heroine sees in it. And, by extension, the hero *is* what his portrait evokes. This fundamental truth is not openly avowed either by the portrait or by masculinity. In fact, if anything it is obscured. Such is not the case in an extraordinary scene from Murat's "Le Roy Porc" that demonstrates just how much masculinity depends upon women's recognition. The hero is taken to the cavernous underworld where the Princess Ondine is held captive. Unseen, he spies her conversing about his portrait with her confidante Miris. Miris objects that the portrait is probably nothing more than the figment of a painter's imagination and that in any event it is impossible to know "s'il a toutes les qualités qui doivent animer sa beauté, s'il a de la naissance, de l'esprit, et surtout un cœur capable de répondre à [sa] tendresse" (if he has all the qualities that should enliven his beauty, if he is of noble birth and has intelligence and especially a heart capable of reacting to [her] tenderness [29]). To this, Ondine responds without hesitation, "il est impossible que l'intérieur d'un objet si accompli ne soit pas aussi parfait que l'extérieur est charmant" (it is impossible that the inside of an object so refined is not just as perfect as the outside is charming [30]), thus reiterating the cliché, often found in literary portraits, that physical and psychological traits are complementary. Of course, the rest of the tale proves that the heroine is right and her confidante wrong. At this particular moment, however, doubt about the portrait's referent threatens to undermine the hero's struggle to overcome his metamorphosis. And theoretically, the stakes are even higher because he himself witnesses this scene. But Ondine trusts her instincts, against Miris's counsel, and Roy Porc is personally reassured of his perfection. Faith in representation defeats skepticism, and the emboldened hero advances toward his predestined bliss.

Contrary to Murat's tale, d'Aulnoy's "La Biche au bois" emphasizes the disruptive effects of portraits. At the beginning of the tale, the hero comes across a princess's portrait and is immediately stricken with love. But so profound is the portrait's effect that love quickly turns to obsession (the prince's passion is even described as "folie"). The only remedy, so his distressed doctors and parents conclude, is to search out the portrait's original. This, however, leads to yet another crisis: when an ugly servant betrays the Princess Désirée and passes herself off as her mistress, the prince assumes that the portrait is a deception and again falls into despondency. What the heroine's portrait seems to show, then, is the extent to which interpretation and self-mastery elude the prince. To be sure, the tale later features his own magical (speaking) portrait and the love it inspires in the Princess Désirée. However, its effects are overshadowed by the trials she must endure before being united with the prince (namely, her metamorphosis into a doe). Later, when she sees the portrait's original, she proclaims the dissemblance between signifier and signified: "ah! que le portrait qu'on m'en apporta est peu fidèle; il est cent fois mieux fait" (ah! how untrue the portrait they brought me is; he is a hundred times more handsome [397]). Of course, Désirée's observation is standard fare in the period's narrative fiction, but it does underscore the status of representation in this tale. Neither the hero's nor the heroine's portrait is the direct, all-powerful extension of its original. Representation is decidedly secondary, if not inferior to ontological presence. It is also a potential threat to the hero's self-control and self-mastery.[28]

By far the most radical subversion of masculine self-sufficiency occurs in a rare anonymous *conte de fées* entitled "Le Portrait qui parle," found in the Bibliothèque de l'Arsenal in Paris. In this dysphoric tale, a portrait that speaks, along with several other magical objects, expose rather than compensate for the hero's fundamental weakness. This tale's entire plot involves a series of attempts by the hero's fairy godmother to avoid the predicted tragic outcome. King Aménophis is consumed by his passion for hunting, which the fairy Impériale divines to be the future cause of his death. To (attempt to) change the course of fate, she envisions a series of contradictory remedies. To tear Aménophis away from hunting, Impériale first proposes marriage to a beautiful princess. But recognizing that marriage does not create a lasting passion, she conceives of a means for the king to hunt safely – a horse with magical diamond horseshoes. Shortly thereafter, she returns to her original plan and creates the speaking portrait that she hopes will prevent the predicted tragic end. Hedging her bet that the king will find an enduring passion, Impériale devises a magic bracelet that, when worn by his future bride, will ensure her eternal "tendresse" and "langueur." In the end, neither enchantment – the magically arranged marriage nor the intrepid horse – can prevent the fatal end. After a greedy lackey replaces the diamond horseshoes with ordinary ones, the king's horse slips on a cliff, killing the hero.

Of all the magical accoutrements created by Impériale, the portrait is most central to the narrative. Highlighted by the title and described in detail by the text, Aménophis's speaking portrait is also a much more direct extension of the hero's being than either his horse or the queen's bracelet. Like its counterparts in literature and art (the literary and painted portrait), the king's portrait is an idealized rendering. Thus, it is no accident that the portrait speaks in alexandrine verse when Philonide exclaims to herself how much she desires "une Conquête aussi illustre qu'est celle de votre cœur" (a Conquest as illustrious as your heart).[29] The highly conventional answer the portrait gives suggests that the portrait is an animate form of the love poems that often appear in seventeenth-century fiction:

> Tout fléchit, tout se rend au pouvoir de vos yeux,
> Et l'on ne voit rien sous les Cieux
> Egal à vos attraits, adorable Princesse;
> Mais en vain de Venus vous avez la bonté,
> L'Amour vous avertit qui n'est point sans tendresse
> De parfaite félicité.

Everything bows, everything surrenders before the power of your eyes, / And nothing under the Heavens / Equals your charms, adorable Princess; / But in vain you enjoy the generosity of Venus, / Love, who is not devoid of tenderness, predicts for you / Perfect happiness. (22)

However literary and stylized, the portrait is nonetheless real, and quite literally so. Not only does the speaking portrait see (cf. above the reference to the princess's eyes), but it also transforms into the flesh and blood of the king. When Philonide admires the portrait in the privacy of her bedchamber, the impatient Aménophis springs to life from his painted image. Fearing for her reputation, the heroine quickly rebuffs him. After declaring his love in person, the hero gives her the magical bracelet and then disappears, with his portrait, in a puff of smoke. Shortly thereafter, the portrait and the bracelet achieve their goal: Aménophis and Philonide are married.

No matter how successful at first glance, the portrait also subtly foreshadows the tale's final outcome, for it is beset with curious shortcomings. The portrait's speech, however amazing, is not an exact duplicate of the king's. The image only speaks when the princess speaks to it and then only to her. Further it always waxes poetic in its answers, to the point of appearing to beg the question. When Philonide asks the portrait if it feels pleasure in seeing and hearing her, the image replies:

> Mon bonheur serait sans égal,
> Et j'aurais des Amants la plus douce aventure,
> Si l'amour me donnait mes douleurs en peinture,
> Mes plaisirs en original.

My happiness would be without equal, / And I would have the sweetest adventure of Lovers, / If love were to render my suffering in painting, / And my pleasures in the original. (26)

The portrait's reply reveals its fundamental ambiguity. Its suffering is real and its pleasures imaginary; it is and is not the king at the same time. In this sense, the portrait is perhaps a concrete expression of the protagonists' evolving passion. But this ambiguity is also part of the portrait's ambivalence. Not only does it advance Aménophis's cause, it also hinders it (albeit only temporarily). When the queen, Philonide's mother, compliments the portrait, it refuses to respond, telling his beloved: "Je ne connais ici d'autre Reine que Vous" (I know here no other Queen than You [28]). This retort is interpreted by the court as an insult, which for a brief moment threatens to derail the impending wedding. After Aménophis springs from his painting to speak with Philonide, the portrait becomes even more of a liability for the plot. The narrator explains that it was Impériale who made the king and his portrait disappear since "elle voulait que toutes choses, jusqu'aux amours qui vont si vite et qui font tant faire de chemin, se passassent dans les formes" (she wanted everything, including a courtship that happened so quickly and covered so much territory, to occur

according to form [48]). Even enchanted love must respect
social convention. And so, the magical catalyst must be with-
drawn before it goes too far.

In "Le Portrait qui parle," neither the portrait, the horse,
nor the bracelet is able to incarnate the marvelous ideal. The
supernatural is not and cannot effect the ideal existence that
the fairy Impériale wants to create. In fact, the question seems
to be whether it can exist at all. The hero is not the
transcendent figure of masculinity that we find in so many
contes de fées. He is, rather, the embodiment of uncertainty and
contradiction, the embodiment of lack that patriarchal masculinity attempts to efface from our imagination. From the very
beginning of the tale, Aménophis is torn between his irreconcilable passions for hunting and for Philonide. Instead of
resolving this tension, Impériale heightens it. Her marvelous
remedies first negate the king's fatal passion for hunting (by
instilling a desire for marriage), and then reaffirm it (by
providing the diamond-shoed horse). On a logical plane at
least, the marvelous cancels itself out. Aménophis, in the end,
is left to his own devices, which is to say, his own weakness.
And it is precisely this weakness that the speaking portrait
helps us to see.

Judged by the standard of the mid-seventeenth-century
literary portraits, the painted portraits in "La Biche au bois"
and "Le Portrait qui parle" are complete failures. Of these two
contes de fées it cannot be said, as the Abbé de Villiers once
quipped, "rien ne déguise mieux l'homme que son portrait"
(nothing better disguises a man than his portrait [quoted in
Plantié, *La Mode du portrait littéraire,* 665]). Quite to the contrary,
these particular fairy-tale portraits are not disguises as much as
they are revelations. They do not show the disparity between
gleaming appearances and unseemly realities, as the literary
portraits of moralist writers do. Rather, they reveal the vital but
tenuous link between subjectivity – particularly masculine subjectivity – and the realm of representation. Whereas d'Aulnoy
and even Murat use the portrait to point out the hero's
dependence on self-representation, the anonymous writer of
"Le Portrait qui parle" makes the hero's self-image the ultimate

symbol of his tragic hubris. All of these tales expose, however timidly, the vulnerability of masculinity.

Perrault seems to make the same point in a salon piece entitled "Le Miroir ou la métamorphose d'Orante" (The Mirror or the Metamorphosis of Orante, 1661). Although not a fairy tale, this text recounts how Cupid transforms the portraitist Orante into a mirror because of his indiscriminately accurate verbal portrayals of women. The moral of the story, so Perrault makes clear, is that the "faiseur de portraits" must learn to "tourner [les petites vérités désagréables] du plus beau côté" (show the most beautiful side [of disagreeable little truths] [217]). The ideal portraitist masters the truth about the subject but divulges only what this same subject wishes to see or hear. Of course, Orante's dilemma does not concern self-portraiture, as does Guerrier's in "La Biche au bois" and Aménophis's in "Le Portrait qui parle." This, however, is not the most significant difference. For, Perrault's salon piece offers a sociable "lesson" (to flatter women is to keep the upper hand), while the *contes de fées* offer no such purported comfort. Their goal is rather to expose the power that representation holds over the hero, to suggest that masculinity is not as self-sufficient as patriarchal myth would have it. Theirs are portraits of lack.

In a sense, the *contes de fées* are themselves portraits depicting a multitude of "truths" about masculinity. Many of them offer the image of a seemingly harmonious masculine subjectivity in which lack is banished by an illusory escape into nostalgia. The conquests of knights offer potential (albeit specious) reassurance to readers of both sexes. And yet, a number of tales paint pictures that do anything but flatter the patriarchal fiction of masculinity. Be they fathers or sons, lovers or husbands, the men of this corpus are not assured of ascending into the plenitude of ideological or psychic transcendence. The *conteuses* especially, and d'Aulnoy first among them, use the fairy-tale genre to deform, as well as to mirror, the patriarchal model. Paradoxically, by portraying what is supposed to be most obvious about the chivalric hero and paternal authority, the *contes de fées* sometimes reveal what is least obvious about them.

Knights are not always assured of victory, and fatherhood does not always incarnate stability. If the vogue is a portrait of masculinity, then there is not just one original, but many. These tales not only blur the distinction between image and original, but make us realize that other portraits and other originals are yet to come.

CHAPTER 6

Imagining femininity: binarity and beyond

It is hardly an exaggeration to say that fairy tales are obsessed with femininity. In an overwhelming proportion of the stories that Western cultures have enshrined as classics, women are central characters. These narratives are concerned above all else with defining what makes women different from men and, more precisely, what is and is not acceptable feminine behavior. Beauty (of "Beauty and the Beast" fame), Cinderella, Little Red Riding Hood, and Sleeping Beauty are simply the most notorious of the fairy-tale heroines who haunt our collective imaginations and, as many scholars have argued, influence our expectations of femininity. More often than not, in their mass-produced varieties these archetypal women have been imbued with highly conservative prescriptions. Beauty exemplifies daughterly love for fathers; Cinderella and Sleeping Beauty demonstrate the "rewards" of submission to the male-lover-turned-husband; and Little Red Riding Hood leaves a warning about the dangers of girls' disobedience or foolishness. The fairy-tale genre has become a powerful tool for making listeners and readers aware of both the ramifications and the conditions of "proper" feminine conduct.

The classic fairy tales mentioned above, among many others, entertain questions that have long haunted patriarchal Western consciousness: "What is Woman?" and Freud's infamous related question, "What does Woman want?" These questions bespeak an extreme uneasiness on the part of both the male subjects who have uttered them and the patriarchal cultures that have conceived them. The universal Woman, who is supposed to define all women of all times and cultures, represents an otherness that threatens to expose the arbitrary nature of patriarchal dominance. If women become the inexplicable beings that patriarchal Western consciousness has puzzled over since antiquity (at least), it is because these representations project masculinist anxiety. By casting Woman as mysterious, patriarchal discourses attempt to redirect attention away from the hegemonic preponderance accorded the male subject. Femininity is reduced to the status of a phallic phantasm and, in this form, provides a stable point of reference for masculinity.

Since they play with the boundaries between the real and the unreal, the imaginable and the unimaginable, folk- and fairy tales have proven to be a particularly apt medium for pondering the seemingly insoluble question of Woman. If, as I have already argued, the implausible marvelous expresses and expels both collective and individual fears, then by portraying unreal, unimaginable women, fairy tales often seek to allay patriarchal fears. But this is not all that they do. Historically, fairy tales have employed the marvelous to unsettle the prevailing order of gender relations, and especially the social and familial lot of women.[1] Fairy-tale fantasy has been used to assuage not only hegemonic desires of patriarchal societies but also desires of subjected individuals or groups.[2] The unreal and the implausible – in short, the marvelous -- can explore the potentially real and plausible realms of different gender identities. But in folk- and fairy tales generally and in the *contes de fées* in particular, this utopian potential is curtailed through the overwhelmingly binaristic portrayals of women. Within the same tale, femininity is repeatedly and relentlessly split into "good" and "bad" entities: the virtuous heroine is contrasted with her unvirtuous opposite or the good (and often dead) mother with the evil (and very much alive) stepmother. To be sure, binary oppositions are a widely recognized component of folk- and fairy-tale narratives.[3] Even so, however, it is striking to note that women of the *contes de fées* are more likely than men to be defined in opposition to their moral and/or physical antitheses. Thus, whereas heroes more often than not struggle with forces or beings totally unlike themselves, heroines are quite often pitted against a negative mirror image of themselves. If Perrault's Petit Poucet tries to outwit the voracious ogre, whose cannibalistic instincts make him only marginally human, the heroine in his "Les Fées" is laudable because her speech and manners are the obverse of her uncouth and downright nasty stepsister's. Even when heroines are not confronted with their reverse images, they are nonetheless very often forced to struggle with other women who are jealous of them.

Explanations of this folkloric phenomenon vary. For psychoanalysis, these binarisms reflect the divisions between the pre-Oedipal and Oedipal stages of development. Bettelheim, for instance, argues that the little girl splits her mother into good and bad entities in order to reconcile the conflicting demands of maternal love and paternal interdiction, but also in order to come to terms with ambivalent feelings toward her mother in the context of the family romance. What this approach does not/cannot explain is why male characters are not similarly portrayed in folklore, especially given the masculine Oedipal model and the fact that the family romance involves fathers as well as mothers. In the final analysis, Bettelheim and other psychoanalytic critics fail to observe that the Oedipal experience as well as the fantasies of the family romance devalue motherhood and exalt fatherhood.

Where psychoanalysis fails, socio-historical readings of folklore would seem to be more helpful. Marina Warner, for instance, finds in the female rivalry of folk- and fairy tales evidence of the conflicts faced by pre-modern female family members.[4] Although this interpretation is quite possibly valid for the early modern period (on which it is based), it does not consider that the structures of female rivalry both pre- and post-date this period. Nor does it take into consideration the difference between the conflictual structures of lower class families and the upper class reception of the literary fairy tale. For, the long-standing binaristic treatment of female conflict and female characterization within folklore is put to historically specific uses. And in the *contes de fées* the late seventeenth-century discourses about women offer insight into the binaristic treatment of femininity.

THE *GRAND RENFERMEMENT* AND THE VALORIZATION
OF MOTHERHOOD

Folkloric mothers hold a dubious distinction. More than all other fairy-tale characters – male or female – they appear in tandem with their binary opposites. Most often, evil stepmothers or mothers-in-law are defined by contrast to dead or absent biological mothers, who are innately good. Recent studies have observed that Western fairy tales have become increasingly obsessed with motherhood, from the Renaissance to the present, to the point of shifting attention away from folkloric tale-types concerning incestuous fathers and toward those involving wicked mothers.[5] The birth of the literary fairy tale coincided with the emerging consciousness of motherhood's power and importance within society. Far from elevating mothers' status, of course, this concern, which became ever more pronounced from the seventeenth through the nineteenth centuries, aimed to control the limits of women's influence within the family and society at large by valorizing, paradoxically, the rights and responsibilities of the maternal role. In this context, one can hypothesize that the recurrent coupling of good and evil mothers in folklore served even more emphatically than before to underscore the virtue of "good" mothers and the horror of "evil" ones. Implicit in this predilection for the good–evil maternal pair would seem to be a specious argument that mothers are inherently of two (good and bad) minds. Splitting the maternal figure into two opposing beings reinforces all the more the radical difference between the two, the polarized distance between two enactments of the same role. The experience of Cinderella, whose (good) biological mother is replaced by a (wicked) stepmother, is potentially that of any and every child. The dangerous ability of mothers to vacillate between good and evil had to be closely watched.

In contrast to the eighteenth and nineteenth centuries, late seventeenth-century France was only beginning to glimpse the ideological and symbolic possibilities of the good–evil maternal pair in folklore. That is, motherhood, as a cultural value inspiring sentimental respect and necessitating codified conduct, was in the embryonic stages of development. Nonetheless, the two final decades of the seventeenth century witnessed a marked shift in both the quantity and quality of the appeals to motherhood as a distinct familial and social role. In the 1690s and early 1700s there was an explosion of "moralist" tracts and/or treatises about marriage, women, and sociability that projected a new vision of motherhood. Works such as *L'Art de rendre les femmes fidelles* (1713), *Caractères divers des femmes mariées* (1694), *Devoirs de la vie domestique* (1706), *Le Portrait d'une femme honneste, raisonnable et véritablement chrestienne* (1693), *La Vie des gens mariez* (1694), to name but a few of the more colorful titles, are part of what recent historical studies have called (borrowing an expression from the Princesse de Palatine) the *"grand renfermement,"* the increasing physical and discursive confinement of women to the familial domestic sphere that occurred during the latter part of Louis XIV's reign.[6] While it is admittedly difficult (if not impossible) to determine to what extent changes may have affected the lives of actual women, there was at the very least a distinctively conservative shift in *attitudes* toward women's social roles.[7] In prescriptive writings, women were granted but one acceptable identity – that of exemplary wife and mother. At the same time as promoting submission to God and husband, careful regulation of household affairs, and care for the moral and physical well-being of husband and children, late seventeenth-century "moralists" denounce the dangers posed by "worldly" (*mondain*) activities. Wives and mothers were to shun *"divertissements dangereux"* (dangerous entertainments), such as card games, novels, plays, and operas that would lead them to neglect their household duties (Liancourt, *Règlement*, 35–37). As one author made clear, women publicly acclaimed as learned and pious were curious oddities and could not serve as general examples of what a "reasonable woman" should be – a woman "[qui] aime son Mari et ses Enfants" (who loves her Husband and her Children) and "se plaît dans son Domestique et prend un soin particulier de son ménage. Ce sont là les premiers traits de son portrait, on peut même assurer qu'ils en sont les plus naturels, les plus vifs, les plus essentiels, et les plus nécessaires, et que sans eux, il ne saurait ressembler" (is proud of her Servant and takes particular care of her household. These are the most important features of her portrait, and one can even affirm that they are the most natural, the most lively, the most essential, and the most necessary, and that without them, it cannot be accurate).[8]

Such proclamations about wifely and motherly duties were hardly original in and of themselves. However, two aspects in particular testify to the dawning of a new interest in mother-hood. First, moralists began to enjoin mothers to display affection for their children, just as they attempted to sentimen-talize the ties between all family members. To be sure, late seventeenth-century prescriptions are still quite timid in com-parison to those of the mid- to late eighteenth century when maternal love, as a social construct, was "invented."[9] Refer-ences to affective ties between mothers and their offspring are still infrequent, which would seem to confirm Jean-Louis Flandrin's contention that family ties among the upper classes of the early modern period were primarily functional and instrumental.[10] As Flandrin himself shows, however, from the early seventeenth century on writers became more and more concerned with the type of attention that parents – and especially mothers – give their children (*Familles*, 136). This was but one facet of the Church's ever intensifying concern with the structure and internal workings of the family from the fifteenth to the eighteenth centuries. By the 1690s and early 1700s, motherhood had become an object of intense interest. The otherwise fairly conventional *La Vie des gens mariez* (1694) stresses the importance of mothers' much more than fathers' attention to raising their children and even devotes a chapter to the benefits of breastfeeding (thus predating by nearly fifty years the eighteenth-century fashion). More generally, this treatise em-phasizes the emotional bonds that tie husband and wife, children and parents: "Il faut que [les gens mariés] aient un grand amour pour leurs enfants afin de les supporter dans leurs premières faiblesses ... [Q]u'ils soient pleins de douceur et de patience afin de les élever chrétiennement et de ne se pas rebuter des peines infinies qui sont comme une suite nécessaire de leur éducation" ([married people] must have a great love for

their children in order to tolerate them in their initial weaknesses ... [M]ay they be full of sweetness and patience in order
to raise them in a Christian way and not to be taken aback at
the infinite pains that are a necessary result of raising them.)[11]
Later, when presenting arguments to promote breastfeeding,
this treatise cites Saint Ambrose's contention that mothers "en
sont elles-mêmes plus affectionnées pour leurs enfants, et ...
elles les aiment avec beaucoup plus d'ardeur qu'elles ne ferait
sans cela" (are themselves much more affectionate with their
children for it and ... they love them with much more ardor
than they would without it [456]). Even if it is considered to be
a learned behavior, affection is an important feature of the
paternal and especially maternal roles.

Paradoxically, at the same time that motherhood was becoming associated with domesticity and intimacy, several
women took pride in their maternal selves, which they and/or
others put on public display. Madame de Sévigné, as Michèle
Longino Farrell has shown, was preoccupied with presenting
herself as an exemplary mother, both through her correspondence and her daughter's words and actions.[12] The Marquise
de Lambert, although purportedly reticent about publishing,
authored several works for her children, among them *Avis d'une
mère à son fils* and *Avis d'une mère à sa fille*, in which the maternal
ego unabashedly imparts moral and practical wisdom for her
children's benefit.[13] In a less well-known text, *Règlement donné par
une dame de haute qualité à sa petite-fille, Pour sa Conduite et pour celle de
sa Maison, Avec un autre Règlement que cette Dame avait dressé pour elle-
même* (1694), republished several times in the following century,
the Duchesse de Liancourt instructs her grand-daughter on the
duties she should expect as wife and mother, how to execute
these, and how to avoid common pitfalls. Whatever these three
women may have felt about becoming public figures, the fact
remains that their maternal examples accrued at least implicitly
an authority for readers.[14] Beyond glorifying the "rights" and
responsibilities of motherhood, these texts perhaps also became
a mechanism for enforcing the ideal of female domesticity.
Offering female readers a virtuous public identity, works such
as Sévigné's, Lambert's, and Liancourt's would seem to make

the constraints of the *"grand renfermement"* appealing. Conversely, they also serve as a subtle reminder that mothers are subject to the scrutiny of society at large. Mothers can be lavished with praise, saddled with criticism, or worse.

In a broad sense, the images of motherhood and family life that appear in late seventeenth- and early eighteenth-century "moralist" works may well be part of a long-term historical process that promotes a nostalgic idealization of those roles. The nostalgia I have in mind here is less one that seeks to recuperate and reinvigorate a past discourse than one that makes it possible for individuals to understand themselves in relation to their own personal histories, and specifically in relation to their own families. In this perspective, the valorization of motherhood might be interpreted as advancing the primal mother (in the Freudian sense) as a culturally imposed psychic construct. Both public and affective, motherhood was beginning to occupy a cultural space that could or was supposed to be appropriated by each and every person. As the sentimentality of the "new" bourgeois family emerged from the indifference of aristocratic dynasticism, the individual was increasingly compelled to create a self based on a master narrative model. And, I would argue, the "good" primal mother, object of nostalgic longings, was a central part of this narrative.

At the end of the seventeenth century, however, this model had not yet achieved the clearer and more elaborate expression that the eighteenth century would give it. In many respects, the *contes de fées* bear witness to the transition that conceptions of motherhood were undergoing at this time. Reading through this corpus, one is struck by the multitude of maternal figures, ranging from those who are prominent and active in the plot to those who are dead (but whose memory lingers on) and from biological mothers to stepmothers and mothers-in-law. Contrary to what would appear to be the case in other corpuses of literary fairy tales,[15] no one maternal type dominates. Furthermore, even if good mothers outnumber their evil counterparts (including stepmothers and mothers-in-law), only in a handful of the *contes de fées* do mothers of any variety have a sustained role in the plot. In the vogue as a whole (with the notable exception of d'Aulnoy, as we will see in a moment), motherhood is neither resoundingly denigrated nor unequivocally celebrated. Mothers are not yet the object of obsessive concern and nostalgia they will become in literary fairy tales of the eighteenth and nineteenth centuries.

It is perhaps not surprising, therefore, that mothers in this corpus (including, again, stepmothers and mothers-in-law) are only infrequently portrayed alongside their binary opposites (virtuous mothers versus wicked mothers). Evil mothers (including stepmothers and mothers-in-law) are just as frequently set against their virtuous (but generally weak) husbands or benevolent fairies as they are against the good mother. For example, d'Aulnoy's "Finette-Cendron" features a malicious mother who, against the wishes of her kind-hearted husband, conceives the fateful plan to abandon their children in a forest. Moreover, good mothers, who outnumber their evil counterparts, are more commonly paired against evil fairies and/or husbands. Murat's "L'Heureuse peine" opposes a kind mother and a vindictive fairy (a common folkloric scenario, of course); and the mother in Perrault's "Le Petit Poucet," based on one of the two tale-types d'Aulnoy amalgamates in "Finette-Cendron," inverts the scenario of the *conteuse* by opposing a virtuous mother and a hard-hearted father.

Compared to the rest of the corpus, d'Aulnoy's tales are exceptional in the amount of attention given to mothers and the recurrence of the binary scheme. Although this may be explained in part by the sheer length of her tales (longer on average than those of most of the other *conteuses* and *conteurs*) and her general propensity for psychological analysis, it is nonetheless noteworthy that she repeatedly highlights wicked and foolish mothers, often developing their role beyond that in specific folkloric tale-types[16] and introducing it into her "invented" tales.[17] The well-known motif of the wicked stepmother who favors her own daughter and persecutes her stepdaughter is extensively developed in "La Biche au bois," "Gracieuse et Percinet," and "L'Oiseau bleu." In each of these tales, the narrator takes particular delight in describing the horrible ugliness and corruption of the stepmother and her daughter, who of course are the perfect antitheses of the incomparably beautiful and kind heroine and, at least implicitly, her deceased mother. After describing how a queen cultivates her daughter Gracieuse's beauty, sweetness, and intelligence (*esprit*), the narrator of "Gracieuse et Percinet" gives the following elaborate description of the stepmother Grognon, who was:

affreuse de tout point: ses cheveux étaient d'un roux couleur de feu; elle avait le visage épouvantablement gros et couvert de boutons; de deux yeux qu'elle avait eus autrefois, il ne lui en restait qu'un chassieux; sa bouche était si grande, qu'on eût dit qu'elle voulait manger tout le monde, mais comme elle n'avait point de dents, on ne la craignait pas; elle était bossue devant et derrière et boiteuse des deux côtés.

awful in every way: her hair was as red as fire; she had a face that was frighteningly big and covered with pimples; of the two eyes she had had long ago there remained only a pus; her mouth was so big one would have said she wanted to eat everyone, but, since she didn't have any teeth, people weren't afraid of her; she had humps in front and in back and limped on both sides.[18]

As is often the case in fairy tales (not to mention other literary forms), ugliness affords more detailed commentary than beauty. In this particular tale, Grognon is the butt of repeated joking descriptions, apparent even in her name, which means "grumpy" or "crabby." Nasty but also ridiculous, Grognon is destined to self-destruct (she is eventually killed off by an evil fairy at the end of the story). Her presence confirms Gracieuse's superiority, already foreshadowed in *her* name (meaning "gracious"). In this way, Grognon, like folkloric evil mothers generally, embodies, on the one hand, an Oedipal and/or patriarchal rejection of the maternal and, on the other hand, an inverted glorification of the "good" mother. Just as much as it departs from the rest of the vogue, d'Aulnoy's penchant for evil maternal figures like Grognon and, especially, the binaristic narrative structure of which they are a part prefigures the representation of motherhood in later literary fairy tales.

D'Aulnoy's fairy tales also display a fascination with foolish mothers. While some of these mothers find themselves in impossible situations (such as the mother in "Le Nain jaune" who cannot avoid promising her child to the dwarf), many others are guilty of overindulgence or quite simply bad judgment (such as the mothers in "Le Prince Lutin," "Le Prince Marcassin," and "Le Serpentin vert"). In "La Chatte blanche," a queen, unable to resist her desire for fruit growing in a garden belonging to fairies, promises them her unborn daughter in exchange. Later, when the princess refuses to marry the fairies' nephew, they change her into a white cat. In the second half of the final moral, d'Aulnoy then links the heroine's metamorphosis to her mother's "folly":

> Tairai-je cette mère et cette folle envie,
>   Qui fait à Chatte blanche éprouver tant d'ennuis,
>   Pour goûter de funestes fruits!
> Au pouvoir d'une fée elle la sacrifie.
> Mères, qui possédez des objets pleins d'appas,
> Détestez sa conduite, et ne l'imitez pas.

Will I be silent about this mother and her foolish urge, / That made Chatte blanche experience so many troubles, / Just to taste some fateful fruit! / She sacrifices her to the power of a fairy. / Mothers, who have charges full of charms, / Detest her conduct and do not imitate it.[19]

From the perspective of this moral, the mother's uncontrollable urge is just as important as the irresistible love that unites the princess and the prince at the end of the tale. To be sure, the mother's urges and fateful promise are cast in highly negative light in the tale itself (including a comparison to Eve in the heroine's autobiography). Yet, the importance that the moral accords to the mother puts her in competition with the daughter–heroine whose adventures by far dominate the story. The mother–daughter bond resurfaces at the end as a conflict that is downplayed in the plot itself. D'Aulnoy draws her readers' attention to ripples that trouble the surface of the tranquil sea of maternal goodness. Through her final imperative ("Mères ... / Détestez sa conduite, et ne l'imitez pas"), she plays into a patriarchal stereotype that she also attempts to empower mothers to overcome. This ambivalence marks d'Aulnoy's corpus as a whole, for in a number of other tales, such as "La Princesse Carpillon" and "La Bonne petite souris" (to which I will turn in a moment), mothers are given resolutely active and highly positive roles. On balance, then, d'Aulnoy's treatment of motherhood exposes its uneasy if not unstable place within the "new" ideal of the family evolving in this period.

In opposition to d'Aulnoy's fairy tales, as I have already noted, the majority of the *contes de fées* do not cast mothers – or fathers for that matter – as central characters. Accordingly, the vogue in large measure might be said to reflect the indifference of early modern family ties. In a few tales, however, maternal figures seem to confirm the emerging desire to sentimentalize motherhood, to make mothers both a source and an object of intense emotional attachment. Moreover, it is significant that in d'Aulnoy's "La Princesse Belle-Etoile et le Prince Chéri," "La Princesse Carpillon," and "La Bonne petite souris" as well as La Force's "La Bonne femme," this sentimentalization of motherhood occurs against the backdrop of pastoral retreats. By withdrawing themselves from court life, the characters seek a simpler, more peaceful existence of nostalgic décor. Included in this nostalgia is a return to a past state of both collective and individual proportions. It is, thus, as if the nostalgic pastoral setting provides a means of tapping into the affective energy (itself nostalgic in a psychological sense) with which motherhood was increasingly being infused. The individual–psychic and collective–cultural varieties of nostalgia seem to feed off each other.

In none of the above-mentioned *contes de fées* are these dual nostalgias a straightforward celebration or sentimentalization of motherhood. In "La Princesse Belle-Etoile et le Prince Chéri" and "La Bonne petite souris," mothers are assisted by fairies who share in their glory, but also complicate the representation of motherhood (a point to which I return in the next section). In "La Princesse Carpillon" and "La Bonne femme," the women who assume the maternal roles are surrogate and not biological mothers, suggesting ultimately that motherhood, as an affective state, is above all a social construction, and not a biological given. However, both tales seem to camouflage this radical conclusion in a discourse that sentimentalizes the maternal. The hero and heroine in "La Princesse Carpillon" are separated from their biological parents in infancy. Even before the initial separation, the tale associates the maternal with intimacy and affection by noting that the mothers of both the prince and princess insisted on breastfeeding their newborns.[20] This detail is significant in a period when the infants and young children of upper class families were still usually cared for outside of the home; yet its melodramatic potential is enhanced further still when the prince's mother dies from a wound inflicted on her breast by a kitten whom her jealous stepson had substituted for her newborn son (233). Both hero and heroine are then raised by surrogate parents. The wife of the tyrant who overthrew Princess Carpillon's parents takes pity on her and decides to raise her. But it is the prince's childhood that most directly accentuates the emotional role of his "mothers." He is first nurtured by an eagle who instinctively understands his needs and loves him with an anthropomorphic passion that surpasses feelings for her own offspring: "l'aigle l'aimait avec une passion surprenante, elle ne lui apportait que des fruits pour sa nourriture, faisant cette espèce de différence entre lui et ses aiglons, à qui elle ne donnait que de la chair crue ... Elle avait ... deux petits aiglons qu'elle nourrissait soigneusement; mais quelque chers qu'ils lui fussent, sa tendresse était encore plus grande pour le jeune prince ... " (the eagle loved him with a surprising passion, she only brought him fruit for his nourishment, distinguishing between him and her eaglets, to whom she only gave raw flesh ... She had ... two little eaglets whom she nourished carefully; but however dear they were to her, her tenderness was even greater for the young prince ... [237]). When the eagle is killed by shepherds, the young prince responds in kind to the affection shown him: "le jeune prince, plein de naturel, voyant tomber sa nourrice, jeta des cris pitoyables, et pleura amèrement" (the young prince, full of spontaneity, seeing his nurse fall, screamed pitifully and cried bitterly [238]). For a second time, then, maternal tenderness, rewarded with death, becomes an object of tragic pity. At the command of the fairy Amazone, the prince is then taken in by the elderly shepherd Sublime, who by raising him as the son he never had, attempts to wrest him from the dominion of women. He does not entirely succeed, as testified by the emotional ties that the prince forms with his new-found mother. One day, for instance, Sublime decides to reprimand the prince for being late for dinner when the prince enters and explains: "Ma *mère* ... l'envie de vous apporter ce chevreuil m'a bien fait courir des monts et des plaines" (My *mother* ... the desire to bring you this venison forced me to run over mountains and plains [273; emphasis added]). As Sublime begins to chide him, his wife intervenes: "Cela suffit, dit la reine qui l'aimait avec une extrême tendresse: mon *fils*, je vous remercie du présent que vous me faites. Venez vous asseoir auprès de moi, et soupez" (That's enough, said the queen who loved him with an extreme tenderness: my *son*, I thank you for the gift you bring me. Come sit next to me and eat [273; emphasis added]). Ultimately, the "tendresse" that links the prince and his "mothers" offers a commentary on the stakes of motherhood itself. Not only is maternal affection absent from most other *contes de fées*, and thus all the more prominent in "La Princesse Carpillon," it is also applied to the prince's surrogate mothers, one of whom is not even human. Motherly love, as an emotional quality, is not the monopoly of biological mothers; and the very role of mother can be fulfilled by virtually any woman. Affection and not biology causes the prince to call his second adoptive mother "*mère*," and causes her to refer to him as her "*fils*."

La Force's "La Bonne femme" (The Good Woman) takes up where "La Princesse Carpillon" leaves off and makes the motif of surrogate maternal love the narrative's central focus. Before becoming an exemplary mother, this "good woman" demonstrates her solid moral character – her "*honnêteté*," "*franchise*," and "*courage*" – by leaving the hypocrisy and dissimulation of court for a pastoral retreat. She tends a flock of sheep to meet her needs, and finds happiness. But when her flock mysteriously disappears, she is grief-stricken and despondent. Yet, her affectionate care for her sheep is a narrative preparation and/or test for a second, more consequential flock. Having lost her means of subsistence and resolved to die, she suddenly happens upon three small children who run to embrace her – one of whom, without hesitation, calls her "*mère*."[21] The good woman devotes herself entirely to raising her new-found family, thinking that "le ciel lui rendait ce petit troupeau en la place de celui qu'elle avait perdu" (the heavens gave her this little flock in place of what she had lost [168]). This vague providential blessing takes the concrete form of Madame Tu-Tu, a fairy who first allays the good woman's worries about the love between her son and one of her daughters (they are cousins and not brother and sister) and who then reveals how this good mother can free these two lovers from the clutches of an evil king. But Madame Tu-Tu reaffirms the good woman's goodness not only because of what she does – she gives supernatural counsel and protection – but also because of what she does not do – she does not love the children as much as their adoptive mother. When Finfin and Lirette are captured by an evil king, Madame Tu-Tu discovers that the only way to rescue them is for someone to sacrifice him/herself to the king. The fairy adds that she cannot do so: "je ne me sens pas assez d'amitié pour eux, ni assez de courage pour aller ainsi m'exposer à sa fureur, et je crois aussi que peu de personnes seraient capables de le faire" (I don't feel enough love for them, nor enough courage to go expose myself to his fury, and I also think that few people would be capable of doing it [196]). When devoted to her children, the good woman's love and courage exceed those of even a fairy, and her efforts are not in vain. She frees the persecuted lovers and comes out alive.

At the end of the tale, her "children" assume their rightful places at court and the good woman returns to her wilderness retreat as the final moral praises her "*grandeur d'âme*" and "*courage*" (200). The final triumph does not offer this protagonist material, social, and political splendor, but rather simplicity and tranquility. Going against the grain of other *contes de fées* featuring parents driven from their kingdoms, La Force's tale questions the ideal of courtly life, at least as a reward for the good woman's maternal virtue. At the end of "La Princesse Carpillon," for instance, the shepherd Sublime and his wife return to their kingdom. Their pastoral existence was a temporary exile proving that they are innately noble and, thus, deserving of royal positions. The good woman's final retreat situates ideal motherhood in an imaginative paradise that rejects the outward trappings of wealth and prestige in favor of inner virtue. The good woman returns to the idealized existence which her children leave in order to inhabit their own world, the real word. She is, we might say, the primal, pre-Oedipal mother who, in the wake of the Oedipal conflict, becomes the object of psychic nostalgia. At the same time, La Force's heroine is perhaps also the reflection of an historically based nostalgia in that she incarnates the affection that children of the aristocracy and upper bourgeoisie often felt for governesses.[22] La Force transposes the affective meaning of motherhood onto a heroine who is not exclusively defined by her maternal persona, which is clear in the title, "La Bonne femme" and the final moral's celebration of universal virtues. To be sure, this *conte de fées* is not a radical departure from cultural discourses that were promoting the "new" ideal of female domesticity. The "good woman" conforms all too easily to the late-seventeenth-century stereotype of the submissive yet hard-working wife and mother. And it is doubtless for this reason that "La Bonne femme" counts among the handful of seventeenth-century *contes de fées* never completely forgotten by editors and publishers.[23] Nonetheless, the good woman's final retreat, like her example throughout the story that bears her name, presents a troubling ambiguity. This heroine retires to a rose house that mysteriously appeared as a symbol of Lirette's and Finfin's love. She retires, in other words, to an idealized if not magical existence, and, significantly, she is joined by the dowager queen, also noted for her "*vertu*" (199), who is the mother of Finfin and another prince who marries the good woman's other "daughter." The good mother and the virtuous queen assume an existence befitting their exemplary motherhood. Yet, they do so, says the storyteller, because they were "rebuté[e]s du monde" (disgusted with society [199]). The rose house seems to symbolize both the consecration of motherhood and the search for something different. Motherhood is rewarded by the tale, but exists outside of the society that this same tale authorizes. It inhabits a never-never land unknown even to the *contes de fées*.

THE REVENGE OF THE FAIRIES

In current definitions of fairy tales, fairies (or *fées* in French) are readily associated with mothers. In English, the very word "fairy" almost effortlessly attaches itself to "godmother." And this association is not without merit: the protection and care offered by good fairies as well as the persecution and spells emanating from evil fairies mirror the binary split of maternity that accompanies its valorization within the patriarchal family. Beyond the resemblance of narrative roles, many fairies in the *contes de fées*, as well as several folkloric traditions, are biological mothers. Murat, for instance, writes three tales featuring fairy-mothers who are important helpers or opponents to their own children.[24] In some early versions of fairy tales such as "Cinderella" the narrative deliberately underscores the continuity between a fairy or some other magical creature and the protagonist's deceased mother (Warner, *From the Beast to the Blonde*, 201–206). Throughout the *contes de fées*, however, the association of fairies with mothers is more complex than it would appear at first sight. The majority of *fées* are not mothers in the biological sense and their narrative roles exceed those of most fairy-tale mothers. At one and the same time, fairies both *are* and are *not* maternal figures.

The alliance of a fairy and a mother is the main focus of d'Aulnoy's "La Bonne petite souris" (The Good Little Mouse). Although this tale is unusual in the amount of attention it gives the mother, the emphatic role played by the fairy is typical of *contes de fées*. What is nonetheless exceptional is this fairy's extraordinary devotion to the heroine's mother, a pregnant queen imprisoned by her husband's murderer. Consequently, the fairy's actions enhance the queen's status as an exemplary mother. In what is an integral part of any fairy's role, the *fée* sets out to test her protégée before offering her protection. She first appears in the prison cell as a mouse and dances until the queen gives it her meager supper of three peas. Rewarding this act of kindness, the little mouse produces an exquisite banquet, and the queen thinks to herself, "en vérité ... un bienfait n'est jamais perdu" (truthfully ... a good deed is never in vain.)[25] The next day, the mouse again appears and, after serving another feast, romps in some straw to suggest that the queen make a basket in which she can lower her soon-to-be born child to safety from the prison tower. What follows is another test of the mother's character. After the queen gives birth to a daughter named Joliette, a crotchety old woman offers to hurry the child to safety if the mother gives her the little mouse to eat. When the queen refuses, the mouse explains, while transforming into a fairy: "j'ai voulu vous éprouver fortement. J'ai pris la figure d'une vieille: c'est moi qui vous ai parlé au bas de la tour, et vous m'avez toujours été fidèle" (I wanted to put you to a harsh test. I took the appearance of an old woman: I was the one who spoke to you at the bottom of the tower and you were always faithful to me [363]).

Alongside this proof of the queen's kindness and fidelity, the fairy assumes a maternal persona of her own. For instance, suspecting that a beautiful girl tending turkeys is the queen's daughter who had been kidnapped at birth, the fairy asks, "ma *fille*, apprenez-moi votre nom" (my *daughter*, tell me your name [367; emphasis added]). When she answers "Joliette," the fairy is overcome with quasi-maternal joy: "à ce mot la Fée ne douta plus de la vérité; et lui jetant les bras au cou, elle pensa la manger de caresses" (at this name the fairy doubted the truth no more; and throwing her arms around her neck she wanted to hug her to death [367]). Later, Joliette confirms the fairy's maternal character by calling her "ma bonne mère" (my good mother [368]). Although her devotion is not unlike that of many other *fées*, this particular fairy reinforces, by duplication, the queen's own maternal sentimentality. Since the text emphasizes the queen's sadness about her daughter's kidnapping and, later, her joy when Joliette is found,[26] the fairy is virtually the queen's alter ego.

In terms of narrative structure, the solidarity between the queen and the fairy serves not only to underscore maternal virtue and affection but also to offset the malice of the Méchant

Roi and the evil fairy Cancaline. Overall, "La Bonne petite souris" details the king's far more than Cancaline's maliciousness; yet the rivalry between the good and evil fairies in this tale, as in many folkloric narratives, echoes the polarization of motherhood that often occurs in patriarchal ideologies.[27] Joliette is caught between two sets of diametrically opposed parental figures. On one level, of course, there are her mother and the Méchant Roi, acting on behalf of his son, who demands Joliette's hand in marriage. On another level, however, the good fairy/little mouse (who defends the ideals of virtuous motherhood) and her villainous counterpart Cancaline (who gratuitously beats Joliette like so many folkloric stepmothers [366]) compete for the princess. Compared to the sadistic Méchant Roi, Cancaline is a minor antagonist. And yet, by making possible the joyous reunion between mother(s) and daughter, she accentuates by negation the maternal goodness of the queen and her fairy protectress. It is as if Cancaline's primary function is to introduce a binary vision of motherhood that would otherwise be absent from d'Aulnoy's tale.

Notwithstanding all these parallels between *fées* and mothers, "La Bonne petite souris," like so many of the *contes de fées*, also differentiates the good fairy from the queen, the godmother–helper from the biological mother. Of course, the most obvious difference between the two is the fairy's supernatural and the queen's ordinary existence. Although the fairy uses her magic to enhance and embellish the queen's maternal instincts, she also uses them to draw attention to herself and her own powers. There is always an element of virtuosic self-display – which should not necessarily be confused with self-aggrandizement – in her good deeds. She, like so many of her counterparts in the vogue, seeks to assist her protégée in a way that will dazzle her at the same time. Thus, having refused to hand over the little mouse to the decrepit old woman, the queen is struck with fear when the little mouse begins to talk: "la reine mourait de peur d'entendre parler la Souris; mais sa peur augmenta bien quand elle aperçut que son petit museau prenait la figure d'un visage, que ses pattes devinrent des mains et des pieds, et qu'elle grandit tout d'un coup" (the queen was frightened to death to

hear the Mouse speak; but her fear was much increased when
she noticed that its little muzzle began to take the form of a
face, that its paws became hands and feet, and that it grew all of
a sudden [362]). This transformation complete, the queen
recognizes the same fairy who had promised to rescue her
earlier in the story. By shedding her mouse disguise, the good
fée simultaneously keeps her promise to the queen and reveals
her own powers. Later, she herself confirms this self-display
when she explains why she had disguised herself as an old
woman to test the queen: "J'ai voulu éprouver votre coeur. J'ai
reconnu qu'il est bon, et que vous êtes capable d'amitié. Nous
autres Fées, qui possédons des trésors et des richesses immenses,
nous ne cherchons pour la douceur de la vie que de l'amitié, et
nous en trouvons rarement ... On ne nous aime que par
intérêt, et cela ne nous touche guère; mais quand vous m'avez
aimée en petite souris, ce n'était pas un motif d'intérêt" (I
wanted to test your heart. I've seen that it is good and that you
are capable of friendship. We Fairies, who possess immense
treasures and riches, are looking for friendship to add to the
sweetness of life, and we rarely find it ... People only like us out
of self-interest, and that hardly impresses us; but when you
liked me as a small mouse it was not out of self-interest [362–
363]). Ironically, as the fairy herself explains, *her* love for the
queen is not without self-interest. And the fairy's double
perspective is confirmed by overall narrative structure. For, "La
Bonne petite souris" draws as much attention to the fairy as to
the queen and Joliette. All three could claim the title of heroine.

The good fairy is more than a maternal persona in another,
more figurative sense, visible in the final moral. Referring to the
queen, it expounds:

> Cette princesse infortunée ...
> Eût d'un destin cruel éprouvé les rigueurs ...
> Si sa juste reconnaissance
> N'eût intéressé dans son sort
> Cette prudente et sage Fée ...

This unfortunate princess ... / Would have experienced the rigors of
a cruel destiny ... / If her just gratitude / Had not made her fate
interesting, / To this prudent and wise Fairy ... (375)

At the end of the moral, the queen's gratitude to her protecting fairy is proclaimed as the tale's principal lesson:

> Tout ceci n'est rien qu'une fable,
> Faite pour amuser quiconque la lira;
> Toutefois on y trouvera
> Une morale véritable.
> A qui t'a fait une faveur,
> Montre une âme reconnaissante;
> C'est la vertu la plus puissante
> Pour toucher et gagner le cœur.

All of this is nothing but a fable, / Created to amuse whoever reads it; / However one will find in it / A true moral. / To whoever does you a favor, / Show a grateful heart; / That is the most powerful virtue / For touching and winning hearts. (375)

Gratitude, then, has very real rewards. In the tale itself, these are symbolized by no one less than the fairy and her favors to the grateful queen. The good fairy/little mouse, the most fictitious of this tale's characters, becomes an emblematic figure of fiction's capacity to purvey "truth." What she represents, more precisely, is the desired effect of gratitude – "touching and winning hearts." In this sense, she ensures, she *is* a form of wish-fulfillment. She symbolizes the unfailing (and magnificent) reward for the effort made to be grateful but also, and more generally, the very possibility that one can find a "true moral" in "nothing but a fable" – in a word, storytelling. In what is a *mise en abyme* of the storytelling act, the fairy rushes to the queen's prison and "tells the whole tale" (cont[e] tout le conte [368]) of how she found Joliette disguised as a girl tending turkeys. Both object of storytelling and storyteller, the fairy symbolizes as well as fulfills wishes. In this regard, d'Aulnoy's good fairy/little mouse is more than a mother. Yet, her own wish-fulfilling storytelling and the storytelling she represents inscribe the power and presence of virtuous motherhood. Significantly, when the queen is reunited with Joliette, she too "tells her the tale of her life" (lui cont[e] le conte de sa vie [373]), thereby imitating the fairy's example. Through her emphatic presence, the fairy crystallizes longings for an all-powerful motherhood, but more generally for a wish-fulfilling storytelling and all it can encompass.

In "La Bonne petite souris," then, d'Aulnoy suggests the utopian potential as well as the ambiguous links between fairies and motherhood. For the good fairy/little mouse, like so many of the *fées* in the vogue, this ambiguity is actually an asset. As fairy godmothers (in the traditional sense of the term), they occupy a liminal space both within and outside of the family unit. Going back to their medieval literary origins, fairies are known to adopt particular families for whom they perform their ritual duties of foretelling the future, bestowing gifts on newborns, and protecting family members from harm.[28] In a number of *contes de fées* this connection to the adopted family is further underscored in the conclusion when, having carried out their prescribed duties, the fairies reappear to share in the final triumph of the protagonist and his/her family.[29] At the same time, of course, good fairies exist outside of the families they aim to protect. Possessing knowledge and powers not imparted to ordinary mortals, they scurry in and out of the "real" world of the protagonists. Fairies may well fill maternal roles, but in ways that allow them to transcend the constraints of death and marriage that weigh upon so many folkloric mothers. Fairies may be mothers in the broadest sense, but in ways that make it possible for them to circumvent to a great extent the "*grand renfermement*" of mothers. They may represent a utopian revenge for mothers by their supernatural deeds, but not without limits. For they also make sentimentality a natural trait of women and mothers. And in this sense, their revenge is only partial.[30]

Compared to other bodies of folk- and fairy tales, the seventeenth-century *contes de fées* make abundant and insistent use of fairies. Even discounting Bernard, Nodot, and Perrault, who feature them either not at all or infrequently, the prominence of fairies is one of the single most defining features of the French literary fairy tale.[31] Be they good or evil, more or less powerful, *fées* are the genre's most often exploited link to folklore and the marvelous. The neologism that was the word "*conte de fées*" in late seventeenth-century France attests to the pronounced role that this character-type played in early conceptions of the genre. Marina Warner has astutely observed that the period's variant spelling "*conte* des *fées*" (as in d'Aulnoy's *Les Contes des fées*, 1697) can be taken to mean "tales *about* fairies" (Warner, 234). Manifestly, the fairy character held an appeal for late seventeenth-century readers and writers.

But what was it that may have attracted this public to *fées* and how might this attraction be interpreted? In the dichotomous population of *fées*, it is the "good" fairy figure who most directly discloses this attraction. "Evil" fairies, of course, abound in the vogue and held a fascination all their own. Yet, their beneficent counterparts, upholding order and protecting the protagonists, on the one hand, fighting disorder and undoing the antagonists, on the other, invite direct readerly identification if not wish-fulfillment. Prime among these good fairies is the archetypal fairy godmother, whose "maternal" qualities offered a means of reiterating and, occasionally, rethinking a dominant cultural discourse. This, however, is only one explanation of the fairies' prominence. In fact, more compelling reasons can be gleaned from these characters' most recurrent traits. As "helpers," good fairies perform (or make possible) supernatural deeds in order to secure the final triumph of moral order and heterosexual union. Reflecting their medieval derivation from classical lore about the Fates, the three goddesses of destiny, and the Sibyls, tellers of oracles, fairies possess a knowledge that exceeds the limitations of the human mind. In the early literary evolution of this character type, the fairy's powers only included the capacity to foretell the future (Harf-Lancner, *Les Fées au moyen-âge*, 17–25). In the *contes de fées*, this remains the one trait common to all fairies regardless of their ability or inability to perform other deeds. More important, by foretelling the future, fairies incarnate one of the basic narrative principles of folk- and fairy tales – the foreknowledge of the ultimate triumph of order over disorder. With the exception of the dysphoric tales, good fairies help to establish and to enact this foreknowledge.[32] They do so through their use of language, by predicting the future outright and/or by announcing the particular gifts they bestow on newborns. On the level of narrative structure, then, fairies' predictive powers are performative. Through their prophetic speech-acts, *fées* act out the etymological meanings of the word that designates them: the French *fée* like the Italian *fata* and the Spanish *hada* can all be traced to the Latin feminine word *fata*, variant of *fatum* referring to a goddess of "fate," but also to *fatum*, past participle of *fari*, "to speak, reveal, bear witness."[33] Speaking the fate that the folk- or fairy-tale narrative acknowledges from the outset, fairies wield considerable power.

This power captured the attention of several of the *conteuses*. As I have already shown in chapter 3, La Force, Lhéritier, and Murat make reference to "*fées*" as fairy-tale storytellers, an association in turn reminiscent of this word's use as a conceit for certain salon women (*salonnières*).[34] By extending the parallel that Murat develops in her dedication letter to "les Fées modernes" (the modern Fairies),[35] it is possible to interpret the proliferation of the fairy character-type throughout the *contes de fées* at least in part as flattering portraits of salon women and, in the case of the women fairy-tale writers, self-portraits. Although difficult to prove in any detail, such an interpretation finds support not only in La Force's, Lhéritier's, and Murat's references to women's tale-telling but also in the fact that the two *conteurs* who rely heavily on fairies, Mailly and Préchac, publish their stories as celebrations, so to speak, of women (Mailly's collection is subtitled *Contes Galans, Dédié [sic] aux Dames* and the end of Préchac's "La Reine des fées" is an *à clef* panegyric of noted aristocratic women and their families.)[36] In another sense, given this period's virulent moralist attacks on polite society, exalting salon women or female powers through the figure of the fairy offered both imaginary compensation and a counter-discourse. Moreover, to the extent that salon culture was perceived to be in decline during this *fin de siècle*, fairies may even have had a nostalgic appeal that recalled the heyday of both the mid-century salon and women's prominent role in cultural discourses. *Fées* may, for instance, have a remote connection to the emerging recognition (and "invention") of a female literary tradition, evident in eulogies by Lhéritier and Vertron, among others. Controlling their own and others' destinies in ways unimaginable for seventeenth-century French women, fairies in their most ideal form project decidedly utopian visions of femininity.

This, however, is only part of the story about the *fées*. Not all fairies are supremely powerful or unequivocally good. Evoking, perhaps, the ambivalence between "fée" as salon woman or fairy-tale writer and "fée" as character-type, La Force does not hesitate to declare, bitterly, at the end of "Plus Belle que Fée":

> Fée en ce temps se fait encore voir,
> Mais on ne voit plus de miracles.

Fairies can still be seen these days, / But we don't see any miracles. (NCF, 7: 35)

Situating the powers of fairy-storytellers and/or fairy-characters in the realm of distant illusion, this remark is emblematic of the limits that several writers impose on fairies. In a common folkloric situation, a good fairy is unable to protect the protagonist from an evil spell, which must run its full course before the tale's triumphant conclusion (cf. Perrault's "La Belle au bois dormant"). In extreme cases, such as Murat's "Anguillette" and "Peine perdue," it is because fairies are unable to assist the protagonist that the tale ends on a dysphoric note. In several other *contes de fées*, the usually obligatory happy ending comes about in spite of the fairy's openly acknowledged limitations.[37] Although not unusual in medieval literature or folklore,[38] the limitation of fairies' powers, especially among the non-folkloric narratives, becomes a means of reflecting on the fairy as a figure of feminine authority.

Nowhere is this more evident than in d'Auneuil's "La Tyrannie des fées détruite." This title has an obvious shock value that can be explained in part as a coy publication strategy for negotiating the already crowded market of literary fairy tales. Yet, d'Auneuil's tale also probes the limits of the fairy character as a figure of wish-fulfillment. The opening clearly reverses the balance of power usually weighted in favor of good over evil fairies:

Le pouvoir des fées était venu à un si haut point de puissance, que les plus grands du monde craignaient de leur déplaire. Cette maudite engeance, dont on ne sait point l'origine, s'était rendue redoutable par les maux qu'elles faisaient souffrir à ceux qui osaient leur désobéir. Leur fureur n'était jamais satisfaite que par les changements des plus aimables personnes en monstres les plus horribles, et si elles ne vous donnaient pas une mort prompte, ce n'était que pour vous faire languir plus longtemps dans une condition misérable, qu'elles vous refusaient le trépas. L'impossibilité qu'il y avait de se venger d'elles les rendait plus impérieuses et plus cruelles . . .

The power of fairies had become so strong that the greatest of this world feared displeasing them. This cursed breed whose origin is unknown had become frightening by the evils they made whoever disobeyed them suffer. Their fury was never satisfied except by changing the most beautiful persons into the most horrible monsters, and if they didn't kill you promptly it was only to make you languish all the longer in a miserable state that they refused you death. The impossibility of getting revenge on them rendered them more imperious and more cruel . . .[39]

Fairies, then, are synonymous with the evil spells and persecution inflicted on "les plus aimables personnes" (the nicest persons), and the plot that unfolds confirms this unequivocally negative image. In this tale, the fairies kidnap the beautiful Philonice and raise her as a bride for their ally, the Roi des monstres (King of Monsters). Shortly before the fateful wedding, the heroine meets the handsome Prince Anaxandre whom, as she discovers, her parents had destined to become her husband. Subjected to the wrath of the fairies for Philonice's refusal to wed the Roi des monstres, the protagonists find consolation in the company of Cléonice, whose lover has been transformed into a dragon, and Mélicerte, whose fiancé is imprisoned in a tomb. Hope for all three couples comes in the form of a divine voice who speaks through Philonice to announce the end of the fairies' tyranny. Immediately thereafter, the fairies, defenseless, see their powers wither away until they themselves are banished by the divine princess, who reunites the heroic couples.

From all appearances, then, d'Auneuil introduces fairies for the express purpose of expelling them from the tale's idyllic closure. Although "La Tyrannie des fées détruite" is an extreme case, the same principle applies here as in other *contes de fées* with prominent evil fairies (eg. d'Aulnoy's and Murat's collections). Evil fairies create the obstacles that allow good fairies and protagonists to triumph. Their defeat is a cathartic expulsion of disorder that enhances the predetermined victory of order. Thus, the tyranny of d'Auneuil's fairies gives way to the equity of the divine princess. At the same time as encapsulating a general narrative principle, the evil fairies in this and other tales comply with a rigid law of patriarchal representation: they incarnate unvirtuous femininity, just as good fairies embody its virtuous opposite. It is striking but hardly accidental, therefore, that the most common form of female rivalry in this corpus is that pitting (good) fairy against (wicked) fairy. Feminine virtue depends upon – is inconceivable without – its antithesis. And in this story as in so many folk- and fairy tales, the importance given to the antagonism between fairies confirms and italicizes this central tenet of patriarchal ideology.

In spite of its title and no matter how much it conforms to the stereotypical representation of fairies, "La Tyrannie des fées détruite" is anything but an unambiguous condemnation of *fées* (which only really occurs in several parodic *contes de fées*.)[40] For, among the tyrannical *fées* exists one fairy, Serpente, whose role in the story is equivocal. With a name that evokes deviousness and deception, Serpente spends the first half of the story trying to play the two sides of the coin. She is charged by her fairy sisters with keeping watch over Philonice, and she initially refuses to defy their authority. Yet she is also moved to compassion at the princess's plight and even tries to convince the other fairies to rescind their fateful edicts. Serpente remains simultaneously helper and opponent in this narrative scheme until she hears the oracle announcing the fairies' downfall. Unable to persuade her sisters to change their ways, Serpente actively but secretly aids Philonice and Anaxandre to elude the fairies' numerous obstacles. However, it is not she but the enigmatic "divine princess" who liberates Philonice, reunites the other two couples, and destroys the fairies' tyranny. Serpente, after all, is a *fée*. Even if the divine princess grants her the honor of being the unique bearer of this title, only the transcendent goddess can reimpose the order to which the fairy-tale narrative aspires. To be sure, in her other works d'Auneuil does not hesitate to rehabilitate fairies to the powerful roles they play in the rest of the vogue, and even in this tale the divine princess possesses curiously fairy-like powers. But "La Tyrannie des fées détruite" nevertheless rejects the *fée* as a figure of unbridled powers and utopian longing.

It does not, however, totally suppress either this figure or her powers. At the end of the story, Serpente does not leave the hero and heroine but stays by their side. Having bestowed "tous les dons qui pouvaient la faire aimer de son aimable maîtresse" (all the gifts that could make her kind mistress love her), Serpente becomes indispensable to Philonice, who "lui fit conter souvent tous les contes qu'elle fait de l'art de féerie, et trouvant la manière dont elle lui en fait le récit galamment tournée, elle lui a ordonné de les écrire" (often made her tell all the tales she told about the art of fairy magic, and finding the manner she tells the stories gallant, she ordered her to write them down [98]). The principal tasks of the sole remaining fairy are to tell and to write down the powerful deeds of women who no longer exist. Serpente is a fairy inasmuch as she is a singular, exemplary storyteller. She transforms her fairy magic into an artform – the *"art de féerie"* – that consecrates the death of the fairies she spins tales about. Hence, Serpente's final appearance in this tale exposes the illusory pleasure of the *"art de féerie"* for what it is. Her storytelling is the mythical beginning of what will become the vogue; she herself prefigures the discursive powers and limits that the *conteuses* in particular discover in the *conte de fées*, the fairy character-type, and perhaps even the salon.[41]

THINKING BEAUTY: THE LIMITS OF VIRTUE

From its inception in the sixteenth century up to the present, the literary fairy tale has been particularly fascinated with defining feminine virtue. In a sizeable number of folk- and fairy-tale plots, heroes are obliged to prove their physical and emotional courage whereas heroines must prove their moral purity, and often, their domestic competence as well.[42] This, of course, is not to say that men are not expected to be virtuous – quite the contrary. On balance, however, heroes are less likely than heroines to have to prove their moral character. Furthermore, as Maria Tatar has suggested, the genre is not so much interested in heroines' virtues as their vices: "It is one of the lesser-known facts of folkloric life that women are rarely as virtuous as they are beautiful" (*Off with their Heads*, 94). And storytellers from time immemorial have consistently delighted in reproving wayward women for vices as varied as pride, disobedience, curiosity, stubbornness, infidelity, gluttony, and sloth.[43] Fairy-tale women seemingly ease the masculinist fears of women's "vices." Meting out punishment on these fictional women makes crystal clear the individual and social consequences of feminine vice.

To be sure, the literary fairy tale's preoccupation with women's "vices" and "virtues" was not born with the rise of the *contes de fées*. Yet, this *fin de siècle* culture was particularly fertile ground for promoting the genre's interest in feminine conduct. The late seventeenth-century *"grand renfermement"* of women not only glorified domestic motherhood, as we have already seen, but more generally promoted a vision of femininity that was hostile to the pursuits of "worldly" (*mondain*) women. During this period, an explosion of "moralist" tracts and manuals dealing with family life, marriage, and women voiced markedly conservative views on femininity.[44] Compared to the proto-feminist opinions expressed by and/or attributed to many mid-century writers and salon circles,[45] the "new" ideals of femininity that prevailed among "moralist" writers of the 1690s and early 1700s are distinctly retrograde. Indeed, the infamous debate of 1694 surrounding Boileau's *Satire X*, was hardly an isolated event but, rather, symptomatic of a broader tendency to revive well-worn anti-feminist topoi from the age-old *querelle des femmes*. And yet, the late seventeenth-century "moralist" discourse on women was far more than a resurrection of the rhetorical flourishes of earlier debates. It acquired a distinctive resonance because of the increasing concern with the economy of family life, combined with the *perception* of a rise in female "libertinism."[46] Accordingly, in the period's moralist writings, women are enjoined to concentrate their energies on their divinely appointed domestic and family duties. To do so, they

must shun the distractions of the outside world and limit their
intellectual efforts to a properly domestic "science."[47] Fénelon
for instance considers that the education of women should be
limited to teaching them about how to raise their children, how
to supervise their servants, how to manage household expenses
– in sum, how to do everything economically and honorably.
He concedes, however, that "une femme curieuse trouvera que
c'est donner des bornes bien étroites à sa curiosité" (an
inquisitive woman will find that this is putting excessive limits
on her curiosity), to which he replies, "elle se trompe; c'est
qu'elle ne connaît pas l'importance et l'étendue des choses dont
je lui propose de s'instruire" (she is wrong because she does not
know the importance and the breadth of the things I propose
she instruct herself in ["De l'éducation des filles," *Œuvres*, 1:
154]). Women, then, must efface themselves and their own
interests in order to think first and foremost of their husbands,
their children, and their servants.[48] In all aspects of women's
appearance and conduct, modesty, simplicity, discretion, and
sincerity become their watchwords so as to guard against those
most "feminine" of vices – affectation, selfishness, and deception. In a versed primer for women entering "*le monde*," we
read: "Fuyez dans vos discours, l'enflure et la bassesse, /
Qu'ainsi qu'en vos habits, rien n'y soit affecté: / Qu'une noble
simplicité, / En fasse l'ornement, la grâce et la richesse. /
Celles dont la témérité / De ces termes savants parent leur
éloquence / Au lieu de montrer leur science / Ne font voir que
leur vanité" (Avoid in your discourse exaggeration and lowliness, / And in your clothing let nothing be affected: / May a
noble simplicity, / Be their ornament, grace and wealth. /
Those women whose recklessness / With learned terms, dec-
orate their speech / Instead of showing their knowledge / Only
show their vanity).[49] As all-encompassing and as all-important
as it proves to be, feminine virtue, in the eyes of moralists,
appears to be both highly tenuous and extremely vital to the
maintenance of family and social order.

Neither this vision of femininity, based on self-denial, self-
effacement, and transparency, nor this late seventeenth-century

preoccupation with women's conduct are foreign to the *contes de fées*. Over and beyond the fact that the heroines in Perrault's "Peau d'Ane" and "Griselidis" are subjected to graphic if not sadistic tests of their patience and virtue, several of the final morals in this corpus specifically concern women.[50]

Compared to such final morals, Bernard's and Perrault's versions of "Riquet à la houppe" and Lhéritier's "Ricdin-Ricdon" explore feminine virtue in even greater depth by connecting it to intelligence. Based on a similar plot scenario, each tale depicts a heroine whose dilemma stems from a promise of marriage she makes to an ugly and (more or less) demonic man. What she actually receives in exchange, as we will see in a moment, differs in "Riquet à la houppe" and "Ricdin-Ricdon"; but in all three stories, the heroine undergoes a sexual initiation through the blossoming of her intelligence. In a scheme such as this where sexuality is knowledge, however, women possess a knowledge all their own. What the tales by Bernard, Perrault, and Lhéritier explore is the specificity of this knowledge or more precisely *esprit* (or intelligence), the mental faculty that regulates knowledge. However, implicit in these *contes* is the recognition that intelligence governs virtue and that any understanding of women's conduct must treat their mental capacities. By endowing a heroine with *esprit*, each storyteller confronts the supposed incompatibility of intelligence and beauty, of mind and matter – of archetypal masculine and feminine properties. From the outset, then, feminine virtue seems to be an oxymoron or at least a profoundly ambiguous (dubious?) notion. And yet, all three tales struggle to resolve the opposition between intelligence and beauty, mind and matter, women and virtue; and they each do so in very different and ambiguous ways.

Of Bernard's, Lhéritier's, and Perrault's *contes de fées*, the two versions of "Riquet à la houppe" are the most dissimilar in spite of superficial similarities. These two fairy tales are linked first of all by their composition. It is possible either that Perrault rewrote Bernard's version or that the two writers engaged in a sort of friendly competition, frequent in salon circles, by executing their own variation of a previously agreed-upon theme.[51] The fact that the story is not of folkloric origin renders either of these hypotheses even more plausible. In both Bernard's and Perrault's plots, a heroine is born with remarkable beauty, but without the slightest trace of *esprit*. Disdained by her peers for her stupidity, she gladly accepts Riquet à la houppe's offer to bestow intelligence on her in exchange for her promise to marry him in one year's time. In the meantime, she falls in love with a handsome prince.

At this point, however, the two versions diverge. After reluctantly agreeing to keep her promise to Riquet à la houppe (and receiving an added dose of *esprit*), Bernard's heroine, Mama, continues to visit her lover Arada. When Riquet discovers this, he first makes his wife "stupid" by day and "intelligent" by night and then, when she continues to deceive him, he gives her lover the same physical appearance as his own. Perrault, by contrast, offers an ostensibly happier conclusion. When she is visited by Riquet at the end of the year, she first attempts to abrogate the agreement, claiming it nul since she was not yet intelligent when she made it. Riquet succeeds in convincing her to marry him by pointing out that she is only displeased by his appearance and not his birth, intelligence, temperament, or manners. The tale ends when Riquet à la houppe appears to the heroine as "l'homme du monde le plus beau, le mieux fait et le plus aimable qu'elle eût jamais vu" (the most handsome, best built, and the most pleasant man she had ever seen [187]).

As their conclusions indicate, Bernard and Perrault give a strikingly different treatment of the relationship between the heroine and Riquet à la houppe. For the *conteuse*, there is never any doubt that Mama is a victim. The King of the Gnomes' physical ugliness and bizarre demeanor, which are emphasized throughout the tale, accentuate the couple's total incompatibility. Mama is united to a husband whom she not only does not love but also finds absolutely unbearable: "elle fut effrayée de s'être donnée à un monstre et à tous moments elle ne comprenait pas qu'elle pût passer encore un moment avec lui" (she was alarmed to have given herself to a monster and at no time did she see how she could spend another moment with him.)[52] The *conteur*, however, imagines a more sympathetic Riquet and, consequently, an almost conventional courtship and marriage. From the very outset, narrative structure indicates the complementarity of the soon-to-be husband and wife. As is often the case in fairy-tale texts, symmetrical oppositions are clearly established. Riquet is born to a queen ugly and deformed, but is endowed by a fairy with the gift of being "aimable parce qu'il aurait beaucoup d'esprit" (attractive because he will be very intelligent) and of giving "autant d'esprit qu'il en aurait à la personne qu'il aimerait le mieux" (as much intelligence as he has to the person he likes the most [181]). The unnamed heroine is born "plus belle que le jour" (more beautiful than daylight) to a neighboring queen, but the same fairy warns the mother that her daughter would be as stupid as she was beautiful and then gives the princess the ability to make "beau ou belle la personne qui lui plaira" (handsome or beautiful the person who pleases her [181–182]). This same symmetry appears later in the couple's first encounter. Deploying all the artifice of *galant* conversation, Riquet asserts that "la beauté ... est un si grand avantage qu'il doit tenir lieu de tout le reste; et quand on le possède, je ne vois pas qu'il y ait rien qui puisse nous affliger beaucoup" (beauty ... is such a great advantage that it should come before everything else; and when one possesses it, I don't think there is anything that can distress us much [183]), to which the heroine responds, with an un-*galant* frankness that nonetheless emphasizes their complementarity: "j'aimerais mieux ... être aussi laide que vous et avoir de l'esprit, que d'avoir de la beauté comme j'en ai, et être bête autant que je le suis" (I'd prefer ... to be as ugly as you and to have intelligence than to have the beauty I possess and to be as stupid as I am [183]). When the two meet up a year later, their wedding occurs as preordained. Without the coercion that marks Bernard's tale (her Riquet threatens to take away Mama's *esprit*), Riquet overcomes the princess's hesitation by reasoning with her and, especially, by revealing her powers to make him beautiful. Bestowing on the other the lacking quality, Riquet à la houppe and the heroine bind themselves together in what is supposed to be a harmonious union.

However, the symmetry that pervades Perrault's tale has nothing to do with a felicitous and unambiguous reciprocity between the sexes. As Patricia Hannon has astutely observed, Perrault's narrative is constructed on the ancient philosophical opposition that associates men with mind and women with matter.[53] And in spite of its apparent resolution, this opposition is only further reaffirmed in the story. Among other things, Hannon shows that the text's often noted inconsistencies are in fact entirely consistent with a patriarchal ideology that limits the intellectual sphere to men and confines women to bodily reality. The fact that the heroine has a twin sister (whereas Riquet is without a sibling) who is her obverse – ugly but intelligent – serves to reiterate the mind / matter dichotomy, and I would add, the binary construction of folkloric women. This task complete, she disappears from the plot, ensuring that her sister will remain in the spotlight. The other seemingly unsymmetrical character, Riquet's rival, also seems to transgress the story's fundamental opposition since he is perfectly "spirituel" (witty) and "bien fait" (handsome [Perrault, "Riquet à la houppe," 184]). Yet, as Hannon suggests, he seems to appear in order to disappear just as quickly from the tale, so as to pay for his deviance (Hannon, "Antithesis and Ideology," 112). The third and most troubling "inconsistency" is perhaps also the most revealing of the lack of true reciprocity within this tale's couple. Whereas Riquet à la houppe is aware of his ability to grant others intelligence, the princess is completely unaware of her power to bestow beauty until Riquet informs her of this at the very end of the tale. Even when she is "intelligent," she must depend on her bridegroom-to-be. It is as if he withholds this decisive information the better to demonstrate the superiority of his knowledge of her, and the superiority of *his* knowledge over *hers*. Perrault casts even more doubt on the princess and her complementarity with Riquet by adding an alternate conclusion. Initially, she pronounces the performative wish that Riquet become "le Prince du monde le plus beau et le plus aimable" (the handsomest and most pleasant Prince in the world) after which Riquet à la houppe appears as just such a man. Perrault then notes that "quelques-uns assurent que ce ne furent point les charmes de la Fée qui opérèrent, mais que l'amour seul fit cette Métamorphose" (some people assert that it was not the Fairy's spells that worked, but that love alone performed this Metamorphosis [187]) and describes how his good qualities helped her to overlook his hunched back, his limping gait, his crossed eyes, and his big red nose, to the point of transforming them into endearing traits. In the end, though, this second conclusion overturns the first. Not only does the alternate ending have the advantage of humorous realism, but the original one never really claims that Riquet à la houppe was himself actually changed ("Riquet à la houppe *parut* à ses yeux l'homme du monde le plus beau, le mieux fait et le plus aimable qu'elle eût jamais vu"). The princess's powers are all in her head, but of course, in Riquet à la houppe's head as well.

Perrault's conclusions expose what is actually at the ideological and structural epicenter of these two versions of "Riquet à la houppe." Both stories demonstrate the dangers of feminine imagination. In women, these stories seem to say, *esprit* only exacerbates an innate penchant for irrationality, if not vice. Granted, both heroines become court celebrities after receiving their gift from Riquet à la houppe. Bernard's Mama is suddenly surrounded by suitors, and Perrault's princess even serves as her father's chief advisor. But there is also another, less flattering side to their *esprit*. Mama, in Bernard's version, not only hides the origin of her new-found intelligence, but also uses it to find ingenious ways to continue to see her lover after their marriage. The princess in Perrault's tale succumbs to amorous casuistry as she attempts to extricate herself from her pledge – she washes her hands of any responsibility and actually blames Riquet for giving her intelligence.[54] *Esprit*, in these tales, incites women to deception.

From this conclusion, Perrault and Bernard develop two different lines of reasoning. For Perrault, the princess's intelligence becomes an object of dismissive humor. Well before her final "transformation" of Riquet à la houppe's appearance, for instance, the narrator explains the heroine's hesitation to marry the handsome and witty suitor with an ironic maxim that intentionally neglects the true reason, her vow to Riquet: "plus on a d'esprit et plus on a de peine à prendre une ferme résolution sur [le choix d'un Epoux]" (the more intelligence one has, the harder it is to make a firm decision [about a Spouse] 184–185). Lacking the reflective distance that characterizes Riquet à la houppe and the narrator, the princess is a comic victim par excellence. Her imperfect *esprit* reaffirms all the more forcefully the validity of the gendered gulf between masculine mind and feminine body.

For Bernard, however, the pessimistic vision of Mama's *esprit* affords a disillusioned commentary on the very nature of love and its consequences for women. As a dysphoric tale, this "Riquet à la houppe" emphasizes the heroine's tragic dilemma. At the end of the year her benefactor had given her to resolve to marry him, she foresees no possibility of happiness: "son esprit, qui lui devenait un présent funeste, ne lui laissait échapper aucune circonstance affligeante; perdre son amant pour jamais, être au pouvoir de quelqu'un dont elle ne connaissait que la difformité, ce qui était peut-être son moindre défaut, enfin quelqu'un qu'elle s'était engagée à épouser en acceptant ses dons qu'elle ne voulait pas lui rendre: voilà ses réflexions" (her intelligence, which became a fateful gift for her, did not let a single distressing circumstance escape her; lose her lover forever, be under the power of someone in whom she only saw deformity, which was perhaps his slightest defect, in any event someone whom she had promised to marry by accepting gifts that she did not want to give back to him: these were her thoughts [273]). When she attempts to keep her lover and her promise of marriage at the same time, the result, as we have seen, is calamitous. Arada takes the same form as Riquet. Yet, the final sentence suggests that this tragedy is a mixed blessing: Mama "se vit deux maris au lieu d'un, et ne sut jamais à qui adresser ses plaintes, de peur de prendre l'objet de sa haine pour l'objet de son amour; mais peut-être qu'elle n'y perdit guère: les amants à la longue deviennent des maris" (saw two husbands instead of one, and never knew to whom she should complain for fear of mistaking the object of her hatred for the object of her love; but perhaps she hardly lost out at all: in the long run lovers become husbands [278]). Not only does "peut-être" (perhaps) add a note of hope to an otherwise despairing conclusion, it also introduces a decidedly feminine perspective. Mama may well have been forced into the self-abnegation that late seventeenth-century moralists demanded of women. But the narrator generalizes from her experience in order to obscure the illusory distinction between lovers and husbands. Women, the narrator points out, lose out in either case. Perhaps even Mama's name, close as it is to "maman," is the means by which the tale denounces the heroine's gradual but no less certain enclosure in maternal domesticity. And yet, by reasserting the point of view of women at the very moment that the heroine is obliged to efface herself and her desires, Bernard's text presents a utopian outlook by negation typical of many dysphoric tales.[55] Exposing the tragedy of Mama's *esprit* expresses the longing for a different *esprit*, in sum a different existence.

Like Bernard's and Perrault's "Riquet à la houppe," Lhéritier's "Ricdin-Ricdon" also concentrates on the heroine's cognition and its influence on virtue. Unlike these tales, however, "Ricdin-Ricdon" is clearly based on a folkloric tale-type (AT500 The Name of the Helper) and is in fact the first literary version of a story immortalized by the Grimms as "Rumpelstiltskin." And yet, when it comes to representing the heroine, Lhéritier's *conte de fées* differs profoundly from later literary versions. Granted, the *conteuse* follows the fundamental outline of this tale-type – an impossible task that involves the heroine's spinning, a supernatural being who proposes to help her if she agrees to a bizarre pact, and the conclusion in which she outwits her helper-turned-antagonist – but "Ricdin-Ricdon" accentuates far more than any of the other literary versions what might be called the heroine's psychological and social *bildung*.[56] It also puts her in a much more positive light. Rosanie, Lhéritier's heroine, is not the clumsy daughter of a boastful peasant whom we find in the Grimms' version. Rather, she is a long-lost princess victimized by an evil stepmother. And even though she cannot spin nearly as swiftly as her stepmother claims, her work is much admired by the queen who employs her.[57] More significant still is the fact that "Ricdin-Ricdon" does not make Rosanie's *esprit* incompatible with either her moral character or her beauty. Instead, she is blessed with magnificent beauty as well as irreproachable "douceur" (sweetness), "modestie" (modesty), and "adresse" (adroitness [60]). Most striking of all, she possesses keen insight into her own ambitions and intuitively senses that she is of a high birth. Although her *esprit* does not draw her to intellectual and cultural pursuits,[58] Rosanie's self-awareness and self-assertiveness are in stark contrast to the heroines' condition in Bernard's and Perrault's versions of "Riquet à la houppe." Even before she discovers her true identity, for instance, she recounts her life-story, assuming that she is of a higher station than her adoptive family:

Malgré le séjour du village et les faibles lumières de mon éducation, je me trouvai des sentiments et des inclinations beaucoup au-dessus de ma naissance, dont la bassesse me désespérait. Les traits de mon visage seuls étaient capables de m'en consoler. Ils me donnèrent de bonne heure de flatteuses espérances pour ma fortune; et je n'avais pas encore douze ans, que déjà je ne trouvais point de fontaine ni de ruisseau par qui je n'aimasse à me faire redire que je ne resterais pas assurément sous une chaumière.

In spite of my stay in the village and the weakness of my upbringing, I found within me feelings and inclinations far above my birth, the lowliness of which made me despair. Only the features of my face were capable of consoling me: early on they gave me encouraging hope for my future, and I was not even twelve years old when, already, at every fountain or stream I encountered, I enjoyed having them repeat to me that I would assuredly not remain in a humble cottage. (42)

More than romantic fantasy, Rosanie's intuition is confirmed when she arrives at court. Immediately she becomes an object of adulation for her extraordinary beauty. Her social graces develop almost effortlessly under the guidance of her appointed tutor and surrogate mother, Vigilentine, whose name denotes the qualities of moral and social control she brings out in her charge. Even her spinning is a sign of her innate nobility.

Rosanie's slow but skillful work is that of a leisure class, unconcerned by the material necessities of productivity.

Compared to Bernard's and Perrault's heroines, Rosanie enjoys an existential plenitude at the beginning of the tale. She is not beset by the lack that characterizes the wives of Riquet à la houppe, but instead possesses an insight and self-assurance that Bernard's Mama and Perrault's princess are never able to attain. True to the laws of fairy-tale structure, Lhéritier's heroine must nonetheless prove her superior essence, including her virtue, through various tests. Struck by Rosanie's beauty and her stepmother's (false) reports of her skillful spinning, Prince Aimant-joie brings the heroine to court. The prince's mother is likewise taken by her beauty and spares no effort to welcome her. This immediately provokes the jealousy of other women at court, who at several points attempt to turn public opinion against her. The motif of jealous courtiers is frequent in Lhéritier's tales[59] and serves here as elsewhere to italicize the heroine's superiority. Thus, one *cabale*'s attempts to misrepresent her beauty as ugliness only backfire: "quelque peine qu'on se donnât à établir ces idées, dès que Rosanie paraissait, elle les dissipait toutes. Ceux qui l'avaient déjà vue, la regardant avec plus d'attention, la trouvaient plus belle que la première fois qu'ils l'avaient envisagée; et ceux qui n'en avaient qu'entendu parler se récriaient en la voyant qu'il y avait bien de la malice ou du mauvais goût dans les peintures qu'on leur en avait faites" (no matter how hard they tried to prove their point, as soon as Rosanie appeared, she proved them all wrong. Those who had already seen her, looking at her more attentively, found her more beautiful than the first time they had seen her; and those who had only heard about her protested at seeing her that there was most certainly malice or bad taste in the portrayals they had been given of her [58]).

Of course, the most decisive of Rosanie's tests occurs when she meets Ricdin-Ricdon, the mysterious forest-dweller who offers her a magic wand capable of spinning thread for her. In exchange, she must agree to return it to him in three months' time without having forgotten his name. If she cannot recall it, Ricdin-Ricdon will enslave her. In the meantime, the wand allows Rosanie to save face with the queen who believes that the young peasant girl is a veritable spinning wheel, capable of spinning the finest thread in no time. The wand enables her to remain at court, to assume the aristocratic persona she senses to be her own and, as she reflects, to confound "l'orgueil de ses concurrentes par le beau fil que la baguette allait filer" (the false pride of her rivals by the beautiful thread that the wand would spin [47]). Victory over her jealous rivals is complete with the other power Rosanie convinces Ricdin-Ricdon to attach to the wand – that of putting "dans la coiffure et dans les habits tout le bon air et toute la bonne grâce qu'il y faut pour plaire" (in hairstyles and clothes all the distinguished manner and grace necessary to please [47–48]).

Even as Rosanie scores her victory, she falls victim to the traditional dichotomy between beauty and intelligence that haunts Bernard's and Perrault's heroines. For, conditioning her acceptance of the wand on its capacity to give her appearance an extra edge, she falls prey to Ricdin-Ricdon's ethic of misogynistic seduction. He grants her request, explaining: "mes camarades et moi, nous ne refusons jamais aux personnes de votre sexe le talent de se bien mettre, dès qu'elles veulent s'entendre un peu avec nous. C'est pourquoi l'on voit dans le monde de petites filles de douze ans, et qui ne peuvent d'ailleurs rien apprendre, se coiffer avec un art admirable et placer déjà une mouche avec d'aussi judicieuses réflexions que les femmes de cinquante ans" (my friends and I never refuse persons of your sex the ability to present themselves well so long as they are willing to come to a little agreement with us. Thus we see little girls twelve years old who are incapable of learning anything do their hair with admirable artistry and already know how to place a *mouche* with as much judicious reflection as fifty-year-old women [48]). Coming from the mouth of the tale's chief antagonist, this commentary offers an implicit criticism of Rosanie's pact with Ricdin-Ricdon. The heroine makes a deal with a creature who incarnates women's irrational waywardness. By accepting the magic wand, she puts beauty before reason and intelligence. Thus, it seems only logical that she should very nearly fall into his trap at the end of the story.

Forgetting his name means losing control of the knowledge and power that issue from the act of naming.[60] Forgetting his name is both the sign and the consequence of privileging beauty over intelligence, body over mind – of letting feminine imagination run away with itself.

At this point, however, Lhéritier moves beyond the irresolvable tension in Bernard's and Perrault's fairy tales. Mind regains control over body as the heroine recollects the fateful name. Consistent with the AT500 tale-type (The Name of the Helper), Rosanie defeats Ricdin-Ricdon whereas Mama and the princess must each resign themselves to life with Riquet à la houppe. Rosanie's *esprit* precedes and endures the encounter with the treacherous man; Mama's and the princess's is inseparable from him. Even more significant, the error of Rosanie's pact is downplayed if not forgotten altogether in the complexities of Lhéritier's plot. At the end of the three months Ricdin-Ricdon has given her, the heroine has been kidnapped by a rival and then rescued by Prince Aimant-joie; she has learned the dramatic story of her birth to a royal family, the separation from her true parents, the adoption by a peasant family; she has been reunited with her biological mother; and, finally, she has been promised in marriage to the prince. The resolution of Rosanie's pact with Ricdin-Ricdon almost appears as an after-thought. And, in any event, the bridegroom-to-be quickly dismisses any fault one might attribute to his bride-to-be as the result of youthful inexperience (119). By contrast with the humorous ambiguity of Perrault's heroine and the tragic fate of Bernard's, then, Rosanie's trajectory is one of seemingly inexorable ascension. And at the end, she finds her predestined place in the tale's royal family.

After the ethereal optimism of Lhéritier's narrative, the final versed moral is surprisingly realistic. Before reciting these verses, King Richard, who tells the story, emphasizes Rosanie's negative example: "j'ai cherché à faire voir les dangers où s'exposent les jeunes personnes qui écoutent imprudemment toutes sortes de gens et prennent avec trop de facilité de la confiance en eux" (I've tried to show the dangers young people expose themselves to when they imprudently listen to all sorts of people and trust them too easily [127]). The moral pursues this didactic reasoning by admonishing young women to be on their guard against malicious influences:

> Belles qu'un triste aveuglement
> D'ambitieux desseins, et le désir de plaire,
> Font faire si légèrement
> Un dangereux engagement,
> Une démarche téméraire:
> Ah! tremblez de l'évènement!
> Souvent sous les dehors d'un doux empressement
> D'un cœur officieux et d'une âme obligeante,
> C'est l'esprit malin qui vous tente,
> Pour vous perdre éternellement . . .
> Soyez donc dans ce temps, jeunes et beaux objets,
> Sur vos gardes plus que jamais.

Beauties whom an unfortunate blindness / Ambitious designs, and the desire to please, / Cause to make so lightly / A dangerous promise, / A reckless reasoning: / Ah! tremble at the thought! / Often underneath the exterior of a sweet pleading / Of an officious heart, and an obliging soul, / It is the malicious spirit who is tempting you, / In order to be your eternal undoing . . . / In these times, therefore, young and beautiful objects, / Be on your guard more than ever. (127–128)

Contrary to what Rosanie's example teaches, it is not what they possess innately but what they learn to do that enables the "belles," the "jeunes et beaux objets" to avoid awaiting dangers. Specifically, they must resist the temptation of listening to those "esprits malins" who appeal to the "esprit malin" within them. They must conquer the type of thinking that leads them to maliciousness or deviousness. To do so, however, they cannot expect to follow Rosanie's lead:

> S'il [l'esprit malin] vous trompait finement . . .
> Vous ne trouveriez maintenant
> Pour réparer de tels dommages,
> Aucuns jeunes héros venus de hauts parages;
> Mais vous trouveriez seulement
> Certains gros financiers, qui, frauduleusement,
> Chercheraient cent moyens pour vous mettre à leurs gages.

If it [the malicious spirit] deceived you craftily . . . / Nowadays you would not find / To repair such damage, / Any young heroes coming from far-off lands; / But you would only find / Certain fat financiers, who, fraudulently, / Would search for a hundred ways to get you in pawn. (127–128)

There is a gulf between the world of the tale and the world of the "belles." While Rosanie exists in a never-never land where aristocratic merit is eventually rewarded on its own – with, of course, a little help from the prince – the "belles" must rely on their own wits to confront the challenges of bourgeois materiality. For the (aristocratic or bourgeois) "belles" of the moral, Rosanie's story is the nostalgic fantasy of aristocratic ascension but also, perhaps, a utopian wish-fulfillment depicting women's victory over female rivalry and over "l'esprit malin" of male suitors. However, the reality principle of the final moral reminds us that Rosanie's adventures are the stuff of a *conte de fées* and that her utopian qualities remain firmly embedded in a nostalgic ethos.

Finally, then, Lhéritier's tale returns to the age-old opposition between women's *esprit* and women's virtue. By accentuating Rosanie's dubious pact with Ricdin-Ricdon, the versed moral contradicts the virtuous portrayal found in the narrative. On the one hand, she is the example of feminine imagination gone awry; on the other, she embodies the apotheosis of feminine noble essence as virtue (*douceur, modestie,* and *adresse*). Moreover, referring back to the narrative as it inherently does, inviting readers to reinterpret the story, the moral only accentuates this contradiction. There is seemingly no easy resolution of the antithesis between mind and body, intelligence and beauty, *esprit* and virtue.

Lhéritier's rewriting of "Rumpelstiltskin" directs our attention to the way this tale-type and the related versions of "Riquet à la houppe" perpetuate these oppositions. So too does a fourth *conte de fées,* Durand's "Le Prodige d'amour," a variation on the "Riquet à la houppe" plot. In this story, however, the quest for *esprit* is undertaken not by a beautiful woman but by a handsome man, Brutalis; and his benefactor is not a demonic man but an amorous fairy, named Coquette. Beyond this fundamental similarity, the differences with

Bernard's, Lhéritier's and Perrault's stories are striking. The hero is not required to conclude a pact with his benefactor in order to receive his share of intelligence (he acquires it when he falls in love with a shepherdess); his *esprit* never leads him into morally unsound territory; and in the end he is granted complete independence from his benefactor. It is obviously no accident that these differences obtain in a plot with a hero in the place of a heroine. Brutalis, who later becomes Polydamour, can have both intelligence and virtue. However different "Le Prodige d'amour" might appear, it in fact recounts the same basic story as "Ricdin-Ricdon" and the two versions of "Riquet à la houppe." The limited virtue and intelligence of Bernard's, Lhéritier's, and Perrault's thinking beauties are the patriarchal counterpart to the thinking beau's boundless virtue and intelligence. They are, then, but four variations on a theme.

The binary perspective that defines women in folklore and the *contes de fées* is the projection onto femininity of the lack within (patriarchal) masculine subjectivity. The rivalries between mothers and daughters, between biological mothers and step-mothers or mothers-in-law, between good and evil fairies, combined with the existential oppositions imposed on folk- and fairy-tale women (mind versus matter, intelligence versus beauty, imagination versus virtue, among others) make femininity a site of bitter internecine and internal psychological conflict. As a group and as individuals, so this patriarchal logic implies, women display tendencies toward self-negation, if not self-destruction. In its extreme form, then, women's sights are turned inward – toward other women, toward themselves; women are unable to contribute to the positive construction of a social order beyond (and sometimes even within) the confines of hearth and home. Fairy-tale heroes are by far more apt to concentrate their efforts on fighting adversaries outside the domestic sphere and even outside the realm of humanity. In this sense, at least, heroes embody positivity and heroines negativity. Women are the deficient flipside of men.

Yet, the femininities imagined by the *contes de fées* are not nearly as bleak as all this might lead us to believe. For, even if binary structures are reiterated, perhaps unavoidable in the folkloric, literary, and cultural discourses that inform the vogue, at the same time certain writers, especially among the *conteuses*, expose just what is at stake for women in these structures. The spectacle of mothers facing off against stepmothers and of fairy godmothers against evil fairies becomes, under their pens, a statement about the difficulty of female bonding within patriarchy. The contradictions between beauty and intelligence and between imagination and virtue are revealed to be as many obstacles to imagining femininity outside of masculinist categories of thought. The implausible marvelous setting makes it possible, paradoxically, to return to and to expose the all-too-plausible difficulties of (re)imagining femininity in late seventeenth-century France.

Afterword

Si t'as pas de nostalgie, t'as pas de futur.
        Advertising slogan for a Parisian radio station, 1995

Literary history teaches us that forms of romance literature such as the literary fairy tale have been especially attractive in moments of social and cultural transition, a peculiarity that has been explained by these forms' status as a "reinvention of a providential vision"[1] or as a "secular scripture."[2] At a time of instability and uncertainty, romance offers the stability and certainty alternatively imparted by religious discourses. At moments of tension between competing socio-economic, esthetic, and/or epistemological systems, then, romance mediates a resolution of contradictory and/or irreconcilable desires. And such is the case of the French literary fairy tales published between 1690 and 1715. During a period when an emerging bourgeois consciousness was beginning to compete seriously with a dominant aristocratic ethos, the *contes de fées* (by and large) projected a worldview that allowed bourgeois and aristocrats alike a retreat into the magnificent wealth of virtuous nobility. As "Ancients" faced off against "Moderns," literary fairy tales set out to demonstrate the didactic and literary efficacy of a nationally "indigenous" genre. At a time when *mondain* culture was closely scrutinized by "moralist" critics, the fairy tale unabashedly proclaimed its roots in salon circles, all the while promoting its *own* moral purpose. At a moment when the discursive groundwork had been laid to exclude women from roles as cultural agents, the vogue proved their ability to fulfill such roles and, indeed, to dominate a literary movement.

220

As sexuality and gender differences were ever more closely regulated if not standardized, these fairy tales proposed a panoply of roles ranging from the most to the least traditional and acceptable.

Of course, what differentiates the *contes de fées* from many other forms of romance literature is their consistent and prominent use of marvelous settings and characters. Thereby, the vogue puts particular focus on the body; for, the marvelous always foregrounds the extraordinary suffering and pleasure experienced by protagonists and antagonists alike. But at the end of most fairy-tale narratives, suffering befalls the antagonists and pleasure greets the protagonists – "evil" bodies are punished and "good" bodies rewarded. In this sense, the marvelous is very much part of the burgeoning regulation and control of the body that Foucault identified in seventeenth- and eighteenth-century educational, religious, and legal discourses.[3] The agonizing punishments imposed on antagonists and opponents on the one hand and the dream-like pleasures afforded protagonists and helpers on the other produce a dichotomy in which "good" and "evil" are given direct equivalents in corporeal terms. The *contes de fées*, then, project a Manichean vision that transforms the body into a simplistic but powerful purveyor of social meaning. And yet, this meaning is far from univocal. If the marvelous often essentializes desires, it can also expose their social construction. Thus, the marvelous forces at work in the *contes de fées* give the illusion that sexual and social longings are a ready-made, biological given arising within an individual based on an innate class and gender. However, these same forces can be used to dispel this illusion by modifying – amplifying or attenuating – the usually stable profile of fairy-tale characters, and especially their gendered and sexual attributes. If these fairy tales provide a way of regulating or controlling the body and its social meanings, then they also show that this regulation/control is never complete.

The dialectic between nostalgic and utopian longings that traverses the corpus of seventeenth-century *contes de fées* plays a decisive, but also ambivalent role in this regulation/control of the body. Nostalgia envelops fairy-tale bodies in an ideal plenitude that is projected onto an uncertain present and future. It obscures the reality of regulation and control with the illusion of transcendence and reassurance. But nostalgia can also serve as a diversionary tactic for the subversive utopian longings expressed through the marvelous. The idyllically remote setting of the *contes de fées* can give the future-oriented utopian critique through reconfigured bodies the appearance of innocuousness, allowing it to pass uncensored. Finally, the body, and along with it sexuality and gender, are at the core of the tensions between nostalgic and utopian longings, themselves the expression of conflicting desires within a moment of socio-cultural transition.

And yet, this does not mean that the vogue as a whole espouses the radical irresolution of these desires, for all in all nostalgia outweighs utopian longings. Only in a couple of subgroups, such as the sexually allusive and dysphoric tales, as well as several individual texts, is this tension or ambivalence maintained and the satisfaction of narrative desire left in suspense and/or projected into the future. Just these exceptional cases seem to confirm Flahault's contention that folkloric narratives abstain from resolving the opposition between satisfying and forestalling desire (*L'Interprétation des contes*, 58) and, further, constitute the satisfaction of desire in and of themselves, without teaching us what this should be (*L'Interprétation des contes*, 174). By contrast, the majority of the *contes de fées* would seem to satisfy nostalgic desires and to present this satisfaction as their "moral" lesson. In another, more oblique sense, however, the entire corpus bears out the validity of Flahault's assertions. Indeed, the quantitative breadth of the vogue testifies to the impossibility of satisfying nostalgic desires. The nostalgic fairy-tale narrative, following the general structure of romance, is circular: its end is the renewal of its beginning, a folding back onto the story, a mythic recreation of itself. As such, this fairy-tale structure cannot satisfy desire except by replicating itself in new, yet-to-be-told stories. If the late seventeenth-century literary fairy tales became a *mode*, a self-perpetuating fashion, it is in part because they demonstrated that nostalgia is in fact a desire and not the satisfaction of desire in and of itself. If so many *contes de fées* were written and published at the end of the seventeenth century, it is in part because these nostalgic desires depended on other *contes de fées* for their satisfaction – without, of course, ever finding it.

In the end, the vogue tells a story we are all too familiar with. Nostalgia permeates so many of the discourses of gender and sexuality that are part of our late twentieth-century world. The phrase "traditional family values," invoked so frequently in our own moment of socio-cultural transition, is an idealized fiction that harks back to a mythic past, a (supposedly) comforting illusion that disdains the messy complexity of an evolving present. However, over and beyond its appeal within particular historical circumstances, nostalgia is a generative aspect of sexual and gender identities. As psychoanalysis suggests, these identities are formed through the incorporation and idealization of a loss (namely the loss of the primal mother).[4] Designated as melancholia when referring to an individual psychic occurrence, this same process obtains in the social and cultural phenomenon of nostalgia. Indeed, collective norms concerning sexuality and gender rely heavily on allusions to an idyllic (because) morally sound past in order to constitute themselves as *norms* and to become enforceable. And yet, nostalgia is not confined to conservative or reactionary forces. In fact, it is a temptation that may be inseparable from any utopian political project, especially when applied to an exploration of the past. Can we examine history from the perspective of gender studies without at the same time transforming it into transcendent meaning? Recognizing the temptation of nostalgia in our own and others' storytelling is the first step toward any utopian outlook. To expose the tyranny of nostalgia is to acknowledge that storytelling, of all types, has its limits. It is not, though, to proclaim the impossibility or the end of storytelling, but rather quite the opposite. There is always something, out there, in the future, left to be said. So many more of the *contes de fées* are worth re-telling. New and different narratives of sexuality and gender need to be told.

Notes

INTRODUCTION

1 The term "literary fairy tale," equivalent to *Kunstmärchen* in German, is used in folkloristic studies to designate those tales that are *written* (as opposed to *oral* folktales – the generic *Märchen* or more specific *Volksmärchen*). Inaugurated by Basile, Straparola, and Sarnelli in sixteenth-century Italy, this genre mimics the stylistics and thematics of "popular" narratives (whether or not they are based on identifiable folkloric motifs), but also freely elaborates on them. For historical overviews of the "literary" fairy tale, see Friedmar Apel, *Die Zaubergärten der Phantasie. Zur Theorie und Geschichte des Kunstmärchens* (Heidelberg: Carl Winter, 1978); Jens Tismar, *Das Kunstmärchen* (Stuttgart: Metzler, 1977); and, especially, Volker Klotz, *Das europäische Kunstmärchen: Fünfundzwanzig Kapitel seiner Geschichte von der Renaissance bis zur Moderne* (Stuttgart: Metzler, 1985).

2 *The Uses of Enchantment: The Meaning and Importance of Fairy Tales* (New York: Random House, 1977).

3 This is especially true of psychoanalytic critics, such as Bettelheim.

4 Notable exceptions include Ruth Bottigheimer, *Grimms' Bad Girls and Bold Boys: The Moral and Social Vision of the "Tales"* (New Haven: Yale University Press, 1987); Maria Tatar, *The Hard Facts of the Grimms' Fairy Tales* (Princeton University Press, 1987) and *Off with their Heads! Fairy Tales and the Culture of Childhood* (Princeton University Press, 1992); and the essays in *Don't Bet on the Prince: Contemporary Feminist Fairy Tales in North America and England*, ed. Jack Zipes (New York: Methuen, 1986).

5 I borrow this term from Gayle Rubin's influential "The Traffic in Women: Notes on the 'Political Economy' of Sex" in *Toward an Anthropology of Women*, ed. Rayna R. Reiter (New York: Monthly Review Press, 1975) 157–210. "A 'sex/gender system' is the set of

arrangements by which a society transforms biological sexuality into products of human activity, and in which these transformed sexual needs are satisfied" (159). Recent feminist work has challenged Rubin's assumption that "biological sexuality" is somehow outside of language. See especially Judith Butler, *Gender Trouble: Feminism and the Subversion of Identity*, Thinking Gender (New York: Routledge, 1990).

6   See, for instance, Butler, *Gender Trouble*, 3–4.

7   Folktales have been catalogued according to "types," "a traditional tale that has an independent existence ... may be told as a complete narrative and does not depend for its meaning on any other tale" (Stith Thompson, *The Folktale* [New York: The Dryden Press, 1946] 415). Tale-types are composed of one or more motifs, "the smallest element in a tale having a power to persist in tradition" (Thompson, *The Folktale*, 415). The standard indexes are: Antti Aarne, *The Types of the Folktale*, trans. Stith Thompson (Helsinki: Academia Scientiarum Fennica, 1981); Paul Delarue and Marie-Louise Tenèze, *Le Conte populaire français: un catalogue raisonné des versions de France et des pays de langue française et d'Outre-mer*, 4 vols. (Paris: Maisonneuve et Larose, 1976); and Stith Thompson, *Motif Index of Folk Literature*. Although this classificational system has been critiqued by a number of scholars (for a cogent overview of these critiques, see Catherine Velay-Vallantin, *L'Histoire des contes* [Paris: Fayard, 1992] 12–23), these indexes remain standard references for folklorists and specialists of fairy tales.

8   Among the studies that examine fairy tales or fairy-tale motifs from feminist perspectives are: Bottigheimer, *Grimms' Bad Girls and Bold Boys*; Andrea Dworkin, *Woman Hating* (New York: Dutton, 1974); Sandra M. Gilbert and Susan Gubar, "The Queen's Looking Glass," *The Mad Woman in the Attic. The Woman Writer and the Nineteenth-Century Imagination* (New Haven: Yale University Press, 1979); Madonna Kolbenschlag, *Kiss Sleeping Beauty Good-Bye: Breaking the Spell of Feminine Myths and Models* (New York: Doubleday, 1979); Marcia Lieberman, "'Some Day My Prince Will Come': Female Acculturation through the Fairy Tale," *Don't Bet on the Prince*, 185–200; Karen E. Rowe, "Feminism and Fairy Tales," *Don't Bet on the Prince*, 209–226; Karen E. Rowe, "To Spin a Yarn: The Female Voice in Folklore and Fairy Tale," *Fairy Tales and Society: Illusion, Allusion, and Paradigm*, ed. Ruth B. Bottigheimer (Philadelphia: University of Pennsylvania Press, 1986) 53–74; Ellen Cronan Rose, "Through the Looking Glass: When Women Tell Fairy Tales," *The Voyage In: Fictions of Female Development*, ed. Elizabeth Abel, Marianne Hirsch, and Elizabeth Langland

(Hanover, NH: University of New England Press, 1983) 209–227; Kay Stone, "Things Walt Disney Never Told Us," *Women and Folklore*, ed. Claire R. Farrer (Austin: University of Texas Press, 1975) 42–50; Kay Stone, "The Misuses of Enchantment," *Women's Folklore, Women's Culture*, ed. Rosan Jordan and Susan Kalcik (Philadelphia: University of Pennsylvania Press, 1985); Kay Stone, "Feminist Approaches to the Interpretation of Fairy Tales," *Fairy Tales and Society*, 229–236; Tatar, *The Hard Facts* and *Off with Their Heads!*; Marina Warner, *From the Beast to the Blonde: On Fairytales and their Tellers* (London: Chatto and Windus, 1994); Martha Weigle, *Spiders and Spinsters: Women and Mythology* (Albuquerque: University of New Mexico Press, 1982); and Jack Zipes, *The Trials and Tribulations of Little Red Riding Hood*, 2nd edn. (New York: Routledge, 1993).

9 See Angela Carter, "The Donkey Prince," *Don't Bet on the Prince*, 62–72, and Anne Sexton, "Briar Rose (Sleeping Beauty)," *Don't Bet on the Prince*, 114–118.

10 The heroines in two of the most recent Disney fairy-tale films, "Beauty and the Beast" and "Aladdin," for instance, are more self-reliant than the studio's earlier versions of "Sleeping Beauty" and "Cinderella." This trend notwithstanding, the latest films continue to idealize marriage.

11 Selected volumes of this collection have appeared in facsimile as *Le Nouveau cabinet des fées*, ed. Jacques Barchilon (1785–1788; Geneva: Slatkine Reprints, 1978).

12 The pioneering study of the *contes de fées* (although devoted exclusively to the first vogue) is Mary-Elizabeth Storer, *Un Épisode littéraire de la fin du XVIIe siècle. La Mode des contes de fées (1685–1700)* (1928; Genève: Slatkine Reprints, 1972). Jacques Barchilon's study, *Le Conte merveilleux français de 1690 à 1790. Cent ans de féerie et de poésie ignorées de l'histoire littéraire* (Paris: Honoré Champion, 1975), considers both vogues from psychoanalytic and stylistic perspectives. Raymonde Robert's seminal *Le Conte de fées littéraire en France de la fin du XVIIe à la fin du XVIIIe siècle* (Presses universitaires de Nancy, 1982) provides rigorous analyses of both vogues and incorporates folkloristic, structuralist, and literary historical approaches. Although devoted primarily to Perrault, Marc Soriano's much-acclaimed *Les Contes de Perrault. Culture savante et traditions populaires*, Collection Tel, 22 (1968; Paris: Gallimard, 1977) provides valuable information about other fairy-tale writers as well. Another stylistic study is Teresa Di Scanno, *Les Contes de fées à l'époque classique (1680–1715)* (Napoli: Liguori Editore, 1975). On d'Aulnoy's tales, see Amy Vanderlyn DeGraff, *The Tower and the Well: A Psychological*

Interpretation of the Fairy Tales of Madame d'Aulnoy. (Birmingham, AL: Summa Publications, 1984) and Jane Tucker Mitchell, *A Thematic Analysis of Mme d'Aulnoy's "Contes de fées"*. Romance Monographs, 30. (University, MS: Romance Monographs, Inc., 1978). Patricia Hannon's *Fabulous Identities: Women's Fairy Tales in Seventeenth-Century France* (Atlanta: Rodopi, 1996) and Philip E. Lewis's *Seeing through the Mother Goose Tales: Visual Turns in the Writings of Charles Perrault* (Stanford University Press, 1996) appeared as this book was going to press.

13 While there are similarities among all the tales of the seventeenth and eighteenth centuries (the use of fairies and the marvelous, an infantilizing tone, a didactic pretext, among others), there are also significant differences. First, there is a much higher proportion of texts with discernible folkloric tale-types and motifs in the first than in the second vogue (Raymonde Robert calculates that one-half of the *contes de fées* of the first vogue are based on folkloric sources as opposed to one-tenth for the second [171]). Structurally, the vast majority of both the seventeenth- and the eighteenth-century *contes* are constructed according to the epic love quest scenario and regularly include "lessons" in the form of moralities, often placed at the end. Yet, there are considerable differences in the ways the two vogues deploy this generic structure. As a group, the tales from the second vogue are considerably more heterogeneous than those of the first, with explicitly didactic or pedagogical, but also exotic, parodic, satirical, and erotic texts. By contrast, the tales of the first vogue refrain from the (often) heavy-handed parody and satire of the eighteenth-century tales, almost never include explicitly erotic descriptions, and, with the exception of Fénelon's tales, were not originally intended for children. For a detailed account of differences between the first and the second vogues in terms of chronological and quantitative production, see Robert, *Le Conte de fées*, 291–320.

14 I include Fénelon's tales in my corpus since they were probably written contemporaneously with the vogue. However, there are notable thematic and structural differences between Fénelon's and the other fairy tales. Thomas Vessely has proposed the term "fairy-tale apologues" to designate Fénelon's corpus since they are narratives "that end in compromise or catastrophe ... [and] whose plot is determined by the lesson to be drawn" from them (*The French Literary Fairy Tale, 1690–1760: A Generic Study*, diss., Indiana University, 1979, 105). As I explain below, Fénelon was also one of the chief opponents of the sociable aristocratic culture that the *contes de fées* sought to defend and preserve.

15 *The Political Unconscious: Narrative as a Socially Symbolic Act* (Ithaca, NY: Cornell University Press, 1981) 148.

16 Paul Hazard, *La Crise de la conscience européenne, 1680–1715* (Paris: Fayard, 1961) 335.

17 Joan DeJean, *Tender Geographies: Women and the Origins of the Novel in France* (New York: Columbia University Press, 1991) 134–158; Timothy J. Reiss, *The Meaning of Literature* (Ithaca, NY: Cornell University Press, 1992), especially 202–215.

18 This term was coined by Maïté Albistur and Daniel Armogathe, *Histoire du féminisme français*, 2 vols. (Paris: des femmes, 1977). See especially 1: 196–200.

19 Madame de Maintenon founded and oversaw, with Fénelon's somewhat secretive counsel, Saint-Cyr and several other schools for girls, and Fénelon penned a treatise on women's education (*De l'éducation des filles*, 1687). See Carolyn Lougee, *Le Paradis des Femmes: Women, Salons, and Social Stratification in Seventeenth-Century France* (Princeton University Press, 1976) 173–208, for an overview of Fénelon's and Maintenon's ideas on education for women as well as the establishment and demographics of Saint-Cyr.

20 Fénelon's and Madame de Maintenon's attacks on aristocratic culture of the time have been well documented (see Lougee, *Le Paradis des Femmes*, for an overview of this literature). Much less so are the effects these had on women's place in the public sphere as well as the state of the salon, if not women's roles in late seventeenth-century France. Studies that suggest an increased exclusion/domestication of women as the century progressed include Albistur and Armogathe, *Histoire du féminisme français*, vol. 1, and Joan Landes, *Women and the Public Sphere in the Age of the French Revolution* (Ithaca, NY: Cornell University Press, 1988). This complex question would be well worth further exploration.

21 Studies devoted to Perrault's *Contes* are numerous indeed. For an overview of recent criticism, see Claire-Lise Malarte, *Perrault à travers la critique depuis 1960: Bibliographie annotée*, Biblio 17, 47 (Paris, Seattle, Tübingen: Papers on French Seventeenth-Century Literature, 1989). The reception history of the first vogue of *contes de fées* suggests that Perrault was not given clear priority until the nineteenth century. Indications from the eighteenth century are that many of the *conteuses* were considered on a par with Perrault and the other *conteurs*. With the exception of Bernard, every *conteuse* had some or all of her *contes de fées* republished at least twice before the Revolution. Indeed, the number of eighteenth-century editions of the *conteuses'* texts outweighs that of the *conteurs'*; and the writers of the second *mode* refer especially to the *conteuses*

when evoking the perfection of the first vogue (Robert, *Le Conte de fées*, 306). Even more significant, both the numbers of republications and critical appraisals of tales confirm that, of all the seventeenth-century fairy-tale writers, d'Aulnoy was just as popular if not more so than Perrault in the eighteenth century (see Storer, *La Mode*, 261–273 and Robert, *Le Conte de fées*, 321–325). Since the nineteenth century, however, critics have celebrated Perrault's tales and ignored – sometimes devalued – the *conteuses'* texts. The editorial practices of the eighteenth century are practically reversed in the nineteenth century (see the bibliography in Storer, *La Mode*, 261–273) when Perrault's became the quintessential French fairy-tale form and, along with La Fontaine's *Fables*, part of a seventeenth-century literary canon for children. Citing Perrault's high profile as a Modern during the *Querelle des Anciens et des Modernes*, Sainte-Beuve stresses the *bon sens* and *raison* of the *Contes* and, thus, implicitly valorizes them as "classical" texts: "... [Perrault] est du pays et du siècle de Descartes." ("Les Contes de Perrault," *Nouveaux lundis*, Deuxième édition [Paris: Michel Lévy, 1864] 311). Perhaps reflecting a Romantic esthetic, other nineteenth-century readers are attracted to Perrault's purportedly faithful treatment of popular sources. "[Perrault] n'a été que l'interprète et le secrétaire très fidèle de la muse populaire dont il a rédigé les récits," declares Emile Montégut. ("Des Fées et de leur littérature en France," *Revue des deux mondes* [1 April 1862]: 665).

22 I also include in my corpus two anonymous tales, entitled "Le Portrait qui parle" (1699) and "Florine ou la belle Italienne" (1713).

23 It has become a commonplace to assert that Perrault initiated the first vogue and that the other fairy-tale writers, and especially the *conteuses*, were his inferior imitators. Typical is the assessment offered by Jean-Pierre Collinet: "less economical in their use of fairy magic, the women who continued and emulated Perrault's example are not always able to protect themselves as well as he was against the abuse of facile wonders" ("Préface," *Contes*, by Charles Perrault, ed. Jean-Pierre Collinet, Collection Folio, 1281 [Paris: Gallimard, 1981] 34). Although most prevalent in twentieth-century criticism, this mythic etiology appears as early as 1703 in an obituary for Perrault that evokes characters in "La Belle au bois dormant": "L'heureuse fiction où l'Aurore et le petit Jour sont si ingénieusement introduits, et qui parut il y a neuf ou dix années, a fait naître tous les Contes des Fées qui ont paru depuis ce temps là ..." (*Le Mercure galant* [May 1703]: 249). Robert

is one of the few twentieth-century critics to debunk this myth (*Le Conte de fées*, 119).

24 To be sure, five of the tales in Perrault's *Histoires ou contes du temps passé, avec des moralités* appear in a manuscript dating from 1695 (see *Perrault's Tales of Mother Goose: The Dedication Manuscript of 1695 Reproduced in Collotype Facsimile with Introduction and Critical Text*, ed. Jacques Barchilon, 2 vols. [New York: The Pierpont Morgan Library, 1956]). However, d'Aulnoy's "L'Isle de la félicité" dates from 1690, and there is evidence that both Bernard's and Lhéritier's tales were composed either before or concurrently with Perrault's (see Soriano, *Les Contes*, 55–71, 190–196).

25 Although the evidence that suggests this is quite scanty–only in two of Sévigné's letters (30 October 1656 and 6 August 1677) and in a list of *jeux* in Scudéry's *Les Ieux* (1667) is there "proof" that this *mode* actually existed as a *salon* game – both Storer (*La Mode*, 13) and Robert (*Le Conte de fées*, 84) (among others) assert that the written fairy tales continued an earlier oral practice.

26 See chapter 3.

27 Patricia Hannon has argued, convincingly, that self-referentiality is a distinguishing characteristic of the women's *contes de fées*. See especially "Out of the Kingdom: Madame d'Aulnoy's *Finette-Cendron*," *Actes de Las Vegas*, Biblio 17, 60 (Paris, Seattle, Tübingen: Papers on French Seventeenth-Century Literature, 1991) 201–208.

28 D'Aulnoy, La Force, Lhéritier, and Murat appear to have attended the same salons. See Renate Baader, *Dames de Lettres: Autorinnen des preziösen, hocharistokratischen und "modernen" Salons (1649–1698): Mlle de Scudéry – Mlle de Montpensier – Mme d'Aulnoy* (Stuttgart: Metzler, 1986) 229.

29 Perrault, for instance, used the fairy-tale form to camouflage his attacks on Boileau. Fénelon wrote his tales as pedagogical devices while serving as tutor to the dauphin, the Duc de Bourgogne. Préchac's "Sans Parangon" is a thinly disguised panegyric of Louis XIV. Finally, Bignon and Le Noble included their *contes de fées* in much longer novels.

30 Notable exceptions to this rule are Perrault's "Les Souhaits ridicules," "Le Petit Chaperon rouge," "La Barbe bleue," "Le Chat botté," and "Le Petit Poucet." That such a high proportion of Perrault's tales (five out of eleven) contravene the conventions of the other *contes de fées* is a sign of their singular position within this corpus, noted in almost every study devoted to the vogue and to Perrault. Other differences include the fact that they borrow only minimally from the novel, dramatically accentuate the

infantilizing pretext of the genre, and employ a succinct, if not laconic, style with limited description.

31 As republished in *Le Cabinet des fées* (1785–1788), the tales by d'Aulnoy, La Force, Lhéritier, and Murat average fifty-six pages against the twenty pages for tales by Mailly, Perrault, and Préchac.

32 "On Fairy Tales," *European Literary Theory and Practice*, trans. Remy Hall, ed. Vernon W. Gras (New York: Delta, 1973) 351.

33 Marthe Robert, "Un modèle romanesque: le conte de Grimm," *Preuves* 185 (1966): 33.

34 François Flahault, *L'Interprétation des contes* (Paris: Denoël, 1988) 12.

35 *Fantasy: The Literature of Subversion*, New Accents (New York: Methuen, 1981).

36 See especially her book, *On Longing: Narratives of the Miniature, the Gigantic, the Souvenir, the Collection* (Baltimore: The Johns Hopkins University Press, 1984) and "Notes on Distressed Genres," *Journal of American Folklore* 104 (1991): 5–31.

37 See chapter 3.

38 See Louis Marin, *Utopiques: jeux d'espaces* (Paris: Minuit, 1973), who insists on utopia's inevitable reinscription of the ideologies of its context(s) of production.

39 In the larger context of Bloch's thought, utopia and his other keyword – hope – lead to an eschatological vision of a classless society toward which the totality of human history is moving inexorably, but elusively. I do not subscribe to this portion of Bloch's thought, nor do I see the texts of my corpus substantiating such an understanding of utopia. Nonetheless, as I will show, Bloch's description of the workings of the utopian function in art and literature are very suggestive and useful, especially for an ideological critique of fantasy and the marvelous.

40 See Zipes, *Breaking the Magic Spell: Radical Theories of Folk and Fairy Tales* (New York: Methuen, 1979), 135–137.

1 MARVELOUS REALITIES: TOWARD AN UNDERSTANDING OF THE *MERVEILLEUX*

1 Lutz Röhrich, *Folktales and Reality*, trans. Peter Tokofsky (1979; Bloomington: Indiana University Press, 1991) 163.

2 "[In the folktale,] wonders are not unbounded; they develop according to a specific typology and logic. We encounter purely subjective, conscious fantasy for the first time in romantic, literary fairy tales. The folktale, on the other hand, has a bounded

imagination, and fantasy does not play as freely as it occasionally
does in the literary tale" (Röhrich, *Folktales*, 3).

3 See Volker Klotz, *Das europäische Kunstmärchen*, 21–24.

4 Rosemary Jackson, *Fantasy: The Literature of Subversion* (New York:
Methuen, 1981) 3.

5 Tzvetan Todorov, *Introduction à la littérature fantastique*, Points, 73
(Paris: Seuil, 1970) 46–47.

6 See introduction, 13.

7 Vladimir Propp, *Morphology of the Folktale*, trans. Laurence Scott
and Louis A. Wagner (Austin: University of Texas Press, 1968)
102.

8 Charles Perrault, *Contes*, ed. Jean-Pierre Collinet, Folio 1281
(Paris: Gallimard, 1981) 176. Throughout this study, quotations
from Perrault's *Contes en vers* and *Histoires ou Contes du temps passé,
avec des moralités* are taken from this edition. Unless otherwise
noted, all translations are my own.

9 I consider the *contes de fées* with unhappy endings, which I call
"dysphoric tales," in chapter 4.

10 I use the French term *vraisemblance* interchangeably with the
English "verisimilitude" and "plausibility." However, I use all of
these in the historically specific meaning defined here.

11 On the relationship between *vraisemblance* and the *ut pictura poesis*
representational system, see Erica Harth, *Ideology and Culture in
Seventeenth-Century France* (Ithaca, NY: Cornell University Press,
1983), especially 27–29.

12 See Aron Kibédi-Varga, "Introduction," *Les Poétiques du classicisme*,
ed. Aron Kibédi-Varga (Paris: Aux Amateurs de Livres, 1990)
38–39.

13 Thomas DiPiero, *Dangerous Truths and Criminal Passions: The Evolution of the French Novel, 1569–1791* (Stanford University Press, 1992)
86.

14 For an incisive review of these critiques, see Georges May, *Le
Dilemme du roman au XVIIIe siècle: étude sur les rapports du roman et de la
critique (1715–1761)* (Paris: Presses universitaires de France, 1963)
1–46.

15 See especially Harth, *Ideology and Culture* and DiPiero, *Dangerous
Truths*.

16 See especially Reinhard Krüger, *Zwischen Wunder und Wahrschein-
lichkeit: Die Krise des französischen Versepos im 17. Jahrhundert* (Marburg:
Hitzeroth, 1986); Ralph Coplestone Williams, *The Merveilleux in the
Epic* (Paris: Honoré Champion, 1925); and Victor Delaporte, *Du
Merveilleux dans la littérature française sous le règne de Louis XIV* (1891;
Geneva: Slatkine Reprints, 1968) 246–279.

17 Perrault provides a resolute defense of this capacity in his *Parallèle des anciens et des modernes* (Munich: Eidos Verlag, 1964) 3: 16, 18; 289.

18 Boileau makes this very clear in "Chant III" of his *Art poétique*, *Œuvres complètes*, ed. Françoise Escal, Bibliothèque de la Pléiade (Paris: Gallimard, 1966) 172–173.

19 Sans tous ces ornements le vers tombe en langueur,
   La Poésie est morte, ou rampe sans vigueur;
   Le Poète n'est plus qu'un Orateur timide,
   Qu'un froid Historien d'une Fable insipide. (*Art poétique*, 173)

20 In this respect, both the Christian epic and the *conte de fées* are "modernist" genres. This is further suggested by the fact that prominent theoreticians of the *merveilleux chrétien*, such as Saint-Evremond and Perrault, were equally prominent polemicists in the Quarrel of the Ancients and the Moderns. Both Bernard Magné (*La Crise de la littérature française sous Louis XIV: humanisme et nationalisme*, 2 vols. [Paris: Champion, 1976]) and Reinhard Krüger ("Perraults Erzählungen und die Metamorphosen des *merveilleux*," *Lendemains*, vol. 14, no. 53 [1989]: 76–88) have suggested that the vogue of fairy tales represents an extension or displacement of the *Querelle du Merveilleux*. To my mind, more striking and ultimately more decisive are the connections of the *contes de fées* to the *Querelle des Anciens et des Modernes*, which I discuss in chapter 3.

21 I discuss the role of the vogue in the Quarrel of the Ancients and the Moderns further in chapter 3.

22 I discuss these criticisms and the infantilizing pretext of the genre further in chapter 2.

23 See Kibédi-Varga, "Introduction," *Les Poétiques*, 41.

24 The *contes de fées* assiduously avoid any explicit appropriation of Christian marvelous elements (saints, demons, angels, etc.). In this respect, they observe the strict separation of secular and religious material common in seventeenth-century literature.

25 Examples of other forms that rely on admixtures of various marvelous traditions include the Christian epics, in which magicians and sorcerers appear alongside saints and angels, and court ballets, some of which feature fairies with nymphs, naiads, and Greek or Roman gods (see Delaporte, *Du Merveilleux*, 246–278).

26 In a detailed and insightful article, Bernard Magné has studied the narrative occurrences of mythological references in the seventeenth-century *contes de fées*. He argues that the use of mythology alongside folkloric material legitimizes the genre's less prestigious *féerie* (fairy-tale magic) and, further, "reflects an incontestable

socio-cultural reality" – the neo-classical culture that dominated the arts in this period (Bernard Magné, "Le Chocolat et l'ambroisie: le statut de la mythologie dans les contes de fées," *Cahiers de littérature du XVIIe siècle* 2 [1980]: 112). Magné also demonstrates that the *conteuses* make more frequent use of mythological allusions than do the *conteurs* and attributes this difference to a desire on the part of women writers to prove their aptitude for literary creation ("Le Chocolat et l'ambroisie," 129–130).

27 See Guy Spielmann, "Chassez le surnaturel, il revient au galop: machines, trucages et merveilleux à l'épreuve du classicisme," *Papers on French Seventeenth-Century Literature*, vol. 19, no. 36 (1992): 23–36.

28 I am using "helper" and "opponent" in the sense outlined by Aldirgas-Julien Greimas, *Sémantique structurale* (Paris: Larousse, 1966) to describe the narrative functions that either advance (helper) or hinder (opponent) the subject's quest for an object.

29 This aspect of Le Noble's "L'Apprenti magicien" is technically an example of metempsychosis, which is also featured in Mailly's "Le Bienfaisant ou Quiribirini."

30 The usual comparison is with the Grimms' tales on this point. See Barchilon, *Le Conte merveilleux français*, 149. On the national specificity of French folklore, see Paul Delarue, "Les Caractères propres du conte populaire français," *La Pensée* 72 (1957): 57–59 and Eugen Weber, "Fairies and Hard Facts: The Reality of Folktales," *Journal of the History of Ideas*, vol. 43, no. 1 (January–March 1981): 93–113.

31 See, for instance, d'Aulnoy's "Le Prince Marcassin," La Force's "L'Enchanteur," Lhéritier's "L'Adroite Princesse," and Perrault's "La Barbe bleue" and "La Belle au bois dormant." On violence in folk- and fairy tales, see among others Tatar, *Off with their Heads* and Warner, *From the Beast to the Blonde*.

32 "Plus Belle que Fée," *Les Contes des contes par Mademoiselle ***, 1698, Nouveau Cabinet des fées*, 18 vols. (1785–1788; Geneva: Slatkine Reprints, 1978) 7: 13. Hereafter all references to tales included in this facsimile edition will appear as "NCF," followed by volume and page numbers.

33 Micheline Cuénin and Chantal Morlet-Chantalat, "Châteaux et romans au XVIIe siècle," *XVIIe siècle* 118–119 (1978): 101–123.

34 Max Lüthi, *The European Folktale: Form and Nature*, trans. John D. Niles (Philadelphia: Institute for the Study of Human Issues, 1982) 37.

35 The last two verses of the final moral emphasize the distance between Plus Belle que Fée and the real "fées" of the salons:

> Fée en ce temps se fait encore voir,
> Mais on ne voit plus de miracles. (35)

2 READING (AND) THE IRONIES OF THE MARVELOUS

1　I use "readability" as defined by Ross Chambers in his consideration of what he calls "readerly" texts: " 'Readerly' texts claim the
power to produce new meanings in ever new circumstances (they
claim the status as artistic discourse), but at the same time they are
concerned, if not to claim a single univocal sense as central to
their meaning, then at least to define the range of possible meanings and relevances. That is what is meant by their 'readability' "
(*Story and Situation: Narrative Seduction and the Power of Fiction*, Theory
and History of Literature, 12 [Minneapolis: University of Minnesota Press, 1984] 26).

2　These ironic pretexts do not necessarily obtain in Fénelon's *Fables
et opuscules pédagogiques* since they were specifically written for a
child, Louis XIV's grandson and heir to the throne, the Duc de
Bourgogne.

3　Several studies discuss the use of irony in Perrault's tales. See
especially, Jacques Barchilon, "L'Ironie et l'humour dans les
'Contes' de Perrault," *Studi francese* 32 (1967): 258–270; Jules
Brody, "Charles Perrault, conteur (du) moderne," *D'un siècle à
l'autre: anciens et modernes*, ed. Louise Godard de Donville (Marseille:
CMR 17, 1986) 79–87; Yvan Loskoutoff, "La surenchère enfantine
autour des *Contes* de Perrault," *XVIIe siècle* vol. 38–4, no. 153
(October–December 1986): 343–350; Claire-Lise Malarte, "Les
Contes de Perrault, oeuvre 'moderne'," *D'un siècle à l'autre* 91–100.
On the use of irony in d'Aulnoy's tales, see Jane Tucker Mitchell,
A Thematic Analysis of Mme. d'Aulnoy's "Contes de fées", Romance
Monographs, 30 (University, MS: Romance Monographs Inc,
1978) 118–120 and Marcelle Maistre Welch, "Les Jeux de l'écriture
dans les *Contes de fées* de Mme. d'Aulnoy," *Romanische Forschungen*
vol. 101, no. 1 (1989): 75–80 and "La Satire du rococo dans les
contes de fées de Madame d'Aulnoy," *Revue romane* vol. 28, no. 1
(1993): 75–85.
　　Robert's thorough and sensitive discussion of fairy-tale textuality, which distinguishes between parodic and non-parodic
tales, falls short of identifying the irony I perceive to be so central
to the first vogue (see especially *Le Conte de fées*, 202–204 and 429–
454). By contrast, she describes a "jeu avec l'écriture" (play with
writing) in all of the seventeenth- and eighteenth-century tales, by
which she means: "the irremediable situation of marginality
peculiar to the marvelous genre in the definition given it at the
time which opens the text to all sorts of manipulations; liberated
from the constraint of traditional models, from the weight of

esthetic norms, from the obligation of a logical meaning, the fairy
tale sees the wide domain of signifying effects open up before it"
(*Le Conte de fées*, 438). As part of this "jeu avec l'écriture," Robert
considers the infantilizing effects of several fairy-tale writers, but
without explicitly connecting it to an irony that determines the
readability of the entire corpus (see *Le Conte de fées*, 436–439 and
"L'infantilisation du conte merveilleux au XVIIe siècle," *Littératures classiques*, "Enfance et littérature au XVIIe siècle," 14
[January 1991]: 33–46). Jean-Paul Sermain perceives parody of
oral storytelling to be a "generic law" underlying the entire first
vogue of *contes de fées* ("La Parodie dans les contes de fées (1693–
1713): une loi du genre?" *Actes du colloque du Mans: burlesque et formes
parodiques*, ed. Isabelle Landy-Houillon and Maurice Menard,
Biblio 17, 33 [Paris, Seattle, Tübingen: Papers on French Seventeenth-Century Literature, 1987] 541–552). Friedrich Wolfzettel
arrives at conclusions similar to my own concerning the importance of irony within this corpus, which he also notes distinguishes
it from the Romantic fairy tales of late eighteenth- and early
nineteenth-century Germany ("La Lutte contre les mères: quelques exemples d'une valorisation émancipatrice du conte de fées
au dix-huitième siècle," *Réception et identification du conte depuis le
moyen âge*, eds. Michel Zink and Xavier Ravier [Toulouse: Université de Toulouse–Le Mirail, 1987] 123–131).

4 Following Ross Chambers, I distinguish between two general
tendencies within irony: it can be negative and/or appropriative.
In negative irony, meaning is a negation of the discourse – it is *not*
that specified by that discourse – yet it necessarily mentions and
acknowledges it. In appropriative irony, the meaning of the text
seizes upon a vulnerability in the discourse and uses it in other
ways – it appropriates and redeploys the discourse. In the *contes de
fées*, irony is both negative, a rejection of the marvelous and all
that is associated with it, and appropriative, a redeployment of
marvelous discourse to ends not specifically foreseen by it. See
Ross Chambers, *Room for Maneuver: Reading (the) Oppositional (in)
Narrative* (University of Chicago Press, 1991) 239.

5 *Les Jeux d'esprit ou la promenade de la Princesse de Conti à Eu par
Mademoiselle de la Force*, ed. M. le marquis de la Grange (Paris:
Auguste Aubry, 1862) 3.

6 Discussions of *contes de fées* within frame-narratives are often light-
hearted if not trivializing. See Durand, *La Comtesse de Mortane*, 2
vols. (Paris: Claude Barbin, 1699) 1: 223–224, for a typical
comparison of a *conte de fées* to storytelling for children. Besides the
famous engraving opening Perrault's *Histoire ou contes du temps passé*,

avec des moralités, the frontispieces to d'Aulnoy's *Contes nouveaux ou les Fées à la mode* (3rd volume, 1698) and a pirated Dutch edition of her *Les Contes des fées* (1698) portray an adult woman entertaining children with stories. See Gabrielle Verdier's excellent discussion of these frontispieces in "Figures de la conteuse dans les contes de fées féminins," *XVIIe siècle* 180 (July–September 1993), 481–499.

7 The infantilizing pretext might also partially explain why the dedication letter opening the *Histoires ou contes du temps passé, avec des moralités* is signed "Pierre Perrault Darmancour," Perrault's son. On the debate about attribution of Perrault's prose tales, see Soriano, *Les Contes*, 13–71; Jacques Barchilon and Peter Flinders, *Charles Perrault*, Twayne World Author Series, 639 (Boston: Twayne Publishers, 1981) 84–90; and Jeanne Morgan, *Perrault's Morals for Moderns*, Series 2, Romance Languages and Literature, 28 (New York, Berne and Frankfurt am Main: Peter Lang, 1985) 7–34.

8 This substitution is made in "Finette-Cendron" when the narrator describes the heroine overhearing her parents' plan to abandon her and her sisters in the forest: "la princesse Finette, qui était la plus petite des filles, écoutait par le trou de la serrure; et quand elle eut découvert le dessein de son papa et de sa maman, elle s'en alla tant qu'elle put à une grande grotte fort éloignée de chez eux" ("Finette-Cendron," *Les Contes des fées*, 1697, NCF, 3: 473).

9 "La Princesse Rosette," *Les Contes des fées*, 1697, NCF, 3: 235.

10 In d'Aulnoy's tales, the narrator's repetition of certain adjectives–especially superlatives – is yet another infantilizing technique. In "La Princesse Rosette," for instance, the storyteller's description of the heroine's amazement at seeing a peacock has just such an effect: ". . . jamais l'on n'a été plus émerveillé qu'elle le fut, de voir dans ce bois un grand paon qui faisait la roue, et qui lui parut si beau, si beau, si beau, qu'elle n'en pouvait retirer ses yeux" (227).

11 "Les Enchantements de l'éloquence," Charles Perrault, *Contes de Perrault*, ed. Gilbert Rouger (Paris: Garnier, 1967) 251.

12 Yvan Loskoutoff has drawn parallels between the infantilization in the *contes de fées* and the mystic devotion to the Christ child in late seventeenth-century France (*La Sainte et la fée: dévotion à l'Enfant Jésus et mode des contes merveilleux à la fin du règne de Louis XIV*, Histoire des idées et critique littéraire, 255 [Geneva: Droz, 1987]). The disciples of the mystical teacher and writer Jeanne Guyon, the "michelins," sought to revert to a state of childhood that imitated the divine perfection of the Christ child, with the "maman mignonne" (as she called herself) as their spiritual guide (See Loskoutoff, *La Sainte et la fée*, part 2, chapter 1). Just as striking, in my view, are the differences between the literary vogue and the

religious movement. Contrary to ironic infantilization in the fairy tale, the fundamental goal of this mystic *repuerascentia* is to break out of the symbolic system and to reach a divine, transcendent state. And in further contrast to the readers of the *conte de fées*, the "michelins" desire to destroy all critical distance from their puerile persona and to become child-like.

13 The Abbé de Bellegarde, *Lettres curieuses de littérature et de morale*, quoted in Storer, *La Mode*, 217–218.

14 Perrault, *Contes*, ed. Jean-Pierre Collinet, 51; Perrault, *Memoirs of My Life*, ed. and trans. Jeanne Morgan Zarucchi (Columbia, MO: University of Missouri Press, 1989) 121. All other references to the *Préface* of the *Contes en vers* are taken from this translation.

15 In the original edition of the *Contes en vers*, Perrault attributes these verses to "Mademoiselle Lhéritier" in a footnote.

16   On y voit par endroits quelques traits de Satire,
                Mais qui sans fiel et sans malignité,
            A tous également font du plaisir à lire:
            Ce qui me plaît encore dans sa simple douceur,
                C'est qu'il divertit et fait rire,
                Sans que Mère, Époux, confesseur,
                Y puissent trouver à redire. (53)

17 Jean de La Fontaine, *Œuvres complètes*, vol. 1: *Fables, Contes et nouvelles*, ed. Jean-Pierre Collinet, Bibliothèque de la Pléiade (Paris: Gallimard, 1991) 297.

18 See Ross Chambers's masterful analysis in *Room for Maneuver*, 59–72.

19 For a different, non-ironic reading of the morals in Perrault especially, see Morgan, *Perrault's Morals for Moderns*, 35–54.

20 See, for example, Nodot: "La vertu y paraît toujours triomphante; le vice condamné ... Enfin tous les différents caractères d'esprits pourront trouver du divertissement dans la lecture de ce Livre, qui est très varié, et profiter en même temps de la morale qu'il renferme" ("Préface," *Histoire de Geofroy, surnommé à la Grand'Dent, sixième fils de Melusine, Prince de Lusignan* [Paris: Barbin, 1699] n.p.). In the tales of the *conteuses*, this cliché often appears in the frame-narratives. In La Force's *Les Jeux d'esprit*, the Princesse de Conty defends the "moral" utility of the *jeux* she proposes for her *salon*: "Je voudrais ... faire un divertissement tout nouveau des divertissements les plus communs, en un mot de ce que nous appelons les jeux. Il n'y a pas un de nous qui ne s'y soit amusé mille fois en son enfance, mais je voudrais que dans ces jeux il y eut de l'esprit et du plaisir. Tant il est vrai qu'on peut ennoblir les choses les plus simples et les rendre en même temps instructives et agréables" (*Les Jeux d'esprit*, 3).

21 Georges May demonstrates the importance of what he calls a "doctrine du plaisir" in the literary esthetic of late seventeenth-century France and cites the *contes de fées* as an example of this tendency (see *Les Mille et une nuits d'Antoine Galland* [Paris: Presses universitaires de France, 1986] 186–191). May also argues that the "plaire et instruire" formula was a tactic used largely to assuage critics (*Les Mille et une nuits,* 181). The one exception, in my view, would be Lhéritier, whose use of this formula as well as maxims and final morals is often strategically literal.

22 *Exemplum: The Rhetoric of Example in Early Modern France and Italy* (Princeton University Press, 1989).

23 The other three, less pertinent to the discussion here, are: iterativity, multiplicity, and exteriority (see Lyons, *Exemplum,* 25–34).

24 The capacity of language to construct power relations is an important theme of Louis Marin's reading of the tale in "La Conquête du pouvoir," *Le Récit est un piège,* Critique (Paris: Minuit, 1978) 119–139. Marin does not, however, deal with the specific role of the marvelous or the final morals.

25 See Paul De Man's famous statement of the problem in "The Rhetoric of Temporality," *Interpretation: Theory and Practice,* ed. Charles S. Singleton (Baltimore: The Johns Hopkins Press, 1969) 173–209. "Far from being a return to the world, the irony to the second power or 'irony of irony' that all true irony at once has to engender asserts and maintains its fictional character by stating the continued impossibility of reconciling the world of fiction with the actual world" (200).

3 THE MARVELOUS IN CONTEXT: THE PLACE OF THE *CONTES DE FÉES* IN LATE SEVENTEENTH-CENTURY FRANCE

1 See Domna C. Stanton, "Classicism (Re)constructed: Notes on the Mythology of Literary History," *Continuum: Problems in French Literature from the Late Renaissance to the Early Enlightenment,* vol. 1: "Rethinking Classicism: Overviews" (New York: AMS Press, 1990): 3–29.

2 Robert refutes Storer's simplistic understanding of escapism as a cause for the vogue (*Le Conte de fées,* 17). She also underscores Storer's imprecise literary chronology: by the 1690s, the *romans* had long been surpassed by the much shorter *nouvelles,* which continued to be published in great numbers throughout the first vogue (*Le Conte de fées,* 18).

3 On several occasions, Robert rejects interpretations of the *contes de fées* as "escape" from reality – such as Storer's (see especially *Le*

Conte de fées, 16–20 and 327–330). However, her own analysis often suggests a more nuanced reading (see *Le Conte de fées*, 328).

4 See especially DiPiero, *Dangerous Truths* and Harth, *Ideology and Culture*.

5 See Velay-Vallantin, *L'Histoire des contes*.

6 On the influence of publication on oral folklore, see especially, Velay-Vallantin, "Le Miroir des contes: Perrault dans les Bibliothèques bleues," *Les Usages de l'imprimé*, ed. Roger Chartier (Paris: Fayard, 1987) 129–185; and Velay-Vallantin, "Introduction," *L'Histoire des contes*.

7 This percentage compares with one-tenth for the eighteenth-century vogue (*Le Conte de fées*, 171).

8 Besides Perrault, d'Aulnoy demonstrates a wide and detailed knowledge of folkloric narratives. Robert finds traces of folkloric tale-types in eighteen of her twenty-five *contes de fées* (*Le Conte de fées*, 127–129).

9 See the "Recensement des contes types folkloriques utilisés par les contes de fées littéraires entre 1690 et 1778" in Robert, *Le Conte de fées*, 127–129.

10 What I discuss as the "indirect" recuperation of folklore has been studied in detail with respect to the German *Märchen* and their rewriting of the seventeenth- and eighteenth-century French literary fairy tales (see Manfred Grätz, *Das Märchen in der deutschen Aufklärung: Vom Feenmärchen zum Volksmärchen* [Stuttgart: J. B. Metzlersche Verlagsbuchhandlung, 1988]). I am grateful to Jack Zipes for this reference.

11 The Abbé de Villiers, a virulent critic of novels and fairy tales, devotes an entire chapter of an anti-novel tract to denouncing the vogue, only to conclude by excusing himself: "mais c'est, ce me semble, assez parler de Contes, je craindrais que si quelque sérieux nous entendait, il ne trouvât notre conversation indigne de nous" (*Entretiens sur les contes de fées, et sur quelques autres ouvrages du temps. Pour servir de préservatif contre le mauvais goût* [Paris: J. Collombat, 1699] 110).

12 Marie-Jeanne Lhéritier de Villandon, "Les Enchantements de l'éloquence," *Contes de Perrault*, ed. Gilbert Rouger (Paris: Garnier, 1967) 256.

13 Marie-Jeanne Lhéritier de Villandon, "Lettre à Madame D.G**," *Œuvres meslées* (Paris: J. Guignard, 1696) 306.

14 My analysis at this point parallels that of Robert, who concludes that "by playing with the material of popular stories, by mimicking their oral character, the *mondains* search for a form of self-affirmation in this confrontation with the alterity of popular

discourse" (*Le Conte de fées*, 384). However, in the course of her analysis, Robert emphasizes not so much the appropriation of popular storytelling by the *conteurs* and *conteuses* (as I do here) as what she calls "the caesura between official culture and popular culture" (*Le Conte de fées*, 384). Moreover, while Robert interprets the *conte de fées* as a form of self-valorization, she does not connect the rise of the vogue with attacks on *mondain* culture.

15 Antoine Furetière, *Dictionnaire universel* (1690; Paris: S.N.L.-Le Robert, 1978).

16 Pierre Richelet, *Dictionnaire françois* (1680; Geneva: Slatkine Reprints, 1970). The *Dictionnaire de l'Académie françoise* (1694) does not give a corresponding definition for "monde."

17 Alain Viala, *Naissance de l'écrivain: sociologie de la littérature à l'âge classique* (Paris: Minuit, 1985) 143–147.

18 In the following passage from the *Traité de la concupiscence*, for instance, Bossuet echoes Pascal in warning about the dangerous diversion from spiritual introspection caused by "sciences" ranging from history and philosophy to novels and poetry: "Pour ce qui est des véritables [sciences], on excède encore beaucoup à s'y livrer trop ou à contretemps, ou au préjudice de plus grandes obligations, comme il arrive à ceux qui dans le temps de prier ou de pratiquer la vertu, s'adonnent ou à l'histoire ou à la philosophie ou à toute sorte de lectures, surtout des livres nouveaux, des romans, des comédies, des poésies, et se laissent tellement posséder au désir de savoir qu'ils ne se possèdent plus eux-mêmes. Car tout cela n'est autre chose qu'une intempérance, une maladie, un dérèglement de l'esprit, un dessèchement du cœur, une misérable captivité qui ne nous laisse pas le loisir de penser à nous, et une source d'erreurs" [Jacques-Bénigne Bossuet, *Traité de la concupiscence*, Les Textes français (Paris: Fernand Roches, 1930) 26]).

19 Antoine Adam, *Histoire de la littérature française au XVIIe siècle*, 5 vols. (Paris: del Duca, 1968) 5: 253, n. 4. On hostility to the theater in late seventeenth-century France, see Adam, *Histoire*, 5: 251–266.

20 I base this observation on Raymond Toinet's extremely useful "Les Ecrivains moralistes au XVIIe siècle," *Revue d'Histoire littéraire de la France* 23 (1916): 570–610; 24 (1917): 296–306, 656–675; 25 (1918): 310–320, 655–671; 33 (1926): 395–407. Roughly half of all the titles inventoried were published in the period 1690–1715.

21 Jacques Revel, "The Uses of Civility," *A History of Private Life: Passions of the Renaissance*, ed. Philippe Ariès and Georges Duby, trans. Arthur Goldhammer (Cambridge, MA: Harvard University Press, 1989) 201–203.

22 I borrow these terms from the Abbé Morvan de Bellegarde, *Réflexions sur ce qui peut plaire ou déplaire dans le commerce du monde* (Lyon: Horace Molin, 1696). See also his *Réflexions sur la politesse des mœurs, avec des maximes pour la société civile* (Paris: J.-F. Broncart, 1699).

23 See Jeanne de Schomberg, Duchesse de Liancourt, *Règlement donné par une dame de haute qualité à sa petite-fille. Pour sa Conduite, et pour celle de sa Maison. Avec un autre Règlement que cette Dame avoit dressé pour elle-même* (1694; Paris: Florentin, 1718), 34.

24 Soriano hypothesizes that Lhéritier and Perrault subconsciously occulted the fact that folklore was addressed almost exclusively to adults in popular settings (*Les Contes*, 96). Whatever the case, the existence of expressions such as "conte de vieille," "conte de ma Mère l'Oye," etc. in seventeenth-century France, attest not only to an undeniable social reality (storytelling by nurses and governesses to upper class children) but also, and more decisively, to a cultural stereotype.

25 Robert, *Le Conte de fées*, 8. Tale-telling was wide-spread in peasant *veillées* until the Revolution. See Edward Shorter, "The 'Veillée' and the Great Transformation," *The Wolf and the Lamb: Popular Culture in France from the Old Régime to the Twentieth Century*, ed. Jacques Beauroy, Marc Bertrand, and Edward T. Gargan (Saratoga, CA: Anma Libri, 1976) 127–140. See also Michèle Simonsen, *Perrault: "Contes"*, Etudes littéraires, 35 (Paris: Presses universitaires de France, 1992) 20–24.

26 Michèle L. Farrell, "Celebration and Repression of Feminine Desire in Mme d'Aulnoy's Fairy Tale: *La Chatte Blanche*," *L'Esprit créateur* vol. 29, no. 3 (1989): 53.

27 See Elias, especially chapter 8, "On the Sociogenesis of Aristocratic Romanticism in the Process of Courtization," *The Court Society*, trans. Edmund Jephcott (Oxford: Basil Blackwell, 1983) 214–267.

28 Again, the obvious exception is Fénelon who figures among the most vocal critics of *mondain* culture.

29 Catherine Durand Bédacier, *La Comtesse de Mortane par Madame ****** (Paris: Veuve de C. Barbin, 1699) 244.

30 See Introduction, 8–9. Tale-telling also existed at court. See Sévigné's letter of 6 August 1677 and Storer, *La Mode*, 12–14.

31 Robert hypothesizes that fairy tales stopped being told in the salons after 1698, the highpoint of the vogue (*Le Conte de fées*, 92–93). However, her own discussion of the second vogue shows that *contes de fées* were both told and discussed in eighteenth-century salons (see especially 342–349). Furthermore, in manu-

script letters dating from 1708–1709, Murat makes reference to salon tale-telling (*Ouvrages de Mme la Comtesse de Murat*, ms. 3471, Bibliothèque de l'Arsenal, Paris, f° 278).

32 This is true for tales by d'Aulnoy (*Le Gentilhomme bourgeois* and *Dom Gabriel Ponce de Léon*), Bernard (*Inès de Cardoue*), Durand (*La Comtesse de Mortane* and *Les Petits Soupers de l'été de l'année 1699*), and Murat (*Le Voyage de campagne*).

33 See Elizabeth Goldsmith, *Exclusive Conversations: The Art of Interaction in Seventeenth-Century France* (Philadelphia: University of Pennsylvania Press, 1988).

34 For a general discussion of the salons' *jeux d'esprit*, see Baader, *Dames de Lettres*, especially 44–61.

35 Pascal is undoubtedly the best known of these critics. In the *Pensées*, *divertissements* refer either to the activities people falsely believe will give them serenity or to those they use to escape a *repos* that has become an intolerable *ennui*. On this Pascalian notion and its relation to the seventeenth-century ideal of *repos*, see Stanton, "The Ideal of *Repos* in Seventeenth-Century French Literature," *L'Esprit créateur* vol. 15, nos. 1–2 (Spring-Summer 1975): 92–93.

36 "Les Ieux servant de préface à Mathilde," *Mathilde d'Aguilar* (1667; Geneva: Slatkine Reprints, 1979) 15.

37 On *l'art de la conversation* in seventeenth-century France, see Goldsmith, *Exclusive Conversations*; Stanton, *The Aristocrat as Art: A Study of the "Honnête Homme" and the "Dandy" in Seventeenth- and Nineteenth-Century French Literature* (New York: Columbia University Press, 1980), 140–145.

38 For instance, in d'Aulnoy's *Dom Gabriel Ponce de Léon*, a frame-narrative containing several of her *contes de fées*, a discussion about the genre's stylistic qualities prompts one character to prescribe the following: "Il me semble ... qu'il ne faut les rendre ni empoulés ni rampants, qu'ils doivent tenir un milieu qui soit plus enjoué que sérieux, qu'il y faut un peu de morale, et surtout les proposer comme une bagatelle où l'auditeur a seul droit de mettre le prix" (*Dom Gabriel Ponce de Léon, Les Contes des fées*, 1697, NCF, 3: 471).

39 Goldsmith, *Exclusive Conversations*, 29–36.

40 See Harth's discussion of Genlis in *Cartesian Women: Versions and Subversions of Rational Discourse in the Old Regime* (Ithaca, NY: Cornell University Press, 1992) 117–118.

41 Even in Perrault's tales, in which the use of such devices is minimal, there is often a play on novelistic expectations (see, for instance, the conclusion to "Le Petit Poucet").

42 Folklorists have often perceived admixtures of oral and patently

literary intertexts as an unreliable "contamination" of the "pure" folkloric tradition. Recently, historical studies of folklore have questioned this assumption and suggested the difficulty of speaking about an oral folklore that does not reflect in some way literary or written sources. See Velay-Vallantin, "Introduction," *L'Histoire des contes*.

43 Quoted in Storer, *La Mode*, 212. "Griselidis" is by Perrault and "La Belle aux cheveux d'or" by d'Aulnoy.

44 Boileau, *Œuvres complètes*, 444. See Georges May (*Le Dilemme du roman*, 16–23) for a discussion of similar criticisms of the novel in seventeenth- and eighteenth-century France.

45 On this ambiguity, see Faith E. Beasley, *Revising Memory: Women's Fiction and Memoirs in Seventeenth-Century France* (New Brunswick: Rutgers University Press, 1990), especially 10–41. See also Harth, *Ideology and Culture*, 129–221; and Marie-Thérèse Hipp, *Mythes et réalités: enquête sur le roman et les mémoires (1660–1700)* (Paris: Klincksieck, 1976).

46 As DiPiero explains, "since it was no longer possible to court an exclusively aristocratic clientele with fictions designed to reaffirm what they already knew or believed, authors needed to invoke multiple and often conflicting political stances in their works ... Noble readers might heed the warning this fiction issued about middle-class upstarts who attempted to usurp their traditional positions of ascendancy and authority, and bourgeois readers could learn ... the contrived nature of the elaborate sign systems they would have to penetrate in order to accede to the ranks of power and privilege" (*Dangerous Truths*, 231).

47 Besides the fairy tales, a group of novels that appeared in the 1690s also recycled the exoticism and extraordinary adventures characteristic of the earlier romances (see Henri Coulet, *Le Roman jusqu'à la Révolution*, 2 vols. [Paris: Colin, 1967] 2: 288–289). Literary fairy tales are doubtless a continuation of and a deviation from this strain of the novel.

48 "La Princesse Belle-Etoile et le Prince Chéri," *Contes nouveaux ou les Fées à la mode*, 1698, NCF, 5: 180.

49 The heroes and/or heroines in Perrault's "Grisélidis," "Les Souhaits ridicules," "Le Petit Chaperon Rouge," "Le Maître chat," and "Le Petit Poucet" and in Le Noble's "L'Apprenti magicien" are the notable exceptions to this rule. Thus, my remarks here apply only partially to these two *conteurs*.

50 See Ellery Schalk, *From Valor to Pedigree: Ideas of Nobility in France in the Sixteenth and Seventeenth Centuries* (Princeton University Press, 1986).

51 Ibid., 213–214.

52 In most folkloric versions of AT707, the princesses in d'Aulnoy's text are commoners who have the good fortune to marry a king. See Delarue and Tenèze, *Le Conte populaire français*, 2: 637.

53 In *De l'éducation des filles*, Fénelon warns: "Celles qui ont de l'esprit s'érigent souvent en précieuses, et lisent tous les livres qui peuvent nourrir leur vanité; elles se passionnent pour des romans, pour des comédies, pour des récits d'aventures chimériques où l'amour profane est mêlé; elles se rendent l'esprit visionnaire en s'accoutumant au langage magnifique des héros de romans; elles se gâtent même par là pour le monde: car tous ces beaux sentiments en l'air, toutes ces passions généreuses, toutes ces aventures que l'auteur du roman a inventées pour le plaisir, n'ont aucun rapport avec les vrais motifs qui font agir dans le monde, et qui décident des affaires, ni avec les mécomptes qu'on trouve dans tout ce qu'on entreprend" (95).

54 Abbé de Villiers, *Entretiens sur les contes de fées, et sur quelques autres ouvrages du temps. Pour servir de préservatif contre le mauvais goût* (Paris: J. Collombat, 1699) 284–285.

55 See DeJean, *Tender Geographies*, 127–158. See also Lewis C. Seifert, "*Les Fées Modernes*: Women, Fairy Tales, and the Literary Field in Late Seventeenth-Century France," *Going Public: Women and Publishing in Early Modern France*, ed. Elizabeth Goldsmith and Dena Goodman (Ithaca, NY: Cornell University Press, 1995) 129–145 and Linda Timmermans, *L'Accès des femmes à la culture, 1598–1715: un débat d'idées de Saint François de Sales à la Marquise de Lambert* (Paris: Champion, 1993) 152–176, 224–236.

56 This collective identity is also evident in Lhéritier's dedication of "L'Adroite Princesse" to Murat and in the *avertissement* preceding Murat's *Histoires sublimes et allégoriques*: "Je suis bien aise d'avertir le Lecteur de deux choses. La première que j'ai pris les idées de quelques-uns de ces Contes dans un Auteur ancien intitulé, *les Facétieuses nuits du Seigneur Straparolle*, imprimé pour la seizième fois en 1615. Les Contes apparemment étaient bien en vogue dans le siècle passé, puisque l'on a fait tant d'impressions de ce livre. Les Dames qui ont écrit jusqu'ici en ce genre ont puisé dans la même source au moins pour la plus grande partie. La seconde chose que j'ai à dire, c'est que mes Contes sont composés dès le mois d'Avril dernier, et que si je me suis rencontrée avec une de ces Dames en traitant quelques-uns des mêmes sujets, je n'ai point pris d'autre modèle que l'original, ce qui serait aisé à justifier par les routes différentes que nous avons prises" (*Histoires sublimes et allégoriques par Mme la*

comtesse D***, dédiées aux fées modernes [Paris: J. et P. Delaulme, 1699] n.p.)

57 Murat, "La Princesse Carpillon," *Histoires sublimes et allégoriques*, 277–278.

58 From all appearances, when the *conteuses* refer to themselves as fairies, they are imitating a practice in the salons whereby certain women were given the title, *Fée*. For instance, Madame de Rambouillet was called "la grande Fée" by Voiture, and the duchesse du Maine insisted on being called "Fée Ludovise" (see Storer, *La Mode*, 12). Moreover, allusions to fairy magic were frequently used in panegyrical works about Louis XIV's reign (see Delaporte, *Du Merveilleux*, 44–46).

59 On this point, see Gabrielle Verdier's "Figures de la conteuse dans les contes de fées féminins," *XVIIe siècle* 180 (July–September 1993): 481–499. Verdier shows how the storytelling figure promoted by the *conteuses*, with all the qualities of a refined salon woman, differs from Perrault's archetypal "popular" female storyteller. However, Lhéritier's position is more complex since she endorses both figures simultaneously.

60 Harth, *Cartesian Women*, 81.

61 See Adam, *Histoire*, 5: 61–66.

62 Ibid., 5: 63.

63 Charles Perrault, *L'Apologie des femmes, par Monsieur P*** (Paris: Veuve Coignard, 1694) 7.

64 Perrault, *Parallèle des anciens et des modernes* 1: 31; 108.

65 Marc Fumaroli, "Les Enchantements de l'éloquence: *Les Fées* de Charles Perrault ou De la littérature," *Le Statut de la littérature: mélanges offertes à Paul Bénichou*, ed. Marc Fumaroli (Geneva: Droz, 1982) 158.

66 See the illuminating discussion of this question in Elizabeth L. Berg, "Recognizing Differences: Perrault's Modernist Esthetic in *Parallèle des Anciens et des Modernes*," *Papers on French Seventeenth-Century Literature* vol. 10, no. 18 (1983): 135–148.

67 In the *Préface* to his *Apologie*, Perrault attempts to preempt the criticism this stance is likely to draw from women inclined toward the Moderns: "Je suis encore persuadé que quelques femmes de la haute volée n'aimeront pas ces mères et ces filles, qui, travaillant chez elles,

> *Ne songent qu'à leur tâche, et qu'à bien recevoir*
> *Leur père ou leur époux quand il revient le soir.*

Elles trouveront ces manières bien bourgeoises, et le sentiment que j'ai là-dessus, bien antique pour un Défenseur des Modernes. Mais quoi qu'elles puissent dire, et quelque autorisées qu'elles soient par l'usage et par la mode, il sera toujours plus honnête pour elles de s'occuper à des ouvrages convenables à leur sexe et à leur qualité, que de passer leur vie dans une oisiveté continuelle" (unpaginated preface).

68 See "Les Enchantements de l'éloquence."

69 See Lhéritier, *Le Triomphe de Madame Deshoulières, Reçue dixième muse au Parnasse* (np: 1694) and *L'Apothéose de Mademoiselle de Scudéry* (Paris: J. Moreau, 1702); Claude Charles Guionet, seigneur de Vertron, *La Nouvelle Pandore ou les femmes illustres du siècle de Louis le Grand,* 2 vols. (Paris: Veuve Mezuel, 1698).

70 Even in elite circles, not all women shared the enthusiasm for fairy tales. In a letter to Huet, an early theorist and apologist of the novel, the Marquise de Lambert writes (probably around 1711): "Je voudrais bien que vous le puissiez guérir [notre sexe] du mauvais goût qui règne à présent. Ce sont les contes qui ont pris la place des romans: puisqu'on nous bannit, Monseigneur, du pays de la raison et du savoir, et qu'on ne nous laisse que l'empire de l'imagination, au moins faudrait-il rêver noblement, et que l'esprit et les sentiments eussent quelque part à nos illusions" (quoted in Roger Marchal, *Madame de Lambert et son milieu,* Studies on Voltaire and the Eighteenth Century, 289 [Oxford: The Voltaire Foundation, 1991] 227). Marchal explains Lambert's disdain for the *contes de fées* as part of a broader rejection of the novel, which was to last until the beginning of Louis XV's reign (*Madame de Lambert,* 228).

4 QUESTS FOR LOVE: VISIONS OF SEXUALITY

1 To be sure, folk- and fairy tales are by no means dominated by the thematics of love. Nonetheless, a high proportion of Western culture's most famous literary fairy tales involve a romantic plot. This is especially true of the tales adapted by Walt Disney Studios, for instance.

2 Juliet Mitchell, "Introduction–I," *Feminine Sexuality: Jacques Lacan and the "école freudienne,"* ed. Juliet Mitchell and Jacqueline Rose (New York: W. W. Norton, 1985) 6. Throughout this chapter, I use "sexual relation" in the sense implied by Lacan, who sees it as the mythic construct that psychoanalytic theory must undo. See, for instance, his "Seminar of 21 January 1975," *Feminine Sexuality,* 162–171.

3 For an overview of these, see Toril Moi, *Sexual/Textual Politics: Feminist Literary Theory,* New Accents (New York: Methuen, 1985).

4 Karen E. Rowe, "Feminism and Fairy Tales," *Don't Bet on the*

Prince: Contemporary Feminist Fairy Tales in North America and England, ed. Jack Zipes (New York: Methuen, 1986) 211.

5 See especially, Ruth Bottigheimer, *Grimms' Bad Girls and Bold Boys* and Maria Tatar, *The Hard Facts of the Grimms' Fairy Tales.*

6 James M. McGlathery, *Fairy Tale Romance: The Grimms, Basile, and Perrault* (Urbana: University of Illinois Press, 1991). Nonetheless, feminist scholarship on Perrault's tales is relatively sparse at present.

7 Studies such as Bottigheimer, *Grimms' Bad Girls and Bold Boys*; Tatar, *The Hard Facts* and *Off with their Heads!*; and Zipes, *The Brothers Grimm: From Enchanted Forests to the Modern World* (New York: Routledge, Chapman and Hall, 1988) show, if anything, the remarkable consistency in gender representations throughout the fairy tales of these and other writers.

8 Claude Brémond, "Le Mécanno du conte" *Magazine littéraire* 150 (1979): 14–18.

9 Jack Zipes follows August Nitschke in defining three forms of action for folktale protagonists: "one can talk about *autodynamics* in a folktale where the fate of a hero depends on himself, *hetero-dynamics* where the hero is dependent on another figure for survival, and *metamorphosis* where the hero undergoes a change to have an impact beyond his life" (*Breaking the Magic Spell: Radical Theories of Folk and Fairy Tales* [New York: Methuen, 1979] 49).

10 A love plot is a secondary concern in a number of tales, such as Le Noble's "L'Apprenti magicien," Mailly's "Le Bienfaisant ou Quiribirini," and Perrault's "La Barbe bleue," "Le Chat botté," "Le Petit Chaperon Rouge," and "Le Petit Poucet." These tales, all of which are derived from folkloric tale-types, are indicative of the thematic heterogeneity of folklore and the thematic homo-geneity of the *contes de fées* as a whole.

11 Many scholars have noted the absence of psychological descrip-tion in folk- and fairy tales. See, for instance, Bettelheim, *The Uses of Enchantment,* 25; Max Lüthi, *The European Folktale: Form and Nature,* trans. John D. Niles (Philadelphia: Institute for the Study of Human Issues, 1982) 11–15; and Tatar, *The Hard Facts,* 79.

12 Murat displays a particular fascination with cabalistic mythology throughout her tales. See Robert, *Le Conte de fées,* 181–193.

13 Eleazar Meletinsky, "Marriage: Its Function and Position in the Structure of Folktales," *Soviet Structural Folkloristics,* ed. P. Maranda (The Hague: Mouton, 1974) 64.

14 Tales with mid-plot marriages confirm this "rule."

15 These novels often feature supernatural characters, who, in contrast to the *contes de fées,* are usually incidental characters.

16 Joan DeJean, for instance, argues that the final volume of Madeleine de Scudéry's *Artamène ou le Grand Cyrus*, which includes the famous "Histoire de Sapho," prefigures the dominance of the conversational style in later prose fiction. See *Tender Geographies*, 55.

17 See Jean-Michel Pelous, *Amour précieux, amour galant (1654–1675): essai sur la représentation de l'amour dans la littérature et la société mondaines* (Paris: Klincksieck, 1980) 460–462. See also Barbara Piqué, *Tra Scienza e teatro: scrittori di fiabe alla corte del Re Sole* (Rome: Bulzoni Editore, 1981).

18 For a discussion of novels in late seventeenth- and early eighteenth-century France, see Henri Coulet, *Le Roman*, 1: 286–317. Coulet cites d'Aulnoy's *Hypolite, comte de Duglas* (1690), La Force's *Gustave Vasa* (1697–1698), and Le Noble's *Zulima, ou l'amour pur* (1694) as examples of this revival of romance at the end of the seventeenth century. Raymonde Robert notes the "medieval decor" in many of the *contes de fées* but connects it to medieval romances and their sixteenth-century rewritings rather than developments in the seventeenth-century novel (see *Le Conte de fées*, 173–176).

19 I explore the gender-specific traits of heroes and heroines, respectively, in chapters 5 and 6.

20 See Coulet, *Le Roman*, 1: 286, 302–315.

21 Untitled fairy tale in *Voyage de campagne, par Mme la Ctesse de M*** – Comédies en proverbes, par Catherine Bédacier, née Durand* (Paris: Veuve de C. Barbin, 1699) 91. I follow Robert and Storer in calling this tale "Le Père et ses quatre fils."

22 On the representation of marriage in the seventeenth-century novel, see DeJean, *Tender Geographies*, 127–158. On the increased number of "misalliances" in seventeenth-century France, especially among members of salons, see Lougee, *Le Paradis des Femmes*.

23 See, for instance, Jean-Marie Apostolidès's discussion of Murat in *Le Roi-machine: spectacle et politique au temps de Louis XIV*, Arguments (Paris: Editions de Minuit, 1981) 141–143. Robert is one of the few critics to recognize the diverse social backgrounds from which the *conteurs* and *conteuses* came (*Le Conte de fées*, 387).

24 On the social background of the *conteurs* and *conteuses*, see Storer, *Un Episode littéraire*. On the rise of literacy in this period, see Roger Chartier, Marie-Madeleine Compère, and Dominique Julia, *L'Education en France du XVIe siècle au XVIIIe siècle* (Paris: Sedes, 1976).

25 The search for authentic identity is a recurrent theme in romance literature. See Leslie W. Rabine, *Reading the Romantic Heroine: Text,*

History, Ideology (Ann Arbor: The University of Michigan Press, 1985) 2.

26 See Pelous, *Amour précieux*, 225–274 and 455–476.

27 *Galanterie* has proven to be notoriously difficult to define. Helpful, but very different discussions can be found in DeJean, *Tender Geographies*, 135–140; Alain Génetiot, *Les Genres lyriques mondains (1630–1660): Etude des poésies de Voiture, Vion d'Alibray, Sarasin et Scarron*, Histoire des idées et critique littéraire, 281 (Geneva: Droz, 1990), especially 97–110; Pelous, *Amour précieux*; Stanton, *The Aristocrat as Art*, 51, 137–138; and Alain Viala, "Introduction," *L'Esthétique galante: Paul Pellisson, "Discours sur les Œuvres de Monsieur Sarasin et autres textes"*, ed. Alain Viala (Toulouse: Société de Littératures Classiques, 1989).

28 "La Puissance d'Amour," *Les Contes des contes*, NCF, 7: 146.

29 See Coulet, *Le Roman*, 1: 211–213; DeJean, *Tender Geographies*, 94–158; and Maurice Lever, *Le Roman français au XVIIe siècle*, Littératures modernes (Paris: Presses universitaires de France, 1981) 167–168.

30 At the end of Scudéry's "Histoire de Sapho," the heroine's companion, Phaon, contests her refusal to marry him before several judges. Sapho wins, and the couple's love remains extramatrimonial and platonic (*Artamène ou le Grand Cyrus*, 10 vols. [1656; Geneva: Slatkine Reprints, 1972] 10: 607). Pelous notes the incompatibility of marriage within several strains of tender love (see *Amour précieux*, 18, 43, 97–100).

31 "La Grenouille bienfaisante," *Contes nouveaux ou les Fées à la mode*, 1698, NCF, 4: 348.

32 Even so, sexual literature flourished throughout the entire seventeenth century. See Roger Bougard, *Erotisme et amour physique dans la littérature française du XVIIe siècle* (Paris: Gaston Lachurié, 1986) and the articles in *L'Esprit créateur*, vol. 35, no. 2 (Summer 1995).

33 A strain of eighteenth-century *contes de fées* is much more explicitly erotic. See Robert, *Le Conte de fées*, 213–221.

34 "Le Prince Roger," *Les Illustres fées*, 1698, NCF, 6: 30.

35 "L'Oranger et l'abeille," *Les Contes des fées*, 1697, NCF, 3: 343.

36 The reasoning the Princesse de Clèves uses to reject the love of the Duc de Nemours is similarly skeptical of men but decidedly more pessimistic: "les hommes conservent-ils de la passion dans ces engagements éternels? Dois-je espérer un miracle en ma faveur et puis-je me mettre en état de voir certainement finir cette passion dont je ferais toute ma félicité? M. de Clèves était peut-être l'unique homme du monde capable de conserver de l'amour dans le mariage" (Marie-Madeleine de Lafayette, *La Princesse de*

Clèves, Romanciers du XVIIe siècle, ed. Antoine Adam, Bibliothèque de la Pléiade [Paris: Gallimard, 1957] 1247).

37 See Delarue, *Le Conte populaire français,* 1: 207.

38 On the frequency of erotic allusions in La Force's tales, see Marcelle Maistre Welch, "L'Eros féminin dans les contes de fées de Mlle de la Force," *Actes de Las Vegas,* Biblio 17, 60 (Paris, Seattle, Tübingen: Papers on French Seventeenth-Century Literature, 1991) 217–223.

39 "Vert et Bleu," *Les Contes des contes par Mlle. de ***,* 1698, NCF, 7: 103.

40 Even before this moment, the heroine had strong inklings that Vert was her ideal mate. When she first hears of Vert, "la princesse Bleu ... ne pouvait s'empêcher en secret de se destiner à un prince si charmant et de souhaiter, au péril de mille travaux, qu'il fût celui qui lui était promis par les destinées" (107). Upon seeing him for the first time, she asks herself, "serait-ce celui dont les qualités communes me doivent rendre si malheureuse? Car les beautés de la personne ne sont rien sans les ornements de l'esprit et les qualités de l'âme" (109–110). Later, after using the *voile d'Illusion* to escape from him, she worries momentarily about his social standing: "Je cède donc à mon destin ... est-il bon, est-il mauvais? J'aime un inconnu qui peut-être n'a point de naissance, et dont le caractère me ferait rougir si je le connaissais. Mais non, reprit-elle, si j'en crois mon cœur, tout répond en lui à une si belle représentation; je ne puis rien aimer qui ne soit digne que je l'aime" (112).

41 D'Aulnoy's "L'Isle de la félicité," "Le Mouton," "Le Nain jaune"; Murat's "Anguillette"; and "Le Portrait qui parle" (anonymous).

42 D'Auneuil, "La Princesse Patientine dans la forêt d'Erimente" and "Le Prince Curieux"; Bernard, "Le Prince Rosier"; and Murat, "Le Palais de la vengeance" and "Peine perdue." In La Force's "La Puissance d'Amour" and Murat's "L'Heureuse peine," the happy ending is tempered by critical comments on love and marriage.

43 These novels are a new inflection of the opposition to marriage voiced in early seventeenth-century salons and feminist writings. See DeJean, *Tender Geographies,* 21, 50. See also Lougee, *Le Paradis des Femmes,* and Ian Maclean, *Woman Triumphant: Feminism in French Literature 1610–1652.* (Oxford University Press, 1977).

44 Perrault's "Le Petit Chaperon Rouge" is the clearest example of a warning tale in the corpus. On "warning tales," see Röhrich, *Folktales and Reality,* 48–50.

45 D'Aulnoy's "Le Mouton" is the other. "L'Isle de la félicité" is a version of AT470B (Friends in Life and Death).

46 Untitled fairy tale, *Histoire d'Hypolite, Comte de Duglas*, 2 vols. in one (1690; Geneva: Slatkine Reprints, 1979) 2: 181. I follow Robert and Storer in calling this tale "Isle de la félicité."

47 "Le Nain jaune," *Les Contes des fées*, 1698, NCF, 4: 141–142.

48 In d'Aulnoy's "L'Isle de la félicité," "Le Mouton," and "Le Nain jaune," the dysphoric ending introduces an element of unpredictability that is usually absent from marvelous settings. The closures in these three tales may indeed represent what Robert calls a "stylistic effect" (*Le Conte de fées*, 35–36).

49 "Le Prince Rosier," *Inès de Cardoue, nouvelle espagnole* (1696; Geneva: Slatkine Reprints, 1979) 42.

50 "Le Palais de la vengeance," *Contes des fées*, 1698, NCF, 2: 366.

51 "Anguillette," *Les Nouveaux Contes des fées*, 1698, NCF, 2: 305.

52 In Lafayette's novel, for instance, Mme de Chartres shows her daughter "quelle *tranquillité* [suit] la vie d'une honnête femme" (*La Princesse de Clèves*, 1113; emphasis added).

53 Other details in "Anguillette" recall *La Princesse de Clèves* as well. Hébé, like the princess, is grief-stricken upon discovering *tablettes* (a letter in Lafayette's novel) she presumes are written by her suitor to another woman (266–269). Later in the tale, Atimir, like Nemours, wears the colors of his beloved in a tournament at which she is present (295).

54 Kaja Silverman discusses Bloch's understanding of utopia in terms of lack and incompletion, which, in his perspective, presuppose a more perfect future. "Although the Blochian future has a way of turning over and over again into the insufficient present, it is endlessly reconstituted through hope. The subject survives by sustaining belief in the possibility of something other than what is and has been, despite mounting knowledge to the contrary" (*Male Subjectivity at the Margins* [New York: Routledge, 1992] 249).

55 "Peine Perdue," *Contes de fées du Grand Siècle*, ed. Mary Elizabeth Storer, Publications of the Institute of French Studies (New York: Columbia University, 1934) 135. In an article that appeared as this book was going to press, Gabrielle Verdier relates the unhappy endings in d'Aulnoy's "L'Isle de la félicité" and Murat's "Anguillette" and "Peine Perdue" to the geographical utopias featured in each tale ("Féerie et utopie dans les contes de fées féminins," *Parabasis*, vol. 7: "Utopie et fictions narratives" (1995): 139–148.

56 See Pelous, *Amour précieux*, especially chapter 1.

5 (DE)MYSTIFICATIONS OF MASCULINITY: FICTIONS OF TRANSCENDENCE

1 See Max Lüthi, *The European folktale*, especially 4–10. I borrow the term "one-dimensionality" from Lüthi.

2 *Nonsense: Aspects of Intertextuality in Folklore and Literature* (Baltimore: The Johns Hopkins University Press, 1978) 120.

3 *Reading the Romantic Heroine: Text, History, Ideology* (Ann Arbor: The University of Michigan Press, 1985) 7.

4 See chapter 1, 40.

5 See René Girard, *Deceit, Desire, and the Novel: Self and Other in Literary Structure*, trans. Yvonne Freccero (Baltimore: The Johns Hopkins Press, 1965) and Eve Kosofsky Sedgwick, *Between Men: English Literature and Male Homosocial Desire* (New York: Columbia University Press, 1985).

6 See, especially, d'Aulnoy's "La Belle aux cheveux d'or," "L'Isle de la félicité," "La Princesse Belle-Etoile et le Prince Chéri," "La Princesse Carpillon," "Le Rameau d'or"; d'Auneuil's *La Tyrannie des fées détruite* and *Les Chevaliers errans, et le Génie familier*; *Florine ou la belle Italienne* (anonymous); Gueullette's *Les Soirées bretonnes*; La Force's "Persinette" and "L'Enchanteur"; Mailly's "Blanche-Belle," "Le Favori des fées," "Le Prince Guérini," "Le Prince Roger," and "Le Roi magicien"; Murat's "Le Prince des Feuilles" and "Le Sauvage"; and Nodot's *Histoire de Geofroy* and *Histoire de Mélusine*.

7 See chapter 1, 28–29; chapter 3, 79–84; and chapter 4, 110.

8 "The tale-hero is essentially a wanderer. None of his responsibilities or adventures have any relation to his home. He finds them much more often far away" (Katalin Horn, *Der aktive und der passive Märchenheld*, Beiträge zur Volkskunde, 5 [Basle: Schweizerische Gesellschaft für Volkskunde, 1983] 6). See also Robert A. Segal, "Introduction: In Quest of the Hero," *In Quest of the Hero* (Princeton University Press, 1990) vii–xi.

9 "Histoire de la Princesse Aimonette," *Inédits et belles pages de l'abbé de Choisy*, ed. Jean Mélia (Paris: Emile-Paul Frères, 1922) 112.

10 "La Belle aux cheveux d'or," *Les Contes des fées*, 1697, NCF, 3: 61.

11 On the links between seventeenth-century opera and the *contes de fées*, see Robert, *Le Conte de fées*, 366–379.

12 As Catherine Kintzler puts it, "a human character must only invoke more powerful forces if he has previously attempted to act on his own" (*Poétique de l'opéra français de Corneille à Rousseau* [Paris: Minerve, 1991] 283).

13 Michael Nerlich, *Ideology of Adventure: Studies in Modern Consciousness*,

1100–1750, trans. Ruth Crowley, 2 vols. Theory and History of Literature, 42–43 (Minneapolis: University of Minnesota Press, 1987) 2: 299–304.

14 See Horn, *Der active und der passive Märchenheld*, 6; Tatar, *Off with their Heads*, 69.

15 See especially Harth, *Ideology and Culture*.

16 See for instance the beginning of d'Aulnoy's "La Princesse Belle-Etoile et le Prince Chéri" and La Force's "La Bonne femme" in which the mother and the good woman, respectively, work to support themselves during their pastoral retreats.

17 Roland Mousnier, *The Institutions of France under the Absolute Monarchy, 1598–1789: Society and State*, trans. Brian Pearce, vol. 1 (University of Chicago Press, 1979) 85.

18 See, among others, Robert Muchembled, *Culture populaire et culture des élites dans la France moderne: XVe–XVIIIe siècles: essai* (Paris: Flammarion, 1978) 292, and Timmermans, *L'Accès des femmes à la culture*, 357–358.

19 See Jonathan Dewald, *Aristocratic Experience and the Origins of Modern Culture: France, 1570–1715* (Berkeley: University of California Press, 1993) 78; and Robert Muchembled, *L'Invention de l'homme moderne: sensibilités, mœurs et comportements collectifs sous l'Ancien Régime* (Paris: Fayard, 1988) 345.

20 See especially Sarah Hanley, "Engendering the State: Family Formation and State Building in Early Modern France," *French Historical Studies*, vol. 16, no. 1 (Spring 1989): 4–27.

21 There are a few exceptions to this rule. In d'Aulnoy's "Gracieuse et Percinet," paternal order is only ambiguously restored at the end since it is unclear what becomes of her father. And in Lhéritier's "Les Enchantements de l'éloquence" a weak father nonetheless stridently defends his daughter when her stepmother persecutes her for reading.

22 Fathers who impose various tests on their children fall into this category. In d'Aulnoy's "La Chatte blanche" and Murat's "Le Père et ses quatre fils," for instance, the father orders his sons to undertake various tasks to prove themselves worthy of him. However, the father/king in d'Aulnoy's tale is an ambiguous character, whose power is superceded by the heroine's (Chatte blanche) at the end.

23 See, for instance, *L'Interprétation des contes*, 91.

24 Compare, for instance, Bettelheim's psychoanalytic (*The Uses of Enchantment*, 114) and Warner's socio-historical explanations (*From the Beast to the Blonde*, 218–240).

25 See Harth, *Ideology and Culture*, especially 102–127. For a detailed

historical overview, see also Jacqueline Plantié, *La Mode du portrait littéraire en France, 1641–1681* (Paris: Champion, 1994).

26 With only a few exceptions (cf. d'Aulnoy's "La Biche au bois" and Mailly's "La Supercherie malheureuse"), portraits of heroes serve as either an object of discussion among the characters or a crucial element in the plot, whereas portraits of heroines are mentioned only fleetingly as part of the courtship ritual.

27 Naomi Schor has developed this line of reasoning in her illuminating article, "The Portrait of a Gentleman: Representing Men in (French) Women's Writing," *Representations* 20 (Fall 1987): 113–133.

28 Such is also the case in Mailly's "La Supercherie malheureuse" in which a stepmother tries to marry off her own ugly daughter by using the portrait of her beautiful stepdaughter. This *supercherie* or hoax for a time estranges the hero, brother of the portrait's original, and his best friend, who falls in love with the portrait but is brought the ugly daughter.

29 *Nouveau conte de fées. Le Portrait qui parle, dédié à Madame la Première Présidente de Metz* (Metz: np, 1699) 21.

6 IMAGINING FEMININITY: BINARITY AND BEYOND

1 This is notably the case of the numerous twentieth-century "feminist" fairy tales in English (see Zipes, *Don't Bet on the Prince*). For a general historical approach to this question, see Warner, *From the Beast to the Blonde.*

2 This thesis has been extensively developed in Zipes's work (see especially *Breaking the Magic Spell* and *Fairy Tales and the Art of Subversion*).

3 See, among others, Brémond, "Les Bons récompensés et les méchants punis: morphologie du conte merveilleux français," *Sémiotique narrative textuelle*, ed. Claude Chabrol and Sorin Alexandrescu (Prais: Larousse, 1973), and Flahault, *L'Interprétation des contes.*

4 See Warner, *From the Beast to the Blonde*, 201–240.

5 Tatar argues that the Catskin tale-type "offers an interesting case study of the way in which rewriters of a tale ingeniously exonerated fathers and shifted the burden of guilt for a father's crimes to the mother" (*Off with their Heads*, 128); Warner notes that "'grandmothers, mothers, and children' could accept an incestuous father placed centre stage in full view, till the eighteenth century ... The story of a father's unlawful love begins to fade from collections of fairy stories as well as from narratives dealing with actual experience" (*From the Beast to the Blonde*, 347).

6 I borrow the term *"grand renfermement"* from Albistur and Armogathe, *Histoire du féminisme français*, 1: 196–200. Their observation deserves more in-depth analysis. An example of the work needed is provided by Hanley ("Engendering the State"), whose analysis of late seventeenth-century judicial *arrêts* as an expression of the "Family–State compact" but also its subversion through a "counterfeit culture" suggests the intensity of public debate about family and gender relations in this period.

7 Of course, the debate that erupted in 1694 around Boileau's *Satire X* ("Contre les femmes") and enlisted the satirist's "ancients" as well as Perrault and his "moderns" illustrates this new conservatism perfectly.

8 Abbé Goussault, *Le Portrait d'une femme honneste, raisonnable et véritablement chrestienne, par Mr l'abbé Goussault, connseiller du Parlement.* (Paris: M. Brunet, 1693), 23. In his preface, Goussault pays homage to learned and pious women only to dismiss them: "Cela est beau, j'en demeure d'accord, mais on en voit tant de l'une et de l'autre de ces manières, que l'on n'en est plus surpris." Instead he lauds domesticity, vowing to portray "un grand nombre de Dames, bonnes, honnêtes et raisonnables, qui rendent leurs maisons également agréables à ceux qui y demeurent avec elles et à ceux qui y viennent" (np).

9 See Elizabeth Badinter, *L'amour en plus: histoire de l'amour maternel (XVIIe–XXe siècle)* (Paris: Flammarion, 1980).

10 Jean-Louis Flandrin, *Familles: parenté, maison, sexualité dans l'ancienne société* (Paris: Hachette, 1976) 118–152.

11 Villethierry, *La Vie des gens mariez, ou les obligations qui s'engagent dans le mariage, prouvées par l'Ecriture, par les saints Peres, et par les Conciles,* 4th edn. (1694; Paris: François Emery, 1709) 9–10.

12 Michèle Longino Farrell, *Performing Motherhood: The Sévigné Correspondence* (Hanover, NH: University Press of New England, 1991), especially 155–186.

13 On Lambert's hesitancy to publish, see Erica Harth, "The Salon Woman Goes Public ... or Does She?" *Going Public: Woman and Publishing in Early Modern France,* 190–192.

14 On the question of women's relation to publicity in early modern France, see the articles in Goldsmith and Goodman, eds., *Going Public.* See also the excellent discussion of Sévigné's case in Longino Farrell, *Performing Motherhood.*

15 See, for instance, the chapters Warner devotes to fairy-tale mothers and stepmothers (*From the Beast to the Blonde*).

16 See "La Chatte blanche," "Gracieuse et Percinet," and "L'Oiseau bleu."

17 See "Babiole," "Le Nain jaune," and "Le Prince Lutin."
18 D'Aulnoy, "Gracieuse et Percinet," *Les Contes des fées*, 1697, NCF, 3: 2.
19 "La Chatte blanche," *Contes nouveaux ou les Fées à la mode*, 1698, NCF, 4: 517.
20 See "La Princesse Carpillon," *Contes nouveaux ou les Fées à la mode*, 1698, NCF, 4: 230 and 248.
21 La Force, "La Bonne femme," *Les Contes des contes*, 1697, NCF, 7: 168.
22 See Wendy Gibson, *Women in Seventeenth-Century France* (Houndmills and London: Macmillan, 1989) 78–79.
23 See Storer, *La Mode*, 266–267.
24 See "Jeune et Belle," "Le Parfait Amour," and "Peine Perdue"; her allegorical "L'Isle de la magnificence" features a fairy who adopts six children – three boys and three girls – and instructs them in the ways of virtuous love.
25 "La Bonne petite souris," *Les Contes des fées*, 1697, NCF, 3: 358.
26 See, for example, the description of her despair (355) and her joy (368–369).
27 Among the *contes de fées* of the first vogue, the anonymous "Florine ou la belle Italienne," Gueullette's *Les Soirées bretonnes*, and Préchac's "La Reine des fées" feature plots dominated by the rivalry between good and evil fairies.
28 Laurence Harf-Lancner, *Les Fées au moyen-âge: Morgane et Mélusine, La naissance des fées* (Geneva: Editions Slatkine, 1984) 27–57.
29 See especially d'Aulnoy's "Gracieuse et Percinet," "Fortunée," "Le Pigeon et la colombe," "La Princesse Belle-Etoile et le Prince Chéri," "La Princesse Carpillon"; La Force's "Vert et Bleu"; Mailly's "Le Roi magicien" and "La Princesse couronnée par les fées," and Murat's "Le Roy Porc."
30 For a more pessimistic interpretation of the fairy's maternal role, see Wolfzettel, "La Lutte contre les mères."
31 Wolfzettel notes that fairies are not nearly as prevalent in the sixteenth-century Italian fairy tales that preceded and, in some instances, inspired the vogue ("La Lutte contre les mères," 125; see also his "Fee, Feenland," *Enzyklopädie des Märchens*, vol. 4 [Berlin, New York: de Gruyter, 1984] 945–963).
32 Even some of the dysphoric tales illustrate a variant of this principle. In Murat's "Anguillette," the fairy repeatedly warns the heroine that her powers cannot prevent tragedies caused by love.
33 See Warner, *From the Beast to the Blonde*, 14–15.
34 See chapter 3, 90.
35 See chapter 3, 89–90, and Seifert, "Les Fées modernes," *Going Public*, 129–145.

36 See "La Reine des fées," *Contes moins contes que les autres*, 1698, NCF, 6: 449–460. Mailly's "celebration" of salon women differs from that of the *conteuses* in that his fairies overwhelmingly come to the aid of heroes, rather than heroines.

37 See especially d'Aulnoy's "La Biche au bois"; La Force's "Vert et Bleu"; "Murat's "L'Heureuse peine" and "Le Roy Porc."

38 See Harf-Lancner, *Les Fées au moyen-âge*, 13–57.

39 Louise de Bossigny, Comtesse d'Auneuil, "La Tyrannie des fées détruite," *La Tyrannie des fées détruite*, (1702; Paris: Côté-femmes, 1990) 24.

40 This is the case of parodic plays by Dancourt (*Les Fées, comédie*, 1699), Dufresny (*Les Fées ou les contes de ma Mère l'Oye, comédie*, 1697) and La Baume (*La Fée Bien-faisante, comédie composée par Mr****, 1708) which ridicule fairies and the entire vogue.

41 Erica Harth notes that the salon's subversion of the socio-political and intellectual order was largely illusory (*Cartesian Women*, 54) and that the salon itself offered women a resolutely circumscribed discursive space (*Cartesian Women*, 63). D'Auneuil's tale might be said to openly acknowledge these limits.

42 See, for instance, the interesting discussion of this question in Maria Tatar's *Off with their Heads*, 94–119.

43 These are the seven sins Maria Tatar discusses in her chapter "Heroines and their Seven Sins," *Off with their Heads*, 94–119.

44 See Toinet's bibliography ("Les Ecrivains moralistes au XVIIe siècle") for a wide-ranging list of relevant titles.

45 See Lougee, *Le Paradis des Femmes*, 11–55; Maclean, *Woman Triumphant*; and Timmermans, *L'Accès des femmes*, 246–318.

46 On this perception, see DeJean, *Tender Geographies*, 149.

47 Timothy Reiss has noted that during the last quarter of the seventeenth century, four recurring arguments were used to exclude women effectively from cultural production: women possessed a reason different from men's; the roles of wife and mother were the dominant model for femininity; women were men's possessions; and they were ideal consumers (as opposed to producers) of culture (*The Meaning of Literature*, 202–215).

48 See Goussault, *Le Portrait d'une femme honneste*, 351–353.

49 "Avis à une jeune personne qui entroit dans le monde," *Lettres d'une dame de qualité sur sa vie mondaine et sa vie pénitente à son directeur, et la réponse du directeur, avec Des Réflexions morales, Dédiées à Mademoiselle P**** (Cologne: Baltazar d'Egmont, nd) 262. See also Liancourt, *Règlement*, 131.

50 See especially the morals at the end of Lhéritier's and Perrault's tales. Of course, Lhéritier's morals are decidedly more pragmatic

– and feminist – than Perrault's, which often single out women for comic jibes. Lhéritier's morals may even be an attempt to find a middle ground between the *mondain* activity of fairy-tale story-telling and the late seventeenth-century "moralist" concern for women's conduct.

51 Taking into account publication dates, Jeanne Roche-Mazon ("Riquet à la houppe," *Autour des contes de fées* [Paris: Didier, 1968] 61–91) argues that Perrault's version (published in 1697) followed and thus imitated Bernard's (published in 1696). Considering the manuscript of Perrault's collection, which was discovered after publication of Roche-Mazon's article, Marc Soriano revises this assertion and proposes that the two versions were written concurrently (see *Les Contes*, 191–196).

52 Catherine Bernard, "Riquet à la houppe" (1696), *Contes de Perrault*, ed. Gilbert Rouger, 275.

53 Patricia Hannon, "Antithesis and Ideology in Perrault's 'Riquet à la houppe,'" *Cahiers du Dix-septième: An Interdisciplinary Journal* vol. 4, no. 2 (Fall 1990): 105–117.

54 "Vous savez que, quand je n'étais qu'une bête, je ne pouvais néanmoins me résoudre à vous épouser; comment voulez-vous qu'ayant l'esprit que vous m'avez donné, qui me rend encore plus difficile en gens que je n'étais, je prenne aujourd'hui une résolution que je n'ai pu prendre dans ce temps-là? Si vous pensiez tout de bon à m'épouser, vous avez eu grand tort de m'ôter la bêtise, de me faire voir plus clair que je ne voyais" (186).

55 See chapter 4, 133.

56 Jack Zipes also notes that "Ricdin-Ricdon" is one of the few literary versions of "Rumpelstiltskin" to attribute a positive value to spinning. See "Rumpelstiltskin and the Decline of Female Productivity," *Fairy Tale as Myth/Myth as Fairy Tale* (Lexington, KY: The University Press of Kentucky, 1994) 67–71.

57 See "Ricdin-Ricdon," *La Tour ténébreuse et les jours lumineux, contes anglois*, 1705, NCF, 7: 37.

58 See the descriptions of her difficulty with writing and her disinterest in tragedies by Corneille and Racine (62–64).

59 See especially "Marmoisan" (reprinted in *La Fille en garçon*, ed. Catherine Velay-Vallantin, Classiques de la littérature orale [Carcassonne: Garae/Hésiode, 1992] 17–54) and "La Robe de sincérité" (*La Tour ténébreuse*, 1705, NCF, vol. 7).

60 See Zipes, *Fairy Tale as Myth*, 51–52, for a discussion of the various functions suggested by the act of naming in this tale-type.

AFTERWORD

1 Fredric Jameson, *The Political Unconscious*, 135.
2 Northrop Frye, *The Secular Scripture: A Study of the Structure of Romance* (Cambridge, MA: Harvard University Press, 1976).
3 See Michel Foucault, *Histoire de la sexualité*, 3 vols. vol. 1: *La Volonté de savoir*, (Paris: Gallimard, 1976) and *Surveiller et punir: naissance de la prison* (Paris: Gallimard, 1975).
4 See the stimulating discussion of this question in Butler, *Gender Trouble*, 57ff.

Selected bibliography

PRIMARY SOURCES

Aulnoy, Marie-Catherine Le Jumel de Barneville, Comtesse d'.
   Histoire d'Hypolite, comte de Duglas. 2 vols. Paris: L. Sylvestre, 1690.
   Les Contes des fées. 4 vols. Paris, 1697–1698; reprinted in vols. 3 and 4
   of *Nouveau Cabinet des fées.*
   Contes nouveaux ou les Fées à la mode. 4 vols. Paris: Veuve de Théodore
   Girard, 1698; reprinted in vols. 4 and 5 of *Nouveau Cabinet des fées.*
Auneuil, Louise de Bossigny, Comtesse d'. *La Tyrannie des fées détruite,
   nouveaux contes dédiés à Madame la duchesse de Bourgogne par Madame la
   comtesse D. L..* Paris: Veuve R. Chevillon, 1702; Paris: Côté-
   femmes, 1990.
   *Nouvelles diverses du temps, La Princesse de Pretintailles, par Mme la ctesse
   D. L..* Paris: Pierre Ribou, 1702.
   L'Inconstance punie, nouvelles du temps, par Mad. la comtesse D. L.. Paris:
   Pierre Ribou, 1702.
   L'Origine du lansquenet, nouvelles du temps, par Madame la Comtesse D*.
   Paris: Pierre Ribou, 1703.
   Les Chevaliers errans et Le Génie familier, par Madame la comtesse D***.
   Paris: Pierre Ribou, 1709.
Beauties, Beasts and Enchantments: Classic French Fairy Tales. Ed. and
   trans. Jack Zipes. New York: New American Library, 1989.
Bernard, Catherine. *Inès de Cardoue, nouvelle espagnole.* Paris: Jouvenel,
   1696; Geneva: Slatkine Reprints, 1979.
   "Riquet à la houppe." *Contes de Perrault.* Ed. Gilbert Rouger. 271–
   278.
Bignon, Abbé Jean-Paul. *Les Aventures d'Abdalla, fils d'Hani, envoyé par le
   sultan des Indes à la découverte de l'île de Borico.* Paris: P. Witte,
   1710–1714; reprinted in vol. 13 of *Nouveau Cabinet des fées.*
Boileau, Nicolas. *Œuvres complètes.* Ed. Françoise Escal. Bibliothèque
   de la Pléiade. Paris: Gallimard, 1966.

Choisy, Abbé de. "Histoire de la Princesse Aimonette." *Ouvrages de Mr. L. de Choisy, qui n'ont pas été imprimés.* Ms. 3186. Bibliothèque de l'Arsenal. Paris. Partially reprinted in *Inédits et belles pages de l'abbé de Choisy.* Ed. Jean Melia. Paris: Emile-Paul, 1922.

Contes de fées du Grand Siècle. Ed. Mary Elizabeth Storer. Publications of the Institute of French Studies, 23. New York: Columbia University, 1934.

Dancourt [Florent Carton]. *Les Fées, comédie.* Paris: Ribou, 1699.

Dufresny, Charles Rivière. *Les Fées, ou les contes de ma Mère l'Oye, comédie. La Suite du Théâtre italien.* Paris: np, 1697.

Durand, Catherine Bédacier. *La Comtesse de Mortane par Madame ***.* Paris: Veuve de C. Barbin, 1699.

Les Petits Soupers de l'été de l'année 1699, ou Avantures galantes avec l'Origine des fées, par Madame Durand. Paris: J. Musier et J. Rolin, 1702.

Fénelon, François de Salignac de la Mothe-. *Œuvres.* Ed. Jacques Le Brun. vol. 1. Bibliothèque de la Pléiade. Paris: Gallimard, 1983.

Florine ou la belle Italienne. Nouveau conte de fées. Paris: C. Jombert, 1713. Reprinted in vol. 8 of *Nouveau Cabinet des fées.*

Goussault, Abbé. *Le Portrait d'une femme honneste, raisonnable et véritablement chrestienne, par Mr l'abbé Goussault, conseiller du Parlement.* Paris: M. Brunet, 1693.

Gueullette, Thomas-Simon. *Les Soirées bretonnes, dédiées à Monseigneur le Dauphin.* Paris: Saugrin, 1712; reprinted in vol. 32 of *Le Cabinet des fées; ou collection choisie des contes des fées, et autres contes merveilleux.* 41 vols. Amsterdam, 1785–1786; Paris, 1788.

Les Mille et un quarts d'heure. 1715. 2 vols. Arles: Picquier, 1995.

Il était une fois. Contes des XVIIe et XVIIIe siècles. Ed. Raymonde Robert. Nancy: Presse universitaires de Nancy, 1984.

La Baume, le Chevalier de. *La Fée Bien-faisante, comédie composée par Mr***.* Grenoble: François Champ, 1708.

Lafayette, Marie-Madeleine Pioche de la Vergne de. *La Princesse de Clèves. Romanciers du XVIIe siècle.* Ed. Antoine Adam. Bibliothèque de la Pléiade. Paris: Gallimard, 1957.

La Fontaine, Jean de. *Œuvres complètes.* Vol. 1: *Fables, Contes et nouvelles.* Ed. Jean-Pierre Collinet. Bibliothèque de la Pléiade. Paris: Gallimard, 1991.

La Force, Charlotte-Rose Caumont de. *Les Contes des contes par Mlle de ***.* Paris: S. Benard, 1698; reprinted in vol. 7 of *Nouveau Cabinet des fées.*

Les Jeux d'esprit ou la promenade de la Princesse de Conti à Eu par Mademoiselle de La Force. Ed. M. le marquis de la Grange. Paris: Auguste Aubry, 1862.

Le Noble, Eustache, Baron de Saint-Georges et de Tennelière. *Le Gage touché. Histoires galantes*. Amsterdam: np, 1700.

Lhéritier de Villandon, Marie-Jeanne. *Œuvres meslées, contenant l'Innocente tromperie, l'Avare puni, les Enchantements de l'éloquence, les Aventures de Finette, nouvelles, et autres ouvrages, en vers et en prose, de Mlle de L'H*** — avec le Triomphe de Mme Des-Houlières tel qu'il a été composé par Mlle L'H****. Paris: J. Guignard, 1696.

La Tour ténébreuse et les jours lumineux, contes anglois, accompagnés d'historiettes et tirés d'une ancienne chronique composée par Richard, surnommé Cœur de Lion, roi d'Angleterre, avec le récit des diverses aventures de ce roi. Paris: Veuve de Claude Barbin, 1705; reprinted in vol. 7 of *Nouveau Cabinet des fées*.

"Les Enchantements de l'éloqence." *Contes de Perrault*. Ed. Gilbert Rouger. 239–265.

Liancourt, Jeanne de Schomberg, Duchesse de. *Règlement donné par une dame de haute qualité à sa petite-fille. Pour sa Conduite, & pour celle de sa Maison. Avec un autre Règlement que cette Dame avoit dressé pour elle-même.* 1698. Paris: Florentin, 1718.

Mailly, Jean de. *Les Illustres fées, contes galans. Dédié aux dames*. Paris: M-M. Brunet, 1698; reprinted in vol. 6 of *Nouveau Cabinet des fées*.

Molière [Jean-Baptiste Poquelin]. *Œuvres complètes*. 2 vols. Paris: Garnier, 1962.

Moncrif, François Augustin Paradis de. *Les Aventures de Zéloïde et d'Amanzarifdine*. Paris: Saugrain l'aîné, 1715; ed. Francis Assaf. Biblio 17, 82. Paris, Seattle, Tübingen: Papers on French Seventeenth-Century Literature, 1994.

Murat, Henriette-Julie de Castelnau, Comtesse de. *Contes de fées dédiez à S. A. S. Madame la princesse douairière de Conty, par Mad. la comtesse de M****. Paris: Claude Barbin, 1698; reprinted in vol. 2 of *Nouveau Cabinet des fées*.

Les Nouveaux Contes de fées par Mme de M**. Paris: Claude Barbin, 1698. Reprinted in vol. 2 of *Nouveau Cabinet des fées*.

Histoires sublimes et allégoriques par Mme la comtesse D***, dédiées aux fées modernes. Paris: J. et P. Delaulme, 1699.

Voyage de campagne, par Mme la Ctesse de M*** — Comédies en proverbes, par Catherine Bédacier, née Durand. Paris: Veuve de Claude Barbin, 1699.

Ouvrages de Mme la comtesse de Murat. Ms. 3471. Bibliothèque de l'Arsenal. Paris. Partially reprinted in *Contes de fées du Grand Siècle*.

Nodot, Paul-François. *Histoire de Mélusine. Tirée des Chroniques de Poitou, et qui sert d'Origine à l'ancienne Maison de Lusignan*. Paris: Claude Barbin, 1698.

Histoire de Geofroy. Surnommé à la Grand'Dent. Sixième Fils de Mélusine. Prince de Lusignan. Paris: Veuve de Claude Barbin, 1699.

Nouveau Cabinet des fées. Ed. Jacques Barchilon. 18 vols. Geneva: Slatkine Reprints, 1978. Partial reprint of *Le Cabinet des fées; ou collection choisie des contes des fées, et autres contes merveilleux.* 41 vols. Amsterdam: 1785–1786; Paris: 1788.

Nouveau conte de fées. Le Portrait qui parle, dédié à Madame la Première Présidente de Metz. Metz: np, 1699.

Perrault, Charles. *L'Apologie des femmes, par Monsieur P**.* Paris: Veuve Coignard, 1694.

 Contes. Ed. Jean-Pierre Collinet. Folio, 1281. 1691–1697. Paris: Gallimard, 1981.

 Contes de Perrault. Ed. Gilbert Rouger. 1691–1697. Paris: Garnier, 1967.

 Memoirs of My Life. Ed. and trans. Jeanne Morgan Zarucchi. Columbia, MO: University of Missouri Press, 1989.

 Parallèle des anciens et des modernes. 1688–1697. Munich: Eidos Verlag, 1964.

Préchac, Jean de. *Contes moins contes que les autres. Sans Parangon et La Reine des fées.* Paris: Claude Barbin, 1698; reprinted in vol. 6 of *Nouveau Cabinet des fées.*

Scudéry, Madeleine de. "Les Ieux servant de préface à Mathilde." *Mathilde d'Aguilar.* 1667. Geneva: Slatkine Reprints, 1979.

Villiers, Abbé de. *Entretiens sur les contes de fées, et sur quelques autres ouvrages du temps. Pour servir de préservatif contre le mauvais goût.* Paris: J. Collombat, 1699.

SECONDARY SOURCES

Aarne, Antti. *The Types of the Folktale.* Trans. Stith Thompson. Helsinki: Academia Scientiarum Fennica, 1981.

Adam, Antoine. *Histoire de la littérature française au XVIIe siècle.* 5 vols. Paris: del Duca, 1968.

Albistur, Maïté and Daniel Armogathe. *Histoire du féminisme français.* 2 vols. Paris: des femmes, 1977.

Apel, Friedmar. *Die Zaubergärten der Phantasie. Zur Theorie und Geschichte des Kunstmärchens.* Heidelberg: Carl Winter, 1978.

Baader, Renate. *Dames de Lettres: Autorinnen des preziösen, hocharistokratischen und "modernen" Salons (1649–1698): Mlle de Scudéry – Mlle de Montpensier – Mme d'Aulnoy.* Stuttgart: J. B. Metzler, 1986.

Bannister, Mark. *Privileged Mortals: The French Heroic Novel, 1630–1660.* Oxford University Press, 1983.

Barchilon, Jacques. *Le Conte merveilleux français de 1690 à 1790: cent ans de féerie et de poésie ignorées de l'histoire littéraire.* Paris: Honoré Champion, 1975.

"L'Ironie et l'humour dans les 'Contes' de Perrault." *Studi francese* 32 (1967): 258–270.

Barchilon, Jacques and Peter Flinders. *Charles Perrault.* Twayne World Author Series, 639. Boston: Twayne Publishers, 1981.

Beasley, Faith E. *Revising Memory: Women's Fiction and Memoirs in Seventeenth-Century France.* New Brunswick: Rutgers University Press, 1990.

Bettelheim, Bruno. *The Uses of Enchantment: The Meaning and Importance of Fairy Tales.* New York: Random House, 1977.

Bloch, Ernst. *The Utopian Function of Art and Literature: Selected Essays.* Ed. and trans. Jack Zipes and Frank Mecklenburg. Cambridge, MA: The MIT Press, 1988.

Bottigheimer, Ruth B. *Grimms' Bad Girls and Bold Boys: The Moral and Social Vision of the "Tales."* New Haven: Yale University Press, 1987.

Brémond, Claude. "Les Bons récompensés et les méchants punis: morphologie du conte merveilleux français." *Sémiotique narrative textuelle.* Ed. Claude Chabrol and Sorin Alexandrescu. Paris: Larousse, 1973.

"Le Mécanno du conte." *Magazine littéraire* 150 (1979): 14–18.

Butler, Judith. *Gender Trouble: Feminism and the Subversion of Identity.* Thinking Gender. New York: Routledge, 1990.

Chambers, Ross. *Room for Maneuver: Reading (the) Oppositional (in) Narrative.* University of Chicago Press, 1991.

Coulet, Henri. *Le Roman jusqu'à la Révolution.* 2 vols. Paris: Colin, 1967.

Cuénin, Micheline and Chantal Morlet-Chantalat. "Châteaux et romans au XVIIe siècle." *XVIIe siècle* 118–119 (1978): 101–123.

DeGraff, Amy Vanderlyn. *The Tower and the Well: A Psychological Interpretation of the Fairy Tales of Madame d'Aulnoy.* Birmingham, AL: Summa Publications, 1984.

DeJean, Joan. *Tender Geographies: Women and the Origins of the Novel in France.* New York: Columbia University Press, 1991.

Delaporte, P. Victor. *Du Merveilleux dans la littérature française sous le règne de Louis XIV.* 1891. Geneva: Slatkine Reprints, 1968.

Delarue, Paul. "Les Caractères propres du conte populaire français." *La Pensée* 72 (March–April 1957): 40–62.

Delarue Paul and Marie-Louise Tenèze. *Le Conte populaire français: un catalogue raisonné des versions de France et des pays de langue française et d'Outre-mer.* 4 vols. Paris: Maisonneuve et Larose, 1976.

DiPiero, Thomas. *Dangerous Truths and Criminal Passions: The Evolution of the French Novel, 1569–1791.* Stanford University Press, 1992.

Di Scanno, Teresa. *Les Contes de fées à l'époque classique (1680–1715)*. Naples: Liguori Editore, 1975.

Don't Bet on the Prince: Contemporary Feminist Fairy Tales in North America and England. Ed. Jack Zipes. New York: Methuen, 1986.

Fairy Tales and Society: Illusion, Allusion, and Paradigm. Ed. Ruth B. Bottigheimer. Philadelphia: University of Pennsylvania Press, 1986.

Farrell, Michèle Longino. "Celebration and Repression of Feminine Desire in Mme d'Aulnoy's Fairy Tale: *La Chatte Blanche*." *L'Esprit créateur* vol. 29, no. 3 (1989): 52–64.

Performing Motherhood: The Sévigné Correspondence. Hanover, NH: University Press of New England, 1991.

Flahault, François. *L'Interprétation des contes*. Paris: Denoël, 1988.

Flandrin, Jean-Louis. *Familles: parenté, maison, sexualité dans l'ancienne société*. Paris: Hachette, 1976.

Fumaroli, Marc. "Les Enchantements de l'éloquence: *Les Fées* de Charles Perrault ou De la littérature." *Le Statut de la littérature: mélanges offertes à Paul Bénichou*. Ed. Marc Fumaroli. Geneva: Droz, 1982. 152–186.

Going Public: Women and Publishing in Early Modern France. Ed. Elizabeth Goldsmith and Dena Goodman. Ithaca, NY: Cornell University Press, 1995.

Goldsmith, Elizabeth. *Exclusive Conversations: The Art of Interaction in Seventeenth-Century France*. Philadelphia: University of Pennsylvania Press, 1988.

Greimas, Aldirgas-Julien. *Sémantique structurale*. Paris: Larousse, 1966.

Hanley, Sarah. "Engendering the State: Family Formation and State Building in Early Modern France." *French Historical Studies* vol. 16, no. 1 (Spring 1989): 4–27.

Hannon, Patricia. "Antithesis and Ideology in Perrault's 'Riquet à la houppe.'" *Cahiers du Dix-septième: An Interdisciplinary Journal* vol. 4, no. 2 (Fall 1990): 105–117.

Harf-Lancner, Laurence. *Les Fées au moyen-âge: Morgane et Mélusine, La naissance des fées*. Geneva: Editions Slatkine, 1984.

Harth, Erica. *Cartesian Women: Versions and Subversions of Rational Discourse in the Old Regime*. Ithaca, NY: Cornell University Press, 1992.

Ideology and Culture in Seventeenth-Century France. Ithaca, NY: Cornell University Press, 1983.

Horn, Katalin. *Der aktive und der passive Märchenheld*. Basle: Schweizer-ische Gesellschaft für Volkskunde, 1983.

Jackson, Rosemary. *Fantasy: The Literature of Subversion*. New Accents. New York: Methuen, 1981.

Jameson, Fredric. *The Political Unconscious: Narrative as a Socially Symbolic Act.* Ithaca, NY: Cornell University Press, 1981.

Kibédi-Varga, Aron. "Introduction." *Les Poétiques du classicisme.* Ed. Aron Kibédi-Varga. Paris: Aux Amateurs de Livres, 1990.

Klotz, Volker. *Das europäische Kunstmärchen: Fünfundzwanzig Kapitel seiner Geschichte von der Renaissance bis zur Moderne.* Stuttgart: Metzler, 1985.

Lacan, Jacques. *Feminine Sexuality: Jacques Lacan and the "Ecole Freudienne".* Trans. Jacqueline Rose. Ed. Juliet Mitchell and Jacqueline Rose. New York: Norton, 1985.

Loskoutoff, Yvan. *La Sainte et la fée: dévotion à l'Enfant Jésus et mode des contes merveilleux à la fin du règne de Louis XIV.* Histoire des idées et critique littéraire, 255. Geneva: Droz, 1987.

Lougee, Carolyn C. *Le Paradis des Femmes: Women, Salons, and Social Stratification in Seventeenth-Century France.* Princeton University Press, 1976.

Lüthi, Max. *The European Folktale: Form and Nature.* Trans. John D. Niles. Philadelphia: Institute for the Study of Human Issues, 1982.

The Fairytale as Art Form and Portrait of Man. Trans. Jon Erickson. 1975. Bloomington: Indiana University Press, 1984.

Lyons, John. *Exemplum: The Rhetoric of Example in Early Modern France and Italy.* Princeton University Press, 1989.

Maclean, Ian. *Woman Triumphant: Feminism in French Literature 1610–1652.* Oxford University Press, 1977.

Marin, Louis. *Le Récit est un piège.* Critique. Paris: Minuit, 1978.

May, Georges. *Le Dilemme du roman au XVIIIe siècle: étude sur les rapports du roman et de la critique (1715–1761).* Paris: Presses universitaires de France, 1963.

Les Mille et une nuits d'Antoine Galland. Paris: Presses universitaires de France, 1986.

Meletinsky, Eleazar. "Marriage: Its Function and Position in the Structure of Folktales." *Soviet Structural Folkloristics.* Ed. P. Maranda. The Hague: Mouton, 1974.

Miller, Nancy K. *Subject to Change: Reading Feminist Writing.* New York: Columbia University Press, 1988.

Mitchell, Jane Tucker. *A Thematic Analysis of Mme d'Aulnoy's "Contes de fées".* Romance Monographs, 30. University, MS: Romance Monographs, Inc., 1978.

Montégut, Emile. "Des Fées et de leur littérature en France." *Revue des deux mondes* (1 April 1862): 648–675.

Morgan, Jeanne. *Perrault's Morals for Moderns.* Series 2. Romance

Languages and Literature, 28. New York, Berne, Frankfurt-am-Main: Peter Lang, 1985.

Nerlich, Michael. *Ideology of Adventure: Studies in Modern Consciousness, 1100–1750*. Trans. Ruth Crowley. 2 vols. Theory and History of Literature, 42–43. Minneapolis: University of Minnesota Press, 1987.

Pelous, Jean-Michel. *Amour précieux, amour galant (1654–1675): essai sur la représentation de l'amour dans la littérature et la société mondaines*. Paris: Klincksieck, 1980.

Plantié, Jacqueline. *La Mode du portrait littéraire en France, 1641–1681*. Paris: Champion, 1994.

Propp, Vladimir. *Morphology of the Folktale*. Trans. Laurence Scott and Louis A. Wagner. Austin: University of Texas Press, 1968.

Rabine, Leslie W. *Reading the Romantic Heroine: Text, History, Ideology*. Ann Arbor: The University of Michigan Press, 1985.

Reiss, Timothy. *The Meaning of Literature*. Ithaca, NY: Cornell University Press, 1992.

Revel, Jacques. "The Uses of Civility." *A History of Private Life: Passions of the Renaissance*. Ed. Philippe Ariès and Georges Duby. Trans. Arthur Goldhammer. Cambridge, MA: Harvard University Press, 1989. 167–205.

Robert, Marthe. "Un modèle romanesque: le conte de Grimm." *Preuves* 185 (1966): 24–34.

Robert, Raymonde. *Le Conte de fées littéraire en France de la fin du XVIIe à la fin du XVIIIe siècle*. Presses universitaires de Nancy, 1982.

"L'Infantilisation du conte merveilleux au XVIIe siècle." *Littératures classiques*. 14 (January 1991): 33–46.

Roche-Mazon, Jeanne. *Autour des contes de fées*. Etudes de littérature étrangère et comparée. Paris: Didier, 1968.

Röhrich, Lutz. *Folktales and Reality*. Trans. Peter Tokofsky. Bloomington: Indiana University Press, 1991.

Rowe, Karen E. "Feminism and Fairy Tales." *Don't Bet on the Prince*. 209–226.

Sedgwick, Eve. *Between Men: English Literature and Male Homosocial Desire*. New York: Columbia University Press, 1985.

Seifert, Lewis C. "*Les Fées Modernes*: Women, Fairy Tales, and the Literary Field in Late Seventeenth-Century France." *Going Public: Women and Publishing in Early Modern France*. 129–145.

Schalk, Ellery. *From Valor to Pedigree: Ideas of Nobility in France in the Sixteenth and Seventeenth Centuries*. Princeton University Press, 1986.

Silverman, Kaja. *Male Subjectivity at the Margins*. New York: Routledge, 1992.

Soriano, Marc. *Les Contes de Perrault: culture savante et traditions populaires.* Collection Tel. 1968. Paris: Gallimard, 1977.

Stanton, Domna C. *The Aristocrat as Art. A Study of the "Honnête Homme" and the "Dandy" in Seventeenth- and Nineteenth-Century French Literature.* New York: Columbia University Press, 1980.

Stewart, Susan. *Nonsense: Aspects of Intertextuality in Folklore and Literature.* Baltimore: The Johns Hopkins University Press, 1978.

"Notes on Distressed Genres." *Journal of American Folklore* 104 (1991): 5–31.

On Longing: Narratives of the Miniature, the Gigantic, the Souvenir, the Collection. Baltimore: The Johns Hopkins University Press, 1984.

Storer, Mary Elizabeth. *Un Épisode littéraire de la fin du XVIIe siècle: la mode des contes de fées (1685–1700).* 1928. Geneva: Slatkine Reprints, 1972.

Tatar, Maria. *Off with their Heads! Fairy Tales and the Culture of Childhood.* Princeton University Press, 1992.

The Hard Facts of the Grimms' Fairy Tales. Princeton University Press, 1987.

Thompson, Stith. *The Folktale.* New York: The Dryden Press, 1946.

Timmermans, Linda. *L'Accès des femmes à la culture, 1598–1715: un débat d'idées de Saint François de Sales à la Marquise de Lambert.* Paris: Champion, 1993.

Toinet, Raymond. "Les Ecrivains moralistes au XVIIe siècle." *Revue d'Histoire littéraire de la France* 23 (1916): 570–610; 24 (1917): 296–306, 656–675; 25 (1918): 310–320, 655–671; 33 (1926): 395–407.

Velay-Vallantin, Catherine. *L'Histoire des contes.* Paris: Fayard, 1992.

La Fille en garçon. Classiques de la littérature orale. Carcassonne: Garae/Hésiode, 1992.

Verdier, Gabrielle. "Figures de la conteuse dans les contes de fées féminins." *XVIIe siècle* 180 (July–September 1993): 481–499.

Warner, Marina. *From the Beast to the Blonde: On Fairytales and their Tellers.* London: Chatto and Windus, 1994.

Welch, Marcelle Maistre. "Les Jeux de l'écriture dans les *Contes de fées* de Mme d'Aulnoy." *Romanische Forschungen* vol. 101, no. 1 (1989): 75–80.

Wolfzettel, Friedrich. "Fee, Feenland." *Enzyklopädie des Märchens.* vol. 4. Berlin, New York: Walter de Gruyter, 1984. 945–963.

"La Lutte contre les mères: quelques exemples d'une valorisation émancipatrice du conte de fées au dix-huitième siècle." *Réception et identification du conte depuis le moyen âge.* Ed. Michel Zink and Xavier Ravier. Toulouse: Université de Toulouse–Le Mirail, 1987. 123–131.

Zipes, Jack. *Breaking the Magic Spell: Radical Theories of Folk and Fairy Tales*. New York: Methuen, 1979.
  Fairy Tale as Myth/Myth as Fairy Tale. Lexington, KY: The University Press of Kentucky, 1994.
  Fairy Tales and the Art of Subversion: The Classical Genre for Children and the Process of Civilization. New York: Methuen, 1983.

Index

Cambridge Studies in French

Printed in the United Kingdom
by Lightning Source UK Ltd.
124338UK00001B/131/A